POLITICAL MAGIC

POLITICAL MAGIC

THE TRAVELS, TRIALS, AND TRIUMPHS
OF THE CLINTONS' ARKANSAS TRAVELERS

BRENDA BLAGG

The Butler Center for Arkansas Studies
Central Arkansas Library System
100 Rock Street
BUTLER
CENTER   Little Rock, AR 72201
BOOKS   www.butlercenter.org

First printing: January 2013

ISBN (13) 978-1-935106-55-5
ISBN (10) 1-935106-55-4

Cover design: David Bailin
Back cover cartoon: George Fisher
Interior book design: H. K. Stewart

Library of Congress Cataloging-in-Publication Data

Blagg, Brenda.
 Political magic : the travels, trials, and triumphs of the Clintons' Arkansas travelers / Brenda
Blagg.
     pages cm
 ISBN 978-1-935106-55-5 (pbk. : alk. paper)
 1. Clinton, Bill, 1946---Friends and associates. 2. Clinton, Hillary Rodham--Friends and
associates. 3. Presidents--United States--Elections. 4. Political campaigns--United States. I.
Title.

 E886.2.B58 2013
 973.929092--dc23

                        2012038137

Printed in the United States of America
This book is printed on archival-quality paper that meets requirements of the
American National Standard for Information Sciences, Permanence of Paper,
Printed Library Materials, ANSI Z39.48-1984.

The publishing division of the Butler Center for Arkansas Studies
was made possible by the generosity of Dora Johnson Ragsdale
and John G. Ragsdale Jr.

THIS BOOK IS DEDICATED TO
ALL OF THE ARKANSAS TRAVELERS.

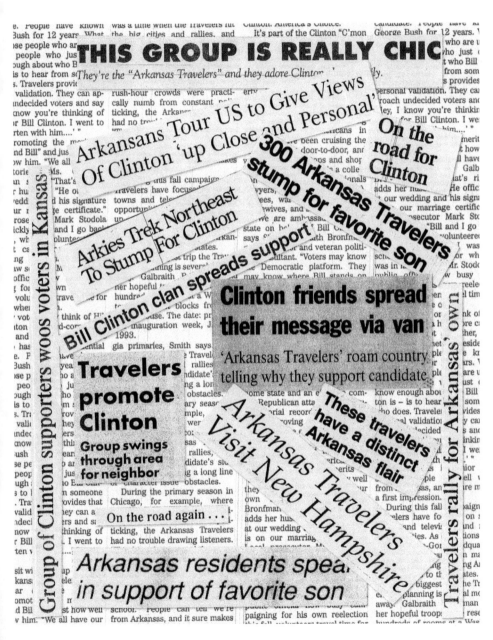

TABLE OF CONTENTS

Foreword
by President William Jefferson Clinton

In 1991, when I decided to run for president, the question I was most often asked back in Arkansas was, "What can I do to help?" Of course we needed funds and to this day I am still amazed at the amount of money we raised in our small state.

But people wanted to do more. They wanted to get actively involved. One day, a group of my longtime friends, led by Shelia Bronfman, came to me with a plan to organize groups of Arkansans to travel to the early primary states on behalf of the campaign. In a campaign short of funds and staff, this built-in group of volunteers seemed like the perfect idea.

The name they proposed for the group was the "Arkansas Travelers," named after our state song, our minor league baseball team, and an honorary award given to visitors who, we hope, enjoy their time in Arkansas, and afterwards say good things about it as they travel the world.

The Travelers provided the organizational boost our campaign needed in those early primary states. As the campaign evolved, they became so much more. They traveled to big cities and small towns, stopping at county courthouses and local radio stations. When the rough and tumble of the campaign got personal, they were there to provide a character reference for me. When people had questions, they had answers. When everyone was tired, they kept pushing. And on those long days, when I was far from home, exhausted and beaten down, they would be there, in some small town, in some other state, cheering me on and giving me the energy I needed to keep going. Thinking back on that campaign, I am not sure I would have survived without them—first in New Hampshire, then in all the states that followed, people everywhere were inspired by their enthusiasm, conviction, and personal knowledge of my life and record.

This book summarizes how they started and what they did back in 1992. In this day and age of billion-dollar campaigns, Super PAC ads, and the Internet, I am not sure that a group like the Arkansas Travelers will ever have as much impact on a future campaign as they did on mine. But back then, they played a vital role in electing a president and for that I will be eternally grateful.

Bill Clinton
September 2012

INTRODUCTION
BY SHEILA GALBRAITH BRONFMAN

The Arkansas Travelers were and continue to be a huge part of my life. I have never met a more dedicated and hard-working group of people who care so deeply about this country. They still walk blocks, hold signs, and give their advice, time, and money to those they believe can make our state and country a better place to live, work, and raise their families. It has been my honor to know, work, and celebrate with each of them.

The Travelers took to the road in 1991 for Bill Clinton and were still going strong in 2008 for Hillary Clinton. In between they have managed to come together to campaign for many other candidates and causes. They are truly a wonderful and special group of people who have brought joy and friendship to my life. I am so proud of each and every Traveler who always answered the call to travel and pay their own way to "Political Camp for Adults." This book is a tribute to them.

I hope this is a book young people will read. I would like for them to come away with the understanding that a few people working together for a common cause can make a difference and have a lot of fun doing it. It is my wish that my grandchildren—Lilly, Maggie, Caroline, Justin, Elizabeth, Sarah, and Stephen—will be inspired by this story to work in their communities and be involved with the world around them. Maybe they will even run for political office! The same goes for your children and grandchildren as well. (You knew I would get those grandchildren in here, didn't you?)

I first want to thank Brenda Blagg for taking on the task of writing this book and preserving the history and memories of this wonderful group of very diverse, talented, politically savvy, and dedicated men and women known as the Clintons' Arkansas Travelers. She has done a marvelous job of capturing the essence of the Travelers and making this book a fun and interesting read. It is a must-read for any political animal.

On behalf of all of the Arkansas Travelers, I want to thank President Bill Clinton and Secretary of State Hillary Rodham Clinton for allowing us to be a part of this incredible journey. You allowed us to participate in very significant ways in your presidential campaigns. It was an experience we will never forget. As you can tell from this book, it was a lot of work but also a lot of fun. Because of the two of you, all of us have developed a strong bond of friendship and have a connection that will last a lifetime. All of us are so proud of both of you and your accomplishments.

This book and the exhibit would not have been possible without the support of the William J. Clinton Foundation, specifically Bruce Lindsey and Stephanie Streett (a Traveler). I also want to thank the William J. Clinton Presidential Library, especially Christine Mouw, Jennifer Wisniewski and Audra Oliver for their work with us on the exhibit and locating material for this book. Without the Butler Center for Arkansas Studies and the Central Arkansas Library Foundation we would not have the book, the exhibit, or their celebratory events. We could not have completed this project without Bobby Roberts (a Traveler) and Madelyn Ganos of CALS Foundation and all they offered us in the way of help and support. A very special thanks to David Stricklin and Rod Lorenzen of the Butler Center for accepting this project with a very short timetable. They made it work and guided us through the world of book publishing. They were calm, patient, and professional. Our editor, Jay Jennings, walked novices through the world of editing and H. K. Stewart did great creative work and was wonderful to work with.

My love and thanks go to my very supportive husband, Richard, who kept the home fires burning while I took off across the United States. Many times, he joined me in those travels. His patience with having numerous people in our home both then and for this project was truly incredible. And through everything, he never "started dating," an inside joke between Skip Rutherford, Richard, and me. As Governor Bill Clinton said when he officiated at our wedding, "Sheila, you are lucky to have found a man who is good enough, self-confident enough to be willing to share his life with someone as strong and independent as you." I am very grateful to have met and married such a wonderful man and such a good Democrat.

During my travels my mother, Joy Galbraith, and my godson Jimmy Davis kept my office up and running. In 1996 and 2008 Marci Riggs was at my side for every aspect of Traveler planning. I can't thank each of them enough.

Gail Goodrum was my fantastic co-leader, and she and her husband, Randy, wrote our famous theme song, "Stand By Your Van." The van leaders and van drivers were all so important to the operation of the Travelers on the road. We would not have been successful without the incredible teamwork shown by this group of folks who took on extra duty.

Speaking of extra duty, a few Travelers went above and beyond in their contribution to this book and exhibit. Without Sherry and John Joyce, and the many months they sacrificed, this book and exhibit would never have been completed. We have very talented Travelers, and our own artist, David Bailin, not only designed the covers for *Political Magic* but also did all of the layout and design for our maps, Traveler names, and all the images needed for the book. He spent countless hours making this book better.

Sue Smith, an excellent photographer, took on the job of selecting photographs from the Hillary trips and gave us a good representative sample for the book and the exhibit. Ann Gilbert, Mary Anne Salmon, Donna Kay Yeargan, and Judy Gaddy helped me narrow down the number of photographs. Yes, we did narrow them down, and it was tough. H. T. Moore and I spent a long weekend together laboring over the final photographs and writing the captions for the book. I promise you that we really did try to include as many Travelers and pictures that would evoke memories of special times as possible. It was not an easy task.

Tyler Thompson is our own James Lipton of the Actors Studio. He elicited some wonderful oral histories that are now preserved at the William J. Clinton Foundation and the Butler Center for Arkansas Studies. Gilbert Cornwell, Mike Malone, and Del Boyette worked tirelessly with me to raise the funds for this project. Rick Watkins, who has made every credential we have ever had, was on hand again to give us one more piece of memorabilia.

Rene de Turenne, Bobette Manees, Sherry Joyce, Wes Cottrell, and Jeff Mitchell all made numerous phone calls and computer searches to track down Travelers. Jeff even had a private detective trying to help us. We did locate all but five of the 521 Travelers. Jan McQuary, Peggy Nabors, Pat Youngdahl, Shirley Montgomery, Stacy Sells, Lisa Powell, Richard Hutchinson, and Linda Ellington searched through documents, worked the computers, proofed copy, and generally did the grunt work needed to make this book and the exhibit a success. And just as they did in 1992, 1996, or 2008, they did it while they took care of work and family obligations. All of these wonderful Travelers joined forces using their special talents to make this project a reality.

Our very generous sponsors have made it possible for us to make history one last time. Without them we could not have written and published this book or been able to celebrate with all of the Travelers coming from all over the United States for the opening of the Traveler exhibit at the Clinton Presidential Center. All of these sponsors care deeply about Arkansas and preserving a small piece of Arkansas political history. They were there for us many times in the past and we are so thankful to have their help again. I know that all of the Travelers join me in my appreciation and thanks to these companies and individuals.

- President Bill Clinton
- Entergy (Home of Travelers James Jones and Ann Pride)
- Insalaco Tenenbaum Enterprises (fellow Travelers Vincent Insalaco and Judy Kohn Tenenbaum)
- McLarty Companies
- Jim and Nancy Blair
- Camrose & Kross
- The Tenenbaum Foundation
- Little Rock Convention and Visitors Bureau
- James Lee Witt and Associates (Home of Travelers Pate Felts, George Kopp and the late Ed Fry)
- Rick Fleetwood
- Brent Bumpers (We appreciate his financial support but we loved his cookies)
- Buddy Young
- Senator Mark Pryor
- Senator Blanche Lincoln
- CDP Strategies, LLC

Most importantly, I want to thank all of the Arkansas Travelers, for entrusting me with the task of leading such an august group and, even more importantly, trusting me with their Social Security numbers and credit cards. In all seriousness, this is the most incredible and committed group of people that I know. I am privileged to be associated with each and every one of them. What a ride!

Any Arkansas Traveler will tell you, "What happens in the van stays in the van," but with this book, we share some of our memories.

I hope you enjoy our story.

Sheila Galbraith Bronfman
Leader of the Arkansas Travelers
September 2012

1.

PRIDE AND PASSION

Pride in Arkansas and unshakable faith in Bill Clinton sent hundreds of his friends on the road twenty years ago to campaign for his improbable presidency. They would become known as the Arkansas Travelers, a committed band of friends who crisscrossed the nation, paying their own way to go places the candidate couldn't or to rally by his side.

With a heavy dose of Southern charm and fierce determination, they stood up for their home state's little-known governor. Their passionate support for a friend helped to carry him through a tough New Hampshire primary and on to the White House.

What they did was "democracy in action," as one Traveler frequently said. The Travelers were living proof of the difference that regular citizens can make in a nation's politics. They came from diverse backgrounds. They were young, old, black, white, straight, gay, doctors, lawyers, farmers, teachers, business owners, beauticians, bureaucrats, and clerical workers. Their common bond was a deep love of Arkansas and their belief in Clinton.

As they prepare to celebrate the twentieth anniversary of Clinton's inauguration, the Arkansas Travelers are recalling their stories and marking the role they played to help elect their friend, Bill Clinton, the first United States president from Arkansas.

The Travelers' numbers grew to more than 500 over five different election cycles, beginning when Bill Clinton first sought the presidency in 1992 and ending with Hillary Clinton's bid for president in 2008.

The Travelers gained experience—and notoriety—as they brought their brand of retail politics to national campaigns. It was the kind of politics they had all practiced in Arkansas, a small state where voters like to look a candidate in the eye and size him or her up for themselves. A handshake can outweigh a promise, conveying more about a candidate than his words.

David Pryor, a populist politician from Arkansas, had practiced retail politics himself, enough to win a state legislative seat, a U.S. congressional district seat, the governorship, and a U.S. Senate seat. When the Travelers first massed in New Hampshire, he schooled them briefly on the distinctions between what they were accustomed to and what they would find there in a New England "town hall" environment. The session helped the Travelers to understand what they would encounter.

The Arkansas Travelers brought to all of the Clinton presidential campaigns an irreplaceable familiarity with the candidate. It was personal, based on real relationships developed by some from childhood and by others during Clinton's long tenure first as attorney general, then governor of Arkansas. They were the "friends of my lifetime," as candidate Clinton first called them, when the Arkansas Travelers flooded New Hampshire in 1992.

Most of them knew his political record firsthand, having followed his public service or worked with or for him or Hillary Clinton. What mattered most on the campaign trail, however, was that these friends really knew the first couple of their state personally. Their lives were inextricably linked by common experiences, mostly in Arkansas. Their children grew up with the Clintons' daughter, Chelsea, as she attended school, played soccer and softball, and did what children do. The Clintons sat in the bleachers with the other parents to watch the kids' games and were there for recitals and such, like other families—although the Clinton family was for a dozen years the state's first family.

Those who were closest politically to Bill Clinton had helped him get elected attorney general and governor time and again.

They geared up with him in 1988, when the Arkansas governor first seriously considered a presidential bid but announced instead that he would not be a candidate. By 1991, when he was preparing to get into the 1992 race, they readily lined up with their friend Bill again. They contributed money, of course, but they also wanted to do something.

That "something" turned into the Arkansas Travelers, made up of people from Arkansas, or with connections to the state, who were willing to pay their own way to go politicking Arkansas-style all across America. Clinton called them his "Arkansas army," these people who went by the dozens into battleground states in the 1992 primary and general elections.

They were back in 1996 to help in President Clinton's reelection campaign. In 2008, U.S. Senator Hillary Clinton (D-NY) summoned the Arkansas Travelers into action again.

The Travelers had a presence in more than half the states in one election or another. They were more critical in some than in others, but the campaign could almost always see some direct benefit to Bill's or Hillary's performance in the states the Travelers helped work. Bill Clinton wrote in his autobiography *My Life* that his friends "probably saved the campaign in New Hampshire," where the first-in-the-nation primary is held. He wrote, too, "They always made a difference, but they were particularly effective in Georgia. The political press said that to go forward I had to win decisively there, with at least 40 percent of the vote. Thanks to my friends and my message, I won 57 percent."

Volunteers flew to campaign states at their own expense. While some traveled alone or in small groups as "SWAT" teams to answer particular campaign needs in certain states, most were organized into cavalcades of vans that crisscrossed a state or focused on a target city. Where they went was often coordinated by that state's campaign workers; but the Travelers sometimes made their own schedules, trying to milk as much campaigning as they could from the few days they would be on the ground in a given state.

Typically, the Travelers worked from early morning until well into the night, doing what they could to help Clinton.

"Bill would do it for us" became a rallying cry for the Travelers. They met shift workers at plant gates in predawn hours, canvassed neighborhoods to hand out literature and videotapes, and sought out voters in shopping malls and on town squares—anywhere people congregated. They worked political events, intersections and over-passes, and, of course, were at the polling places on election days, always looking for another opportunity to swing a vote.

The strategy was pretty much the same whether Travelers were in New Hampshire, where presidential candidates stack up like cord-wood, or on some desolate stretch of highway in rural Kansas, South Dakota, or any other sparsely populated place where presidential hopefuls seldom, if ever, go.

The Arkansas Travelers proved to be particularly effective surrogates in 1992, helping to acquaint the nation with the young governor. Initially seen by Clinton's national campaign staff as bodies to augment the paid staff in an underfunded campaign, the Travelers soon served a more critical role, vouching for his character.

The Travelers are widely credited with helping Bill Clinton survive in New Hampshire. Questions about his military draft status and allegations of womanizing threatened to end the young campaign. Clinton miraculously managed a second-place finish but sounded like the winner, famously declaring himself the "Comeback Kid."

Mike Stafford, a consultant in Washington DC and an Arkansas Traveler, summed up the Travelers' role in Bill's election: "The New Hampshire primary was and always will be retail politics on steroids, which is at the very heart of what the Arkansas Travelers were. As Dale Bumpers used to say, 'You don't have to be broke out with brilliance' to understand the key was the Travelers." Bumpers was the state's other U.S. senator in 1992 and, like Pryor, a strong supporter of Clinton's candidacy for president.

You didn't have to be "broke out with brilliance" to see the Travelers' impact on Hillary's New Hampshire win sixteen years later either.

The Arkansas Travelers for Hillary brought the same kind of personal connection to her campaign, helping their friend and former first lady win the critical primary. She prevailed in New Hampshire and some other states but lost the Democratic nomination to Barack Obama. After the U.S. senator from Illinois won the presidency, he chose Hillary for secretary of state. She has since been the nation's chief diplomat, logging more miles than any past secretary.

James L. "Skip" Rutherford of Little Rock helped coordinate Traveler activities from Bill Clinton's national campaign office there in 1992. The group became a powerful force. Their techniques were effective and, he said, "made a big difference" in the campaign. How big is difficult to discern, but that phrase is repeated by many who know the Travelers' history.

As Skip said, the Travelers became a movement with an aura of its own. They certainly helped the campaign and drew a lot of national attention to a proud state. Much of that came on local radio stations and in small daily and weekly newspapers scattered from coast to coast. The Travelers worked in large city neighborhoods, too, but focused their efforts on smaller towns where they piled up free media that delivered a positive message for their friend Bill.

The Travelers went places the Clintons didn't go and provided moral support in places they did go. That moral support was a major value of the Travelers. A tired Bill Clinton or Hillary Clinton on the road in some far-off place could look up and see this brigade from Arkansas. "It was a big uplift." Bill and Hillary both knew, Skip said, "I'm not out here on this road alone. These people ... don't want anything. They care about me as a friend and a human being."

By the fall campaign for Bill Clinton, after the Travelers were better known, the campaign's demand for them increased enormously. Clinton backers in some other states even formed groups to travel within their borders. Rutherford joined a group of people from Maine on a bus tour and spoke on Clinton's behalf at Kennebunkport, the site of President George H. W. Bush's vacation home. All Skip had to do, he said, was stand up and say, "I am a friend of Bill," a phrase that gained popularity during the campaign. Like many of the Travelers, Skip's relationship with the Clintons was long-standing, going back to the 1970s. The Batesville native is still their friend and dean of the Clinton School of Public Service in Little Rock.

In the spring of 1991, Skip got the first hint that Bill Clinton might be running for president. He was at a Little Rock park, sitting with Hillary as they watched his daughter and hers playing softball. Rutherford commented that it looked like President Bush would coast to reelection. "She looked at me and said, 'What the Democrats need is the right message and the right messenger.' ... I thought to myself, 'Very wise.'" He wondered then if that messenger could be Bill Clinton.

Later in the summer, Rutherford was walking in his neighborhood when Craig Smith tracked Skip down and took him to the governor's mansion, sweaty clothes and all. Bruce Lindsey and both Clintons were in the mansion kitchen. Like Rutherford, Smith and Lindsey were also longtime friends and supporters of the Clintons. They also lived in Little Rock.

Bill Clinton had a question for these three Arkansans, his most trusted political advisors. What did they think about his running for president?

"In my brilliance, I say, 'I don't see a way this time. George Bush is so popular. ... I just don't see it,'" Skip answered. The conversation continued. It became apparent to them all that Clinton was running. Bruce asked, "What if we win?" Hillary said, "We will serve," Skip recalls.

Clinton's top advisors were his contemporaries like James L. "Skip" Rutherford and Craig Smith.

When he returned home, Skip's wife, Billie, couldn't believe he'd been to the governor's office unshaven and dressed as he was. "What was so important that you had to go to the governor's mansion looking like that?" she asked. He told her he thought Clinton was running for president and that he'd advised against it. All that mattered, Skip said, was that Bill thought he could run and win. If Clinton did run, Rutherford told Billie, "None of our lives will ever be the same again." They have not been the same—not for the Rutherfords, not for Smith or Lindsey or any of Bill's other friends.

2.
"Political Magic"

At the heart of the Arkansas Travelers was, and is, Sheila Galbraith Bronfman, a Clinton volunteer from Little Rock who helped conjure up the group and led it through all the presidential campaigns of both Bill and Hillary Clinton. It was she, Skip Rutherford would say, who turned the hard-working Travelers into "political magic."

Sheila was one of the first volunteers in the door of Clinton's national campaign office when it opened in mid-August 1991. Clinton wouldn't officially announce his candidacy until October 3rd, but his Arkansas supporters knew the announcement was coming.

Craig Smith was the first person hired for the campaign staff. His initial instruction from Governor Clinton, as they met briefly at an old, vacant paint store located on 7th Street in downtown Little Rock, was, "I need you to do two things. Raise me a million dollars as fast as you can. And I need you to sweep this place up." This first headquarters was a humble stop on what Clinton has called his "improbable journey" to the presidency. The old paint store was filthy and dusty from disuse. No one had been there in years.

So Craig swept the place up. Then he called on his good friend, Sheila, and other volunteers to help set up shop. Both Sheila, who owned a political consulting business, and her husband, Richard, a Little Rock podiatrist, were active in the state Democratic Party and longtime Clinton supporters. With a check from the brand-new campaign in hand, the two headed to the local Sam's Club to buy essentials like toilet paper, coffee, and office supplies.

Sheila Bronfman would later be renting office furniture and file cabinets and setting up the correspondence system for the office. She volunteered there in those first months. The campaign staff grew rapidly with the addition of out-of-staters, many of whom would become household names during and after the Clinton administration.

Among Sheila's early tasks was finding local people to house the growing campaign staff. George Stephanopoulos, a Massachusetts native, became a key campaign deputy and later White House press secretary, presidential advisor, and successful television news journalist. He moved in with the Bronfmans. So would many others over the course of the campaign. "We had an open house for a year," she said. Eventually, the campaign secured apartments for some of the staff; but a great number continued to stay with Sheila and Richard and other Little Rock hosts.

The Bronfman home became a campaign hub. Not only were the spare bedrooms housing campaign staff, Sheila moved the Arkansas Travelers headquarters there and called in help. These were the days when there were few cell phones, only landlines, and no electronic mail. As Bronfman said, a fax machine was "fancy" for the time. She set one up in a closet for the expanding Traveler operation. It took a lot of faxes and a lot of phone calls to line up a Traveler trip, so Bronfman recruited her own crew of volunteers to help get Arkansans on the road. Rene de Turenne and Sherry Joyce, both of Little Rock, volunteered at Sheila and Richard's home regularly. Many others came in and out on a daily basis.

This whole idea of putting Clinton's friends on the campaign trail for him originated in September 1991. Bronfman had been working at the paint store-turned-campaign headquarters when she and fellow volunteers, Rutherford and Robin Reynolds Armstrong, another Clinton friend and supporter, gathered outside on the loading bay amid stored campaign signs. They had slipped outside the din of the headquarters to discuss what to do with the large numbers of Arkansas people who wanted to be involved in the campaign. All three were accustomed to working with volunteers and knew they needed to give the Arkansas folks something specific to do. While

Getting the 1992 Travelers ready to go on the road took lots of work, and every room in the Bronfmans' home was called into action. Top left, Randy Goodrum types up lists in the library while Gail Goodrum, top right, is shown reviewing a fax in the bedroom. Bottom left, Rene de Turenne sorted packets in the dining room while George Kopp, bottom right, was stuck in a closet faxing. They had no e-mail or cell phones.

Arkansans ably answered phones and made calls from headquarters, Sheila knew they could do more. She didn't want to waste their collective political skills.

Bronfman had heard about the Peanut Brigade, a group of Georgian friends of former President Jimmy Carter who traveled America during his 1976 campaign. Arkansas was among the stops on one of their tours, according to Ron Oliver, who had managed Carter's presidential campaign in Arkansas. "They helped us to campaign for a few days," said Oliver, who told Bronfman how the grassroots campaign helped acquaint the nation with Carter and put that Southern governor in the White House. Carter's surprise breakthrough in New Hampshire's Democratic primary helped establish that state's reputation as a major player in primary races and as a predictor of primary results.

"I thought this could work," said Skip, who would become the Clinton campaign's primary liaison with the Travelers, first as a volunteer and later as part of the paid campaign staff. "Arkansas," Rutherford explained, "is a small state. We do retail politics. People call their politicians by their first names." Arkansas people commonly know the politicians who win state office. People could live in Fayetteville or Eudora, Piggott or Texarkana and they really knew the governor, Skip said. "Everybody knew him." Skip saw the potential to capture that spirit by sending Arkansas volunteers into voters' living rooms and onto their town squares as surrogates for Clinton.

Bronfman took the concept and made it "into a real political force," he said. Agreement came quickly on the name, Arkansas Travelers. Readily recognizable in Arkansas, the name identifies a minor league baseball team in Little Rock, as well as a state song, a famous painting, a popular 170-year-old story, and more. Successive governors, including Clinton, have awarded Arkansas Traveler certificates to visitors, assigning them to be ambassadors of good will beyond the state's borders.

Bronfman made sure Bill Valentine, the general manager of the Arkansas Travelers baseball team, had no problem with the group using the name. He did not object and instead offered them Traveler ball caps and other insignia.

The campaign recognized these traveling Arkansans as potential ambassadors for Clinton and began planning to send them to Florida, New Hampshire, and elsewhere.

Bronfman meanwhile called Dorothy "Dot" Padgett, the longtime Carter supporter from Douglasville, Georgia, who had organized the Peanut Brigade, to learn more about their experience. She offered plenty of advice, including the suggestion, as Bronfman remembers, to be "more of a dictator" with the Travelers. "That fit perfectly with my style." Sheila took the advice to heart and became affectionately known by the Travelers as "The General" and "Attila the Hen" for the way she barked orders and whistled them in and out of their travel vans and buses.

Padgett advised Bronfman to keep her Travelers focused on the campaign. "You've got to get them thinking they can't just stop and visit Aunt Mabel along the way," she said. Bronfman planned rigorous schedules for her Travelers that allowed little variance. Padgett specifically encouraged the Arkansans to travel as a group, not in private cars. She also discouraged putting too many people on a bus because of the time lost getting them on and off. Most often, the Travelers rented 15-passenger vans. When they did travel by bus, Bronfman had them practice getting on and off quickly.

Anywhere the Georgians had traveled, they sought out the radio stations. By the time they got to the town square or a shopping center, Dot said, the local people would know they were there campaigning for Carter. It was one of many strategies emulated by the Travelers, who similarly sought out interviews with local media wherever they went. They amassed newspaper clippings all across America and were often followed by broadcast and print reporters, who found the Traveler story engaging.

When they could, the Peanut Brigade tried to meet up with Carter on the campaign trail, providing them and him a morale boost. The Travelers also looked for opportunities to be where Clinton was, especially during his campaign's darkest days in New Hampshire. Clinton thrived on such confidence-boosting interaction.

The greatest similarity between the Peanut Brigade of 1976 and the Arkansas Travelers in 1992 was in their makeup. Both groups were largely professional people who had typically worked in campaigns for their governors and knew them personally. And they were adults, not the college-age kids presidential campaigns traditionally rely upon for manpower. Plus, they were willing to pay their own way.

The Travelers would visit twelve states in the 1992 primary and twenty-seven for the general election. They went to four for President Clinton's 1996 reelection and four for Hillary Clinton's presidential campaign.

Sheila was well suited to lead the Arkansas Travelers. A political dynamo by the time the Clinton campaign tapped her to lead the Travelers, Bronfman hadn't really taken any interest in politics until 1972, when then U.S. Representative David Pryor challenged U.S. Senator John McClellan.

A 23-year-old Sheila Galbraith, just out of college with a degree in psychology, walked into Pryor's headquarters to volunteer. His campaign staff gave her some handout cards and told her to walk an assigned block. She did and went back to the office two or three times, only to be told they'd call her when they needed her. "They never called me again." Sheila drew on that experience over the years, never making the same mistake, as she managed dozens of campaigns and learned to wring all she could from every volunteer. Pryor lost that race against McClellan.

Sheila's connection with Bill Clinton came when he was attorney general. By then, she had a master's degree in education with special emphasis in counseling and spinal-cord injury and had gone to work for a related state agency. She met the attorney general when he came to participate in a barrier-awareness day to highlight issues for the disabled. A friend later invited her to go to Clinton's 1978 announcement for governor. Clinton, who had met her just once, "remembered me, shook my hand, looked into my eyes, and asked me to volunteer in his campaign," Sheila said, laughing. "I took it as a direct invitation, not realizing he was saying that to several hundred people that day." She ended up on his campaign staff, unpaid, answering phones. It was the start of a lifetime of political activism, much of it for Clinton.

Bronfman left state government to take a position with a private rehabilitation company. After a shakeup in the company, she lost the job. Fired on a Friday, she was hired the following Monday when David Pryor asked her to work with Henry Woods, Pryor's volunteer coordinator, on his Senate campaign. It was her first foray into full-time politics.

She had an offer from Governor Clinton's office as well, but it was conditioned on curtailing her personal relationship with the first couple. She turned down the offer, telling Betsey Wright, the Clinton aide who had offered the post, that she valued the friendship more than the job.

By 1987, after a stint as a marketing director in the private sector, Sheila Galbraith opened her own business doing political campaigns, lobbying, and special events. Her business was up and going. First known as Creative Exchange, it has since become Southern Strategy Group.

In 1989, Galbraith married Dr. Richard Bronfman. Both Sheila and Richard were friends with the Clintons, so much so that Hillary Clinton and State Treasurer Jimmie Lou Fisher hosted her bridal luncheon at the governor's mansion. Among officiates of the Bronfman wedding was Governor Bill Clinton.

It was in the late 1970s when many of the Travelers' friendships were cemented. Ann Henderson (now Gilbert) drew Sheila into active participation in the Arkansas Young Democrats. Sheila also became close friends with Jan McQuary and later Rose Crane. All were young professionals, close in age and dedicated to the same political ideas. Henderson was a lawyer, McQuary a kindergarten teacher, and Crane a public relations professional.

All of them were veterans of many political campaigns, including Clinton's, when he started calling around in 1991 and asking what people thought of a potential run for president. "He called me, like he was calling hundreds of people," Sheila said. "I said, 'If that's what you want to do, let's do it.' We were all young, thinking we could do anything." By August, she was down at the old paint store-turned-campaign headquarters, volunteering and organizing.

Bronfman's organizational skills surfaced really early in life. "I know that my mother said I was 'bossy' from a young age." Sheila remembers organizing her kindergarten band. She told her classmates what instruments to play and how to march.

Fast forward to 2007, when Travelers were getting ready to board their vans in Iowa. They were campaigning for Hillary Clinton. Lisa Powell from Batesville was new to the Travelers. She retrieved her bag from the plane and listened to Bronfman lay out the rules about how they'd be on a need-to-know basis and not to be asking a lot of questions that would slow the Travelers down. Bronfman was like a drill sergeant commanding her troops, said Powell, admitting she might have been a little bit afraid at first. She gained instant respect for Bronfman's ability to lead such a diverse group of accomplished people. Clearly, they all respected Sheila and willingly followed, as they did that day in Iowa.

"I look back, and all of us are walking in single file with our luggage, like in kindergarten," volunteered Powell. Sheila had said, "Follow me," and they did, Powell recalled, "like a bunch of little ducks following the momma duck."

When the idea of the Arkansas Travelers came about, Bronfman naturally turned to friends made through Arkansas Young Democrats and the Democratic Party of Arkansas for help.

Mary Anne Salmon, a state legislator from North Little Rock, was a key leader for the Travelers. "She was always my sounding board, my partner in crime," Bronfman said. Salmon was also the field director for Arkansas in the Clinton presidential campaign.

A Little Rock native who then lived in California fell into a Traveler leadership role instantly. Gail Goodrum, who met Bronfman in New Hampshire, became a trusted cohort. So did Sue White, a Democratic friend from Conway who made nine Traveler trips. They all helped Shelia with Traveler leadership responsibilities.

The three of them and other Arkansas friends like Rose Crane, Myra Jones, Wanda Northcutt, Henry Woods, H. T. Moore, Randy Laverty, and Wes Cottrell served repeatedly as van leaders. They would ramrod crews of Arkansas Travelers as they campaigned in distant locales. The way the assignments worked out, van leaders were usually women and the drivers men. "I don't know if I thought women had more organizational skills, or just listened better, or could ramrod everybody easier and get away with it," Sheila said. "But it worked."

Gail Goodrum and her songwriter husband, Randy, were among the flood of Arkansans who showed up in New Hampshire. Randy had played in a high school combo with Clinton in Hot Springs. Back home in California, he and Gail heard about Clinton's troubles and wanted to help him. "We'll figure it out when we get there," Randy told her. Like so many others, they were propelled by a sense of urgency, Gail said.

Bronfman was working in the Super 8 Motel in Manchester, the Travelers' base of operations, when the Goodrums got there. While Randy visited with old friends in the lobby, Gail slipped into the room where Bronfman, Ann Henderson, and David Matthews were plotting strategy. Henderson was yet another longtime friend of Bill's. By then, the Hot Springs native and attorney lived in Little Rock and headed the Arkansas Transit Association. Matthews was a former state representative from Northwest Arkansas. He had been Bill's strong ally in the Legislature. Both had known Bill since the 1970s and volunteered in his first political campaign, a failed 1974 bid to represent Arkansas's Third District in the U.S. House of Representatives.

Gail "went in that room and everything in the world changed," said Randy.

"I was intrigued with what was going on," said Gail. "I got along instantly with people in the room." The energy was right, she said, "and Sheila incorporated me in her little tribe."

Like Sheila, Gail would spend most of 1992 engaged in the presidential campaign. She basically moved into the Bronfmans' Little Rock home to help plan, organize, and lead Traveler trips for the primary and general elections. Randy returned to work in California but joined Gail for several Traveler trips. Randy jokingly said Gail went to New Hampshire in February and ended up coming home a year later.

As he explained, Gail and Sheila shared the belief that "every little thing that could be done mattered." They had a sense of mission, he said.

"This was such a disparate group of people you can't even imagine," Gail said. "But we spoke with one voice. And then everybody had their own personal stuff to add. That's what made it special." She credited Bronfman with holding the group together. The Travelers "very much respected her," Gail said. "Everybody got tired. And nobody likes to be told what to do." They were working with doctors and lawyers and other people not used to being told when they could go to the bathroom, she said. "But they all fell into line because we could all sense where it was going, and I don't think there was anybody on any of those trips that wasn't dedicated to that."

Randy emphasized the support and encouragement Hillary gave the Travelers. She knew how having kindred spirits around would affect Bill. "She did that to bolster Bill."

Gail remembered those New Hampshire days when, at the end of the day, some Travelers would gather in a coffee shop around Bill to talk. "She thought it was good for him."

As the campaign intensified, he didn't get to meet as often with his friends. Security would also tighten as his chances for election improved.

Randy Goodrum and Billy Clinton, as he was called in high school, were pals who hung out at each other's Hot Springs homes and knew each other's parents. Their moms made peanut butter sandwiches for their band. The jazz band, The Three Kings, was Goodrum on piano, Clinton on sax, and Mike Hargrave on drums. After Hargrave graduated, Joe Newman, another Traveler, took his place on drums.

Gail and Randy, who met at Hendrix College, left Arkansas in 1973 to pursue his music career in Nashville and later in New York and Los Angeles. They kept in contact with Clinton. "I would get a call from him once in a while," Randy said. Clinton called just to check in or to congratulate Randy on a song, Gail added.

When Clinton appeared on the *Tonight Show* and played the saxophone, Gail said he mentioned Randy, whose hit songs include "You Needed Me," "Foolish Heart," "Oh Sherrie" and "Bluer Than Blue."

"'Poor Bill,' I told Randy, 'You're the most famous person he knew at that time.' Now he knows everyone in the world."

Some Travelers had known Bill his whole life. Others just loved him for what he represented and because he was from their state, Randy said. "If you wanted to support him, there was a place for you in the Travelers."

For much of his Arkansas political career, Clinton served two-year terms. In all, Clinton ran for Arkansas offices eight times from 1974 to 1990, losing only twice. One was a failed congressional bid. The other was his infamous loss in 1980, when the one-term governor failed to win reelection. All those elections gave his supporters plenty of opportunity to learn retail politics. The Travelers "wouldn't have happened," Gail said, without the connections that Bronfman had made in all those years in Arkansas politics.

"We'd just call them up, tell them we wanted them to go and we wanted them to pay for it and we needed their credit card numbers. And they just all did it," she said, because of Sheila's history with Clinton supporters. Sheila said they responded mainly because of their loyalty and friendship with the Clintons.

3.

THE FLEDGLING CAMPAIGN

Patty Howe Criner and Dale Evans Jr. were the first of the road warriors for the Arkansas Travelers.

The group itself hadn't yet been named or organized when these two were dispatched in September 1991 to New Hampshire by the fledgling Clinton campaign.

U.S. Senator Tom Harkin (D-IA) was sure to win the Iowa caucuses, which came first; so the Clinton camp decided not to compete there and focused on New Hampshire's February primary.

Patty was a childhood friend of Bill's who lived and worked in Little Rock. They had been friends since they were first-grade classmates in Hot Springs. Bill recruited her for the mission. Sheila Bronfman recommended Evans, whom she had gotten to know through the Young Democrats of Arkansas. Evans first met Clinton when Clinton ran for Congress. Dale was a Fayetteville lawyer and a former law student of both Bill and Hillary Clinton at the University of Arkansas. Like the Travelers to follow, these two Arkansas friends of Clinton were unpaid volunteers. Evans later signed on as a paid member of the staff.

Bill's official announcement wouldn't come until October 3rd, but Patty and Dale slipped quietly into New Hampshire two and a half weeks earlier to start the campaign.

"You're late," George Bruno, an attorney in Manchester, New Hampshire, told them when they first arrived at his office. Bruno's was one of three names in the otherwise empty file the Clinton campaign headquarters had provided Patty about New Hampshire.

Patty thought maybe they were late for the appointment, but Bruno meant the campaign was late getting started. Other hopefuls, like

Harkin, former Senator Paul Tsongas of Massachusetts and California Governor Jerry Brown already had a presence in New Hampshire.

"Bruno wanted action and he wanted it fast," Evans said, remembering how New Hampshire's Democratic national committeeman barked orders at him and Criner. "Patty and I looked at each other and thought, 'Boy, this is going to be tough.'" The two would be in New Hampshire for six months with only brief trips home to Arkansas.

Their journey ended in jubilation when they, with more than a hundred others from Arkansas, jammed into an election-night party as Clinton secured a second-place finish in the New Hampshire primary.

Clinton's comeback came after a torturous campaign in which he was first challenged because of his youth and experience as the governor of such a small Southern state, and then attacked on character issues involving his draft status and accusations of womanizing.

The New Hampshire headquarters for Clinton's campaign had opened quietly with just the two Arkansans. The national headquarters in Little Rock was busily alerting supporters in Arkansas and elsewhere about Clinton's impending announcement. They readied the Old State House for the October 3rd event.

Patty watched the announcement on a motel TV and cried because she was not in Little Rock with her friend. "I'm in some foreign country called Manchester, New Hampshire," she said. It was a place she'd never been, where few people knew Bill Clinton or even how to find Arkansas on a map. Clinton would soon be in New Hampshire himself, making the first events and home visits set up by his tiny campaign field team.

Two paid campaign workers joined the operation. Mitchell Schwartz and Wendy Smith were a New York couple who had worked together in other presidential campaigns. They were "seasoned operatives who could put together a twentieth-century campaign," said Craig Smith, who became political field director of the national campaign and later White House political director.

Schwartz was the campaign director and Wendy the full-time scheduler in New Hampshire. Evans focused more on research and tracking Clinton's numbers while Patty was "the people person," serving as political director until the campaign hired someone from New Hampshire to do that job.

Dale and Patty, and all those who would follow, quickly learned that New Hampshire is unique when it comes to voters' expectations of presidential candidates. They needed to be wooed.

Once, when Governor Clinton was walking down one side of a street, Evans ran across the street to invite someone to come meet the governor. The man declined, saying he'd wait "until Clinton came on his side of the street." Evans was stunned. The guy wouldn't cross the road to meet a presidential candidate. The campaign had to beg people to come to events set up for Clinton.

While people in Arkansas might feel privileged to be invited to a gathering with a high-profile politician, people there were not. New Hampshire's high-maintenance voters expect personal contact with all the presidential candidates, some more than once.

Clinton's second trip to New Hampshire came in early December for the Democratic state convention. It was there, Patty believes, that Bill really started to separate himself from the large primary field with a "stem-winder" of a speech. "People were taking off their Tom Harkin buttons and putting them on the stage," she said. They wanted Clinton buttons. "We had none, because we had no money." The Clinton campaign had only paper lapel stickers.

The campaign had a few friends then, no more than ten. The motley crew included a guy named Flash, who danced in front of the gymnasium and lived on the street. After the response to Clinton's speech, the field staff grew a little and started building support.

Hillary had told Skip Rutherford many months before, to beat President Bush, the Democrats needed the right message and the right messenger. Bill "did the work" in New Hampshire, Dale said. His campaign was candidate-driven. As Schwartz told Evans, "We just have to show up." The two of them also made a habit of going to hear the other candidates when they held events. "It was obvious real quick," Dale said, "there wasn't anybody in the same category."

Eventually, Schwartz would head a paid staff of about fifteen members, including Dale, who estimates that more than 500 people worked in that New Hampshire campaign. Of the volunteers, 137 were Arkansas Travelers, who swarmed into New Hampshire when the campaign was most challenged.

Not only was the New Hampshire campaign late getting started, it did have seriously limited funding in those earliest days.

"We were sent with no money," Patty said. They improvised, made do, or paid for what they needed themselves, even buying the coffee and donuts for the house parties. Unlike in Arkansas, where hosts for political functions normally donate food and drink, the New Hampshire people expect the campaigns to pay.

The cash-strapped campaign got a helping hand from some of the Arkansas Travelers. J. T. Rose, among the first to join Criner and Evans there, took note of the near-empty Clinton headquarters in New Hampshire. "It was just awful." The staff had little in the way of supplies. Rose demanded a full wish list and got help to fill it. When the supplies arrived, the staff acted like kids at Christmastime. But Charlie Varner, another Traveler, was having a little heartburn.

Rose, a wealthy nursing home owner from Rogers, and Varner, an affable but not-so-wealthy Alcoholic Beverage Control enforcement officer from Fort Smith, would become close friends as Travelers, sharing a room and many experiences. But this trip to a Manchester Costco came early in their association for what followed. They, along with Sheila Bronfman, had filled three big carts with the requested office supplies, which added up to a pretty hefty total. Costco wouldn't accept any of Rose's credit cards, so J. T. convinced Charlie to put it all on his Discover card. Charlie reluctantly paid the bill but worried his wife Merle would be upset if he didn't get the money back. Much to Charlie's relief, J. T. wrote him a check when they got back to the hotel after delivering the supplies.

On another occasion, George Jernigan, a former Arkansas secretary of state and the chairman of the Democratic Party of Arkansas, delivered a box of fruit to the headquarters in New Hampshire.

"You would think everyone had scurvy," Patty said, the way they consumed the fruit.

Jernigan had realized the staff was eating all meals at a nearby pizza place. He later sent more fruit.

"Money was tight right off the top," confirmed Craig Smith. The campaign was raising OK money but didn't have much to spread around.

The campaign initially relied entirely on the Arkansas volunteers, Criner and Evans, and the seasoned political operatives, Schwartz and Smith, to run the New Hampshire operation. The paid staff in New Hampshire, even at its largest, was one of the smallest staffs up there. Rival candidate and U.S. Senator Bob Kerrey (D-NE) had fifty staff members "just to knock on doors," Smith said. "We didn't have fifty people on our whole staff."

The Clinton troops had the added disadvantage of having a relatively unknown candidate, compared to others who were nationally known figures. "No one really knew who we were," Smith said.

"Early on, my job was to find us some friends," Patty said. She worked the phones day and night to build a list of supporters. When she had identified 200, she celebrated. New Hampshire people, accustomed to being courted by presidential wannabes, don't commit quickly. Identifying 200 who would commit was big.

She asked them to be on the "steering committee." Someone said, "What is that?" Patty answered, "I don't know but that's what they're on." Those people were early contacts for the Arkansas Travelers in New Hampshire. They would later host house parties to let Bill meet their friends and neighbors. Or they would guide the campaign to

Staff members' limited diet prompted George Jerningan, Arkansas Democratic Party chairman, to supply fresh fruit for the team. Shown are Patty Criner in front of George Jernigan in the center of the photograph and Dale Evans to the far right of the photo.

George Bruno and John Broderick, early New Hampshire Clinton supporters, visit with Arkansas Traveler Patty Criner.

well-connected New Hampshire people who should host parties in the different towns.

The campaign also named ten state co-chairs for the New Hampshire campaign. "We determined early on that we couldn't appoint one chairperson. Not there," said Patty. "They needed more variety."

New Hampshire is small and some of these people had aligned themselves previously with other candidates, she explained. They came with political baggage.

If the campaign had "a bowtie liberal" like George Bruno for a chairperson, she said, it also needed a John Broderick, a more conservative lawyer. The point was to build a coalition with diversity.

The result was multiple co-chairs, some of whom would later become Travelers, joining the Arkansas people to travel elsewhere for Clinton and forge lifelong friendships.

Terry Shumaker was one of Bill's first three supporters in New Hampshire in 1991. A lawyer in Concord, he and Broderick had met Clinton through the Democratic Leadership Council (DLC). They heard him speak and told him in August 1991 they would support him if he decided to run. Bruno, Patty and Dale's first contact in New Hampshire, was the other person to sign on early with Clinton.

"Nobody knew who the hell he was," Shumaker said of Clinton, who had just three percent name recognition when he got into the race.

"The Travelers arrived at just the right time," Shumaker said, to help overcome that anonymity. In this group, he included the earliest of the arrivals, those Travelers who helped get the New Hampshire campaign going, not just those who responded when Clinton faced trouble there.

When trouble did come, the Travelers' loyalty and dedication helped keep Clinton's New Hampshire supporters on board, he said.

Alice Chamberlin, a New Hampshire woman who met Clinton while he was studying in England and she in Paris, was also among his early backers.

Some people were concerned, she said, about his being young and from a small state. "Oddly, it was his character that overcame those criticisms, because when people met him, or heard him, they realized they were not worried about his youth or where he was from," she said.

Memorably, Shumaker said, Clinton held up one event in New Hampshire. "He's trying to talk some kid out of dropping out of high school," said Shumaker. Clinton brought the kid into the campaign van and wouldn't let him go until he promised not to drop out. "There was no press, nothing for show," he said. "It was the real deal."

The Clinton campaign purposefully attracted supporters from a wide spectrum in New Hampshire. Nancy Richards-Stower, self-described as "very, very liberal" and a civil rights lawyer who had been backing former U.S. Senator George McGovern, was one. By contrast, Shumaker and Broderick were involved with the more centrist DLC. Clinton was national chairman of that organization, while the New Hampshire men were establishing a state affiliate.

After McGovern pulled out of the Democratic race, Nancy found not having a political candidate was "like not having a date to the prom." Her mentor, Bruno, persuaded her to consider Clinton. He asked her, "Wouldn't you for once in your life like to work for a winning candidate?"

Still unsure of Clinton's positions on issues that mattered to her, nuclear power and abortion, she called the Clinton headquarters in Arkansas to find out where he stood. Sheila happened to answer the phone and sold Nancy on Clinton.

The personal stories Sheila told about Clinton were what persuaded Nancy to get on board with the campaign, including the fact that the governor had a regular lunch with two of his kindergarten friends. "I liked him for that," Nancy said. The conversation was precisely the sort of message that the Arkansas Travelers carried to New Hampshire and other states in Clinton's campaigns.

Richards-Stower was a co-host for Clinton's first primary appearance in New Hampshire, held at a Nashua restaurant. Had Sheila treated her differently on the phone, Nancy said she "wouldn't have had the ride of a lifetime" with Clinton's candidacy and presidency.

That ride included an early encounter with Hillary Clinton. At an event in New Hampshire, she volunteered to Hillary that the people there "don't do wives very well," stressing that they want the candidate, not the spouse, at events.

Hillary looked at her, pinched the skin on her own hand to make the point and said, "My skin is this thick. Don't worry about my being insulted. You all tell me what to do and I'll do it. You're from New Hampshire. You know New Hampshire."

What Richards-Stower said she didn't know was about Hillary's charm and ability to draw a crowd. It was unusual for New Hampshire people to pay to go to political events, but Hillary had one and it sold out.

"She is a better campaigner than I could have imagined," Nancy said. "My remarks were stupid." From then on, she said the campaign was "just a rocket ride."

Among her memories is a time when Bill Clinton visited a senior center where a sobbing woman collapsed in his arms, saying she couldn't afford both medicine and food. Richards-Stower said the event demonstrated how Clinton "really does feel your pain."

Afterwards, she talked with Clinton in the campaign van and confirmed that people there were choosing "between their second pill and their second meal." The phrase became a frequent campaign line.

David Matthews, the longtime supporter from Northwest Arkansas, was with Clinton when photos of him embracing the woman in the senior center aired on all three major networks.

"Well, Bill, you're leading the national news. I can't tell if it's a good story or another sex scandal," Matthews commented, "but you're leading the news." Everyone in the van died laughing, Matthews included.

4.

FLORIDA STRAW POLL

In December 1991, traveling Arkansans helped pull off Clinton's first major showing in Florida in what was then a six-man Democratic field for president. They didn't have the buttons yet that labeled them as Arkansas Travelers, but a number of Travelers went to help. Several would become mainstays of the group.

Florida Democrats were preparing to assemble for a state convention and would be holding a mock election. The straw poll wasn't binding, but the Clinton camp wanted to make a good showing.

Craig Smith saw the Florida straw poll as "the first big battle" of the campaign. The Clinton campaign brought in a team of political operatives from elsewhere. The Arkansas people, paid and volunteer, went to supplement the effort.

Larry Crane took leave from his job as state assessment coordination director to work in the Florida campaign during the two weeks leading up to the straw poll. Crane, who had lived across the street from Clinton when they were boys in Hot Springs, had never worked in a presidential campaign but had been volunteering as a fundraiser in Little Rock when he found himself at the core of the early 1991 Florida campaign.

With him was Larry Grisolano, a political strategist who had worked in Mayor Richard Daley's campaign organization in Chicago. Crane got to Tallahassee on December 1st and was soon joined by John Yates, a recent University of Arkansas graduate, and Texan Jeff Eller, who headed Clinton's Florida campaign.

Crane was sent to pick up a new press person at the airport. He met "a very stressed-out, disorganized, disheveled woman" there. It was Dee Dee Myers, who handled press for the campaign and eventually for the Clinton White House.

When the core group first gathered, Clinton had only single-digit name recognition (nine percent) among the Florida convention delegates. Job one was to recruit straw poll voters for Clinton from among the 2,000 Democrats who would gather in convention a couple of weeks later in Orlando.

Every Democrat in the Florida House and Senate was a delegate, as were all the Democratic constitutional officers. They were in Tallahassee, the state capital, which is where the Clinton campaign initially set out to meet with the leaders and start swinging votes.

Within days, the campaign sent boxes of videotapes for distribution to the delegates. The taped message introduced Clinton to the delegates. Florida legislative leaders arranged to have copies of the video delivered to each Democratic representative and senator. That first video was not of the quality of a video created later by Harry Thomason, a Hollywood producer and friend of the Clintons. Crane called the use of videotapes "cutting-edge politics at the time."

Slowly, delegate by delegate, Clinton gained support. Arkansans kept coming to join the effort, some from the staff and some as volunteers. They brought an intimate knowledge of Bill Clinton based on years of working together in Arkansas and gave the Clinton camp a significant edge over other candidates' teams, who were mostly campaigning for someone they had recently met.

Two Arkansas teachers, Jan McQuary and Peggy Nabors, both Travelers from Little Rock, were there to focus on the educators who were delegates to the convention. The two proved to be workhorses for Clinton's Florida team. They helped to deliver those Clinton videotapes to delegates and spent days calling other delegates, particularly the teachers among them. They even made signs for the delegates to wave for Clinton at convention.

Everyone was learning on the job, said Jan, a kindergarten teacher who had first gotten acquainted with Clinton when he was attorney general. McQuary's strength was that she could answer any education-related questions about Clinton and about education reforms made in Arkansas during his administration. The reforms, specifically the reduction in Arkansas' kindergarten class sizes from twenty-eight pupils to twenty, had changed her life a lot, as they changed the lives of many Arkansas teachers and their students.

She was teamed with Nabors, a former president of the Arkansas Education Association and, in 1992, an AEA staff member. Peggy had worked for all of Clinton's past elections save one. That was when she was president of AEA and Governor Clinton had pushed a controversial teacher-testing bill her organization fought.

She startled Clinton when he first saw her in the convention center in Florida. "I could tell he really did not know whether I was there to help him or hurt him." Nabors put him at ease, telling him she had been speaking on his behalf to a higher-education caucus. "You could see a sense of relief on his face."

Some of the delegates in higher education were opposing Clinton because of teacher testing. Peggy told them that, while she and Clinton disagreed about that, other things were more important than the testing. Clinton had been good for public education in Arkansas, and Peggy, his foe on teacher testing, proved a strong witness.

When Clinton got to Florida, he vigorously campaigned among the delegates himself. "We kept Bill literally walking the halls and advanced him as he went," Crane said. "No one is better at making those 30-second impressions."

Marianne Maffia, a non-committed delegate from Broward County, was among the Floridians who met Clinton in those halls. Jan first approached Maffia, introducing herself as a fellow teacher. She wanted Maffia to know about her governor and his educational stance. "She discussed how, as governor, Mr. Clinton supported public education stronger than anyone before or since," Maffia remembers. Then Jan asked if the Florida woman would like to meet him. "I turned around to see Governor Clinton coming up behind me. It was a moment I'll never forget. I was shaking hands with one of the most formidable people I had ever met, and I was introduced to him by someone he calls 'my friend.'" Out of that encounter grew a friendship between McQuary and Maffia that has continued ever since. So have many other acquaintances made between Travelers and the people they met campaigning for Clinton.

In the time leading up to the Florida state convention, Arkansans were working in Tallahassee and Orlando and elsewhere, trying to build support for the still-new campaign. One Arkansan didn't necessarily know what others were doing in Florida.

J. T. Rose worked independently from most of the others, circulating among wealthier Floridians, including retirees. He and Traveler Rocky Wilmuth, a Batesville businessman, also hosted a hospitality room for delegates while other Travelers worked the halls and receptions. J. T. had met Clinton when he ran for Congress in the state's Third District and had worked closely with the governor on legislation affecting nursing homes. "He helped me," said J. T., who wanted to return the favor. A colorful character and a Democratic national committeeman from Arkansas, J. T. became a popular interview subject for the national press in Florida.

Also working the straw poll were Travelers Woody Bassett, a Fayetteville lawyer; Bill Wiedower, a Little Rock architect; Greg Joslin, a grad student from Little Rock; Gregg Burgess and Wayne Gruber, both Little Rock lawyers. Like the others, they sought out delegates, trying to answer their questions and to let them know who this Bill Clinton was.

To win that straw poll required appealing to political insiders. But the campaign specifically needed to reach out to labor, teachers, African Americans, Hispanics, and retirees.

Crane told headquarters that the African American delegates weren't responding well to the white Clinton staff. Headquarters dispatched two notable Arkansans to help. Carol Willis and Rodney Slater were in Florida within a couple of days.

Both African American, Willis was a Clinton staffer and political adviser and Slater was a former Clinton staffer whom Clinton had named to the Arkansas Highway Commission. They easily turned their target delegates around and illustrated the diversity in Governor Clinton's administrations. Slater would later serve President Clinton as United States Secretary of Transportation.

Just when the campaign needed added manpower, a busload of college students from Arkansas arrived. They provided more visibility for the campaign and, most importantly, extra hands. The students had traveled by bus for several days, arriving on Friday before the Sunday straw poll. They helped Jan and Peggy get the Clinton video-tape out to every delegate. The students did chores, too, such as leaving a surprise by every plate for a banquet the night before the Sunday vote. The campaign had shipped fortune cookies in from Chicago. The message inside for everyone at the banquet was, "Bill Clinton is in your future!"

The next morning, delegates who had left a wake-up call with the hotel were greeted with a personal message from Clinton. Such touches caused staff of other candidates to say they had never seen such an organized campaign. "Neither had we," Crane admitted. "It was all made up as we went along."

It worked. Clinton came out of the straw poll with fifty-three percent of the Democrats' votes. The next closest was U.S. Senator Tom Harkin (D-IA), with thirty-one percent. Travelers believed the vote legitimized Clinton, showing the Arkansas governor as a credible candidate. Clinton's success "put him out there as a contender and made us all realize he could actually win this thing," Peggy said. Jan also sensed the possibilities. They would occasionally see another candidate walking the halls with a few people hanging around him during the convention. "When Bill Clinton would show up," she said, "there would be mobs of people following him." That was Jan's signal that he would do well.

"When the results came out," Jan said, "those of us from Arkansas just looked at each other and thought that this was really going to happen. I'll never forget that moment." Crane counts the two weeks he spent there as the best political experience of his life, surpassing even his own 2010 election as circuit and county clerk for Pulaski County, Arkansas's largest county.

The Florida campaign operated "on a shoestring," J. T. observed. After Clinton won the straw poll, money opened up. Bill was showing he could win and the campaign came away from Florida with millions in new money.

When they got back home, Arkansans raised $1 million for him, the most ever for a political fundraiser in Arkansas. That was the "Winner Wonderland" fundraiser chaired by Skip Rutherford and coordinated by Sheila Bronfman. Raising that kind of money for a

This cartoon by Milton Davis appeared in Conway's *Log Cabin Democrat* and depicts Bill Clinton's win in the Florida Straw Poll. (Reprinted with the permission of Milton Davis.)

political campaign was simply unheard of in Arkansas at the time, according to Rutherford.

That money and the millions generated because of Clinton's Florida surge carried the Clinton campaign on to New Hampshire.

5.
WHO WERE THESE ARKANSAS TRAVELERS?

When Bill Clinton described the Arkansas Travelers as his "friends of a lifetime," he meant it.

They do, too. In their collective responses to a survey, Travelers poured out the way they felt about both Bill and Hillary Clinton, people they have shared their lives with for decades. Almost 300 Travelers answered the online survey.

They emphasized the gifts they received because of his campaigns, including exposure to many parts of the country they had never seen. The greatest gift, however, was the close alliances they built with one another during their travels.

Certainly, Bill became acquainted with larger numbers of them in adulthood, mostly through his political and family life. But others come from the same Arkansas roots. Many of the Travelers first connected with him in childhood or as teens in high school in Hot Springs.

Born in Hope, Billy Blythe moved to Hot Springs at age four with his mother, Virginia, and her new husband, Roger Clinton. Billy soon took the Clinton name. "I sat by Bill Clinton in the first grade at St. John's Elementary School in Hot Springs," said Patty Howe Criner, who would become one of the first Arkansas Travelers. "We went all through school together," she said. "Our families have been friends as long as I can remember."

David Leopoulos, who would be one of Clinton's most ardent champions in the presidential race, met Clinton when they were in the fourth grade at Ramble School in Hot Springs. They have been lifelong friends, always there for each other. He readily told voters about growing up with Clinton, "the things we did, where we lived, how we all took up for each other, and how our parents were involved."

"I met Bill when he moved into the home across the street from my family when I was three or four years old," Larry Crane recalled. "He was in many respects the brother I never had." Crane would work for and with Clinton when he was attorney general and governor.

Rose Crane also remembered the neighbor boy she befriended when they were nine years old, recalling a lifetime of card games with her competitive pal. The former president gave the eulogy for Rose at her 2012 memorial service. As with several other Travelers who have died, she wanted her role as an Arkansas Traveler to have prominent mention in her obituary.

Crane is one of sixty-eight Travelers who are no longer living as of August 2012. Many of their obituaries mentioned their Traveler association. Among them were former state Representative Myra Jones of Little Rock, Cynthia Beshear of Salt Lake City, and Ed Fry, whose obituary not only referenced his being a Traveler but also said he was a lifelong "yellow dog Democrat." Fry served three consecutive Arkansas congressmen in his long career in Washington DC. These individuals were all so proud of having been an Arkansas Traveler and helping to elect their friend president, Sheila said.

Mack McLarty, an Arkansan who served as White House chief of staff, read a letter from President Clinton at Myra's memorial in Little Rock: "I will always be grateful for her support in 1992 and for all she did for Hillary and me. I have an enduring memory of showing up at a rally in a horse barn in South Dakota in 1992 and seeing Myra smiling and working the crowd."

Clinton's most famous friend from his high school band days was Randy Goodrum, the songwriter who would later provide the musical score for part of the Clinton campaign.

Clinton's band connections also produced a couple more Travelers. Bill Lawson, a tenor sax player from Marked Tree, met him during a high school band competition in Hot Springs, as did Tyler Thompson from Little Rock.

One of the Travelers had an even earlier connection. "Our mothers were good friends in Hope, Arkansas, and I've known him ever since I was born," said Joe Purvis, who went to kindergarten in Hope with little Billy Blythe and later worked as a deputy attorney general for his childhood pal.

Joe and Bill both attended Arkansas Boys State, a weeklong summer camp sponsored by the American Legion that immerses selected high school juniors in civics education. Don Richardson, who is an environmental advocate for the Pew Charitable Trusts, was another Traveler who first knew Clinton as an Arkansas Boys State delegate. Don is from Clinton, the Van Buren County seat.

Bill himself was elected as an Arkansas delegate to Boys Nation. It was there, in 1963, when the future president was famously photographed shaking hands with President John F. Kennedy. The next year, he would return to Arkansas Boys State as a counselor and meet yet another corps of friends, including Harry Truman "H. T." Moore. of Paragould. He crossed paths with Clinton again in Fayetteville a decade later, when Clinton taught at the University of Arkansas School of Law. Mark Stodola, a future mayor of Little Rock, Arkansas, was attending law school when Clinton was hired. Both Bill and Hillary taught numerous future Travelers.

Moore and Stodola were among several future Travelers who would work in Clinton's 1974 congressional campaign against U.S. Representative John Paul Hammerschmidt. Clinton lost to the incumbent Republican but gained sufficient name recognition to mount a successful bid for state attorney general two years later. Stodola was the campaign's full-time volunteer scheduling coordinator.

That congressional campaign was the start of many of the future Travelers' association with Clinton. Among them was Ann Henderson, then a student at the University of Arkansas. She had grown up in Hot Springs and knew Clinton's mother and brother. When she learned Roger's brother was running for Congress, she volunteered to work on his campaign. She was so convinced Clinton would succeed that Henderson transferred to George Washington University anticipating a chance to work in Clinton's Congressional Office. She made it to Washington and he didn't until 1993.

Another Traveler, Susan Jones of Royal in Garland County can claim the oldest connection to him, sort of. She wasn't there, but her great aunt was the delivery-room nurse when the future president was born. Susan and her mother, Charlene Clark of Hope, traveled together supporting Clinton.

Numerous Travelers have had lasting, long-term friendships with Bill and Hillary.

Ann Henry, a community activist, and her husband, Morriss, an ophthalmologist and a state legislator, hosted the Clintons' 1975 wedding reception in their Fayetteville home. And it was Ann Henry who helped pack up the Clintons' personal belongings for shipment from the governor's mansion to the White House. Another Traveler, Marian Alford Hodges, a mutual friend, helped with the move and even went to the White House to unpack.

David Matthews was a law student when Clinton was teaching at the law school in Fayetteville. Matthews volunteered initially to take Clinton around Benton County and became one of Clinton's regular drivers for the Third District race. The criterion to be a driver, Matthews said, was "to own a car and have a tank of gas."

Carl Whillock of Fayetteville, then an electric cooperative executive, drove Clinton on his first round of visits in the district to help him make political connections.

Sid Johnson was president of the Fort Smith Classroom Teachers Association when he was being bothered to put a candidate for Congress on a program agenda. He said no, but eventually gave in to allow the guy fifteen minutes. "Two hours later, we were still there listening to and having a conversation with Bill," said Johnson, who had to schedule another meeting to do the association's work.

Jo and Jerry Parker owned a restaurant in Waldron that served up burgers and fries late at night to Clinton and his driver, whoever it might be, as they were heading back home from campaign trips.

Many Travelers met Clinton, worked with him or were his students at the University of Arkansas Law School in Fayetteville, where many also first got to know Hillary Rodham Clinton.

Kay Goss, a political scientist who was working as a congressional legislative assistant, met Clinton in 1973. After a long visit over coffee, she returned to her office to say she had just met with "a future congressman, governor, and president." She was right about two out of three.

Ann Pride, another of the Travelers, was a student in Fayetteville when Mack McLarty, the student government president, introduced her to a visiting friend, Bill Clinton. McLarty and Clinton are both from Hope. "Funny, for years, I thought Mack was going to be president of the United States," said Pride. Mack was President Clinton's chief of staff.

For dozens of Travelers, connections came in their professional lives while Clinton held state office. Many of them were also officeholders, some in statewide positions, others in the state Legislature. Several were lobbyists and business people.

Among them was Percy Malone, an Arkadelphia pharmacist who still carries a laminated business card of Clinton's. It has the handwritten name of a governor's office contact that Clinton told Malone to call for help with a business-related problem. Malone made the follow-up call. He and Clinton straightened out the situation. Later elected to the state legislature, Malone remained a strong supporter and was one of the first Travelers in New Hampshire along with his wife, Donna.

Many Travelers aligned with Clinton politically. Others developed personal friendships. A few Travelers, notably some lobbyists, became

Travelers because they knew, if Clinton lost the presidency, he'd still be governor. They didn't want to be seen as not being supportive.

Del Boyette, the director of the Arkansas Industrial Development Commission, went to New Hampshire to campaign for Clinton and to defend Arkansas. "I felt that he was being attacked because he was an Arkansan," Boyette said.

Several of the Travelers were children when they met Clinton, either at official functions when he was governor or through politically involved parents.

A few of those, like Mike Malone of Fayetteville, not only became Travelers for Clinton's presidential campaign but also followed him to Washington DC to work in the White House. Malone had met the governor through his father, a state lawmaker, and was a political science student at Hendrix College when the opportunity to travel to New Hampshire in 1992 came up. "That was the center of the political universe," he remembers of the New Hampshire experience. As the youngest in his van, he was called upon to talk about the improvements that had been made to Arkansas education under Clinton.

Ragan Hoofman Milner, who met Governor Clinton when she was five, remembers his having tea with her and her dolls during a fundraiser being held at her home.

Sarah Argue of Little Rock said the Clintons where always part of her life. "My first memory of Bill Clinton is at a Halloween Party at which he was wearing a crazy scary mask. He terrified me," she said. Her first memory of Hillary Clinton was at an Earth Day celebration on the state capitol grounds.

Kimball Stroud remembers sitting at her family's kitchen table and having breakfast with the governor, who had stayed with them on a campaign swing to Texarkana. "My fellow ninth-grade classmates were so envious," she said.

Rhonda Jones McCauley read Clinton's 1991 announcement speech and wanted to be involved. "I was very impressed with his talk about the value and dignity of blue-collar work, having grown up the daughter of a bricklayer," she wrote, noting her father always gave more than was expected of him for a day's pay.

Clinton's ability to connect instantly with people also snagged Travelers. "Clinton did not meet any strangers. He made everyone feel as if they knew him," said Roosevelt Coleman, who met Clinton at a Democratic Party function. "He just walked up and said, 'Hi, I'm Bill Clinton,'" and started to talk, said Coleman, who worked for the state Department of Veterans Affairs.

Eleanor Coleman, a public school teacher in Little Rock, met Clinton at the same time, when he was attorney general. "He went around the room and spoke to everyone," she said. "It did not matter if they were black, white, or whoever. He would shake your hand and talk to you."

Clinton made an impression on Democratic Party regulars early. Jimmie Lou Fisher of Paragould recalls meeting him in 1974 when he was campaigning for Congress in Russellville at a Democratic rally. "Bill Clinton made the most compelling speech of the evening. Many in the audience compared him to John F. Kennedy," she said, "and most take credit for predicting that one day he would be president of the United States."

Judy Tenenbaum of Little Rock, who traveled for Hillary Clinton in 2008, had known the Clintons since the 1980s. Tenenbaum was in the fitness business and did walking groups and private home training. Hillary joined a walking group in Little Rock's Heights area, and Judy also did personal training for Hillary at the mansion.

And then there were other Arkansas Travelers, like the handful of New Hampshire people who got so close with the Arkansas crew that they later went on the campaign trail with them. Terry Shumaker, a Concord lawyer, and Alice Chamberlin, a New Hampshirite who met Clinton when he was a student at Oxford,

Ricia McMahon, Nancy Richards-Stower, Debbie Crapo, and Barbara and Bob Baldizar all became Travelers for Hillary.

The Travelers were "a dedicated group of extraordinary people of so many personalities, professions, ages, races," Pat Morrow of Little Rock, who has moved to Pennsylvania, said. All of the Travelers had the same determination to elect and reelect Bill Clinton and to try to do the same for Hillary.

6.

ON TO NEW HAMPSHIRE

"Let me tell you about my governor," the Arkansas Travelers asserted, as they knocked on doors in the New Hampshire snow and looked for any opportunity to help voters there know Bill Clinton the way they did. Traveling at their own expense to support Clinton's candidacy, these people poured into the state in ever-growing numbers in 1992.

Initially, they were there primarily to assist the paid campaign staff, assigned to help raise the profile of a little-known Arkansas candidate. The Travelers arrived in waves, numbering well over 100 in the 1992 campaign. Still more Arkansas people went to campaign in New Hampshire that year, but 137 took their orders from Sheila Galbraith Bronfman, the Travelers' leader.

She first led a small group of Travelers into the state in early January to volunteer and to advance the arrival of others. Another wave of Arkansans went in early February, and the largest contingent gathered in New Hampshire about a week out from the February 18th primary.

Dale Evans and Patty Criner, who had slipped into New Hampshire in September, were well embedded in the campaign headquarters in Manchester when Bronfman arrived to start work.

Sheila was there to lay the groundwork for the first of the Arkansas Traveler trips and to schedule activities for Arkansas Travelers such as Gilbert Cornwell, Clinton's cousin; Percy Malone, David Matthews, and Jay Bradford, all past, present, or future state lawmakers; and Sid Johnson and Peggy Nabors, both Arkansas Education Association representatives. All arrived with Sheila or were soon to arrive in New Hampshire.

Sheila and other Travelers were staying in Manchester at the Super 8 Motel, which she would eventually pack with Arkansans. She also took over a small conference room in the hotel as her office.

She shared connecting rooms with Dale, the Arkansas Democratic Party friend she had recommended to help set up the New Hampshire campaign. "I had the coffee pot and the microwave in my room," Bronfman said. "He had the refrigerator for the beer in his room. The door stayed open so both of us could get to each." The arrangement continued the whole time the two were in New Hampshire. Dale and Sheila, needless to say, became close friends and are today. She's his "other Sheila." His wife is also named Sheila.

Bronfman spent two weeks in New Hampshire in January, returned for almost all of February, staying until after the primary vote. Her frequent travel prompted Skip Rutherford to ask, "Has Richard started dating yet?" The joking reference to Bronfman's husband continued, but she said Richard didn't lack for company.

Remember, their Little Rock home was a campaign hub, filled with out-of-state campaign staff living there and in-state volunteers working on Traveler arrangements and preparing materials. Plus, Sheila would pop in for a couple of days to do laundry and plan another trip. Her supportive husband had agreed, she said, "that this was an experience that I could not pass up and that I needed to do this for our friend." He did get bored once, went to an auction, and bought an oriental rug that would not fit anywhere in their house. But he never did start dating. The rug was donated to the Arkansas Governor's Mansion and now sits under the governor's desk.

For Bronfman, New Hampshire is "the pinnacle" of presidential politics.

"If you don't go to New Hampshire, you haven't experienced a presidential campaign," she said, joining an almost universal defense by Travelers of that small state's holding the first presidential primary every four years.

"The people in New Hampshire take this so seriously," she said. Bronfman recalled attending a town hall meeting in Bedford, where Clinton was speaking. The Travelers were working the crowd.

She noticed a woman there taking notes in a reporter's notebook. Not wanting to miss an opportunity for the Travelers to get quoted, she asked the woman what newspaper she was with. "She went, 'I am not with the paper. I'm an interested citizen,'" Bronfman said. That summed up for her the level of engagement the New Hampshire people have in the primary. The woman was taking her own notes on the candidates, learning about policy.

James Jones, who was economic development manager for Entergy Corporation in Little Rock, said he was surprised to see New Hampshire people show up for rallies in frigid conditions. They came, he said, and stood outside in line, waiting to get in. Unlike political rallies in Arkansas, which tend to be more like social events, the New Hampshire town halls are opportunities for voters to gather information on the various candidates. Jones was impressed with the locals, who went to learn and ask questions, not necessarily to show support for any candidate.

Evans was impressed with the political savvy of the people there. "You didn't find anybody that didn't know the issues and have an opinion on it and want to know what each of those presidential hopefuls' position was," he said. "It was just like a different world … where everybody is interested."

He's not talking about party-affiliated people only. The desk clerk, the cabbie or someone behind a convenience-store counter may ask pointed questions to or about a presidential candidate. It's something they start learning to do as schoolchildren, when teachers impress upon them the role New Hampshire plays in selecting the American president.

The practice fits the political tradition Senator Pryor explained in his civics lesson for the Travelers about the contrast between New Hampshire politics and Southern politics. While New Hampshire politics derive from the New England "town hall" tradition where issues matter and are resolved by the community, Southern politics is founded on the Scottish tradition of family, or clan, where relationships matter most.

Joel Buckner of North Little Rock related to what Pryor said. In the South, Joel said, "If your cousin is running for sheriff and you don't vote for him, don't even think of coming to Sunday dinner at Grandma's. In New England, issues are the most important thing. In the South, it is relationships."

Ann Henderson was one of about a dozen Arkansans who first followed Bronfman to New Hampshire. Henderson, executive director of Arkansas Transit Association, joined Bronfman to help set up travel schedules and event appearances for individual Travelers, including Dale Bumpers and David Pryor, the state's U.S. senators then; George Jernigan, chairman of the state Democratic Party and a former Arkansas secretary of state; and others who functioned as surrogate speakers for Clinton. As testament to how well these Travelers knew their homegrown politicians, Henderson remembers a day when New Hampshire people expected them to stop what they were doing to go meet Bumpers when he entered the room. "It's just Dale," Ann said to incredulous New Hampshire people who had never met their senators. Ann and Sheila continued their work until Dale came up to say hello.

Peggy Nabors, a leader with the Arkansas state teachers' union, was summoned to New Hampshire by the campaign. "Bill needed her there," Sheila said, recalling a forum when he pointed Nabors out in the crowd and said, "That woman made my life a living hell and she's here now supporting me. It shows how we can work together, what we can do together." Nabors got up and responded, "Well, I may have made his life a living hell but he didn't exactly make mine fun either."

Governor Clinton and Nabors, representing teachers, had butted heads over his legislation for teacher testing in Arkansas. Theirs was a high-profile fight, waged in part on national television. Yet, almost a decade later, she was supporting his candidacy for president. Nabors was such a strong advocate for Clinton's election that a video of her speaking for him was distributed nationwide to National Education Association (NEA) members.

She and another Traveler, Eleanor Coleman, were also among featured Arkansas teachers in an NEA brochure about Clinton's education policies. "Just as he's not a single-issue candidate, we're not a single-issue organization," said Nabors, then employed by the Arkansas Education Association. While teachers might still disagree on teacher testing, the brochure quoted her as saying, "We have seen so many changes under his leadership, so many positive changes in the teaching environment, that they cannot be ignored."

Coleman, then president of the Little Rock Classroom Teachers Association, said much the same. "It doesn't matter whether we agree on every issue if we have the same goal. We've worked together. Even when in our judgment he had the wrong solution, he was always involved in trying to find one."

Meanwhile, Bronfman was preparing for the arrival of other Arkansans, booking rooms and lining up transportation. Travelers Larry Vaught and Larry Crane, both of Little Rock, flew in early to help at campaign headquarters advancing the Travelers.

Among the new arrivals was George Fisher, a popular political cartoonist in Arkansas, who had frequently cartooned Clinton's career during his gubernatorial years. The cartoonist famously advanced the governor's mode of transportation as he matured. A baby-faced Governor Clinton first had a tricycle. George later gave him a bike and eventually a pickup truck. George drew similar cartoons to warm up the crowd and introduce Clinton speeches.

In the evenings, after the Travelers had done their work, they'd relax in J. T. Rose's "suite." It served as a hospitality room only because he had a room with a couch. One night, Sid Johnson and

Jay Bradford found themselves stretched out on the same bed. Sid said, "Someone came in and needed to sit, so Jay moved over, reducing the space between us quite a bit." Then, Jay announced, "I have been accused of being in bed with the AEA before, but this is the first time I can remember it."

Sheila was busy renting vans for the incoming masses. "We took every van they had in New Hampshire, including what we called 'the van from Hell,' which had no heat," Bronfman said. The Travelers were competing with news outlets and other campaigns for transportation. "I'd already booked all these vans, knowing Arkansas people were coming," she said. Besides, she figured they could ditch the vans if they weren't needed. They were needed, even the one without heat.

The vans held fifteen passengers, although sometimes only thirteen people could ride, if the people were large or wore bulky clothing. Those in "the van from Hell," including Bronfman, also brought along the covers off their motel-room beds. "We'd just wrap up in our blankets to get from place to place," she said.

"The higher we went in the polls," J. T. Rose noticed, "the better our vans were. The first ones were awful." He, too, had been assigned to the one with a broken heater in New Hampshire. The Travelers went from "the van from Hell with no heat to limos at the White House," he said.

Adjusting to the cold in New Hampshire was challenging to pretty much all the Arkansans.

As Sid Johnson said of the experience in zero-degree weather, with sharp wind and deep snow, "Little Rock cold ain't New Hampshire cold." Johnson said he had not dressed for the biting weather and had the misfortune of being ferried to his speaking engagements in a car with a broken heater. Sid said, "I almost froze to death because it was in January in New Hampshire, and the coldest front of the year had moved in. Below zero, folks, with wind. ... That is also when I realized that Bill was running a campaign on a tight budget."

One group of at least ten Travelers made a quick trip to a Manchester shoe store to buy boots and hand and foot warmers when they first got to New Hampshire. None of them, not even Gregg Reep, then the mayor of Warren, who had bragged about bringing his duck-hunting gear with him, could keep warm. Apparently, duck blind cold isn't New Hampshire cold either.

The most recognizable piece of the Travelers' cold-weather gear, however, was probably David Matthews's hat, which the former state lawmaker from Lowell wore all over New Hampshire as he traveled with Governor Clinton.

Matthews said the wide-brimmed, light gray hat—a favorite—was a Borsalino Alessandria that he has had since 1982. "You can shape it any way you want to," he said. "I still have it. I still wear it. And it's principally because I'm bald-headed and my head gets cold."

Matthews, a frequent contact for the media, said the hat made it to national TV and the *New York Times*, where the caption identified him as "unidentified man." When he got home from New Hampshire, Matthews told Mary Beth, his wife, about his time there and that he felt he had played a significant role. She kind of said, "Yeah, right," he remembered. The next year, during the inaugural, Matthews was wearing the hat when the two were walking on the National Mall. A stranger stopped them and asked if he was David Matthews and said he had heard him introduce Clinton in New Hampshire. "I just wanted to shake your hand," the man said. "It was the hat that he remembered," Matthews said.

Most of the Travelers have cold-weather stories from New Hampshire or Illinois or some other winter exposure.

When J. T. Rose, the Rogers nursing home owner, first arrived in New Hampshire, he was wearing just a suit jacket. Bill Clinton greeted him, "J. T., you're as big a hayseed as I am." By then, Clinton had donned a heavy overcoat and advised Rose to get one, too.

David Matthews and Congressman Ray Thornton show off their hats in New Hampshire, 1992.

The Travelers' most inexplicable experience with the cold came when they were invited to a pig roast in Meredith, New Hampshire, at the home of an Arkansas native, Jan Paschal. Clinton was there to speak. And the small contingent of Travelers who were in the state at that time went, too.

To their surprise, the guests were expected to remain outside the whole time in freezing temperatures. The day's high temperature was fourteen degrees and the low just five, not considering wind chill. The only time Travelers were allowed in the house was to use the bathroom. Most sought refuge there as often as possible.

David Matthews lightens the mood at a late night strategy session at the Super 8 by demonstrating the versatility of his hat.

Jan McQuary, the kindergarten teacher from Little Rock, remembers having gone to "the middle of nowhere" for the January 19th event. "People were roasting this pig in ten feet of snow," she said. It was so unbearably cold, Gregg Reep couldn't take his gloves off even to eat. "There was no way that pig was cooked, and I nearly froze my feet off," said Donna Malone, a Traveler from Arkadelphia. "I asked myself, 'Would I do this for Percy [her husband]?' Answer, '*No*.'"

J. T., who said it was "the coldest I have ever been," sneaked into the Paschal house, where the Travelers were specifically told not to go. "I decided they were going to have to throw me out of that house—and away from that fire," he said. While there, he said he saw a young boy ask Clinton why he was so popular. Clinton, bending down to the boy's level, responded, "Let's just hope that continues." Rose said he was glad the traveling press noticed the exchange because it showed the way Clinton connects with people.

Larry Vaught and Larry Crane doing advance work for the Travelers in the Manchester headquarters, early February 1992.

Getting headquarters up and running in Manchester, New Hampshire, 1992.

Despite the miserable conditions, McQuary said the Travelers were able to visit with other attendees, answer their questions and set the stage for Clinton to speak, as they would many times.

Many of the Travelers' trail stories come from New Hampshire. Although they had done door-to-door campaigning many times at home, this was a new environment for almost all of them and they piled up memories about each other, if not themselves.

Del Boyette recalled being at a rally in Keene, New Hampshire, when he happened upon Bill Clinton and someone who was "in Bill Clinton's face" yelling at him. "It's the economy, stupid! That's all these people care about," said the man, whom Boyette later learned was James Carville, a key Clinton adviser. A sign conveying the same thought famously decorated the Clinton campaign's War Room in Little Rock.

Another memory Boyette shared was of Traveler Maria Haley, a native of the Philippines who worked with him at the Arkansas Industrial Development Commission (AIDC) and later headed the renamed Arkansas Economic Development Commission (AEDC). Because of her accent, Boyette said he had to vouch for her being from Arkansas. She told New Hampshire voters to be for Clinton "because he believes that everyone should have a chicken in their pot," he remembered with a laugh. The proverbial phrase is "a chicken in every pot." However she said it, she got their interest.

Charlie Varner stories are common among Travelers. Donna Malone described Varner as a big man who wore Razorback apparel, Bill Clinton buttons and stickers and who was loved by the media. He was also loved by the Travelers for his funny reactions, like one Malone recounted about Charlie's being offered littleneck clams. The waiter had just explained how to eat them to Woody Bassett, the Traveler who ordered the clams. "I don't want anything to eat that I have to have OJT (on-the-job training) for," Varner said.

J. T. Rose regularly roomed with Varner on Traveler trips. He described Varner as "100 percent loyal" to Bill Clinton. Varner was

Senator Jay Bradford "in bed" with the Arkansas Education Association (Sid Johnson). From left to right are Ann Bradford Mourning, Jay Bradford, Mary Beth Frazer, Sid Johnson, and Wayne Gruber at the Super 8 Motel in Manchester, New Hampshire, 1992.

More togetherness and debriefing after a long day of campaigning. Shown left to right are Donna Malone, Charlie Varner, Lewis Frazer, J. T. Rose, and Woody Bassett in New Hampshire, 1992.

The Travelers debut their road show in New Hampshire, January 1992. From left to right are Margaret Compton, Charlie Varner, Dale Evans, Sheila Galbraith Bronfman, Percy Malone, Donna Malone, and J. T. Rose.

one of the people who was first up and last to quit when the Travelers were campaigning, Rose said. "A lot of people thought we were up there playing," he said. But the Travelers worked long, hard days, then came back to the hotel to unwind and plan the next day.

The Travelers, explained Patty Criner, were adults who had opinions and could talk knowledgably with the New Hampshire people, who ask penetrating questions. "I think the Travelers made a huge difference," she said, adding that people there were astounded at the Travelers' abilities, who they were, how smart they were, and that they represented such a cross-section of people who had given up time in their lives to be there.

7.
LOGISTICS

The Travelers were pretty well organized from the get-go, according to Sheila Bronfman, their leader. The organization they developed for New Hampshire worked elsewhere.

She and her leadership team planned who would be in which vans, assigning individuals to provide a mix of skills and backgrounds in each group. Typically, a van might have a teacher, a lawyer, a farmer, a state agency employee, a state legislator or other public official, a student, a retiree, a banker, a lobbyist, a heath care provider, and a business owner on board. They were of varying ages and income levels, but the common denominator was that they knew the candidate personally.

By mixing the different professions in a van, they knew they had a spokesperson for any issue that might come up, Sheila said. They tried to stay focused on the personal connections with Clinton, but many times had to talk issues, particularly in New Hampshire.

The campaign trusted the Travelers with daily talking points, which were sent to them on the road, and the Travelers tried to stay on message. But, as Sheila said, "The Travelers knew their stuff and were a wealth of knowledge on a variety of topics."

Once assigned a van, Travelers stayed together for the duration of a trip. It was all by design, intended to allow them to get to know each other better and develop camaraderie within the van and to learn the motto, "What happens in the van, stays in the van." Already cramped quarters were made worse because luggage was traveling with them from town to town.

Life in the vans, Sheila said, forced close relationships that led to such friendships. "You are living in the van," she said of the close quarters. "You're eating in the van, sleeping in the van. ... You get close when you're doing that." Plus, they talked to kill the time between stops, learning about each other's lives.

The drivers would get up extra early, get the vehicles fueled, and pull them around front. There was luggage to load on the cross-state trips when the Travelers were moving from town to town. The passengers would pile in. Women might be putting on makeup or fixing their hair. Van mates were in many ways like families.

That's why Sheila didn't want strangers riding with the Travelers. "You throw off the dynamics of that van when you suddenly stick a new person in it." That proved especially true on a Travelers' general election trip to South Dakota. The campaign field staff put someone in one of the vans with the Travelers.

The chemistry and the amount of space for each person would get thrown off when anyone new got aboard. What's worse, the campaign staffer who got into Wanda Northcutt's van kept trying to tell the Travelers what to do and how to do it.

Northcutt, a state representative from Stuttgart, was the van leader. She had "just had it" with the interloping staff member. The van stopped at an Indian reservation to campaign. When it was time to leave, she had her Travelers get in the van. Then she walked up to the young staffer and told him, "We're leaving you here. I hope you can get somebody to come get you." Bronfman was with other Travelers on the opposite side of the state. Wanda had notified her of the plan. Sheila told her to "do what she needed to do."

"The interloper didn't last long," said Bronfman, who explained that the vans were "safe havens" where Travelers could talk freely. Once in their vans, the Travelers could "yell and gripe and bitch about everything that goes on," she said. Then, when they got out, they would smile and turn on the Southern charm.

Van partners didn't have much trouble relating to each other. "Being the small, incestuous state that we are, everybody has some

Life on the road.

connection," Sheila said, either through the Democratic Party, their respective professions, family, or friends.

Mostly, they were there for a common goal. "We were in the midst of a presidential campaign for a friend," she said. "There is nothing like that. It wasn't for a candidate that we just happened to believe in and support. It was for a friend."

While Traveler trips were always fun, they were also challenging. The Travelers were dealing with the physical demands of long days of campaigning and the mix of personalities on a van. "Amazingly enough, we all got along most of the time," she said.

Bronfman recalled one rare "blowup" on a van in New Hampshire in 2008. Some strong personalities were involved and they were making life miserable for the van leader. Sheila solved the situation on a later trip by making the most vocal complainer a leader, which turned out extremely well. She also put into van rules that, if someone had a problem, he or she needed to take it up with the leader and not incite the rest of the van's riders.

For the most part, the Travelers followed Bronfman's strict lead. She knows of one vanload in 1992 that "went off kind of renegade," escaping to nearby Maine for a lobster dinner. "I did not find out about it until later, which was a good thing." Sheila was not happy about their taking time off. Ark Monroe, a Little Rock lawyer, and his wife, Nancy, were the leaders for the vanload of people who snuck off from campaigning to eat seafood. Bobby Hargraves, a Hot Springs lawyer, drove the renegade van. According to Ark, "It was like summer camp for adults. We had attorneys, doctors, congressional staffers, insurance agents, and housewives in our van. We did not follow instructions the day before the election and went to Portsmouth, New Hampshire, to campaign for Governor Clinton. He was campaigning in Portsmouth that day. We put up signs, knocked on doors, met the motorcade, and enjoyed a good lobster dinner in York, Maine, that night. For our good work, we were assigned to a polling place in New Hampshire very early the next morning. We had 100 percent attendance that morning to work the polling place and no complaining."

Sheila said, "It didn't happen again, not that I know of." At least no one else ever owned up to similar adventures.

The Travelers' schedules were so tight there really weren't many opportunities to tarry. The vans made bathroom breaks and stopped at night at convenience stores where the Travelers could load up on fruit and snacks. Mostly, they moved from destination to destination and tried never to burn daylight.

Travelers regularly snacked in the vans or got by on a fast-food stop for lunch. The usual van fare was cheese and crackers—and cookies, donated by Brent Bumpers. Unable to travel himself, Bumpers kept the Travelers stocked with Brent and Sam's cookies all over the United States. Not everything the Travelers snacked on was welcome in the van. Elmo Wolfe, a retiree from Fordyce, "Miss Elmo" to the Travelers, famously popped open a can of tuna for a snack. The fishy smell filled the van and caused some Travelers to ask Sheila to intervene.

The Travelers always managed to have dinner, although it might not come until eight or nine p.m., when Sheila would arrange for them to take over an available restaurant after walking neighborhoods or working phone banks. "That would be our time to tell war stories," Bronfman said, explaining that the evening outings were part of the plan to build camaraderie among the Travelers. The exchanges also let them learn what was working or not working with prospective voters. "You've got to have the fun. Or they won't want to go out and do it the next day," she said of the grueling pace. Having a bar and/or restaurant on the premises or nearby was a requirement for getting the Travelers' bookings.

Coordinating those people, where they went and what they did was Bronfman's primary job, although she also canvassed and campaigned

Leaders Bill Trice, Bob Ridgeway, and Richard Bronfman get up early to plan the day for the Travelers.

We are the Arkansas Travelers
Help us re-elect President Bill Clinton

We are all Arkansans who know President Bill Clinton. Some of us have known him since first grade, some since high school, some as a friend in our community, and all as a capable governor and president. All of us support his re-election because we know him to be honest, fair and an excellent leader. President Bill Clinton has been a good friend to us and to the American people and we want to tell the people of your great state that he is a man we are proud to know and proud to support.

We are working and retired men and women, small business owners, lawyers, teachers, homemakers, health care providers. We have taken time from our jobs and families to travel in support of our President.

We travel at our own expense and operate as volunteers. Thank you for the opportunity to ask for your support to re-elect our friend and president.

Re-elect Bill Clinton President
Paid for by Clinton Gore 96 Primary Committee, Inc.

The Travelers passed out hundreds of thousands of these cards with similar messages in 1992 and 1996.

along with them. Bronfman herself made fourteen Traveler trips for Bill Clinton and another four trips for Hillary Clinton, always serving as van leader when she did.

Her total count for Travelers is 521 with 452 who traveled for Bill Clinton and 141 for Hillary. Seventy-two traveled for both. Eighteen were Travelers in both the 1992 and 1996 elections for Bill Clinton and for Hillary's primary election run: Jay Bradford, Richard Bronfman, Sheila Bronfman, Charlie Cole Chaffin, Gail Goodrum, Jean Hervey, Elaine Johnson, Myra Jones, Susan Jones, Lorene Leder, Jan McQuary, Pat Morrow, Peggy Nabors, Sarah Jo Parker, Gregg Reep, Mary Anne Salmon, Sue White, and Pat Youngdahl.

Initially, Sheila was putting together the trips from Little Rock, inside the national campaign headquarters, where David Watkins, David Wilhelm, Mickey Kantor, and Craig Smith appreciated the abilities of these Clinton surrogates. Interaction with the field staff in New Hampshire proved altogether different.

When the New Hampshire field staff heard the Travelers were coming, Patty Criner said, "the staff just really didn't get it." They wanted to blow these people off; but the staffers were getting pressure from Sheila, who called constantly to say the Travelers were coming and wanted to know what the campaign wanted them to do. Patty remembers the reaction of the press secretary, who wanted to control the message coming out of the campaign. "What do you mean they want to be on the radio?" the staffer asked, when she learned the Travelers planned to offer themselves for interviews. The Travelers also wanted to meet with the *Union Leader*, the dominant newspaper, and otherwise interact directly with voters.

The staffers, Criner explained, were young and energetic and thought they knew more about campaigning for Clinton than these visiting Travelers could. Most of the young staff didn't know Clinton. Only two had ever met him, she said. "These are young people who worked in campaigns because they wanted a job in the White House," she said. "They didn't want to get hitched to a candidate who might go by the way early on."

Most of the Arkansas Travelers weren't shopping for jobs in the campaign or in a Clinton administration. They were there to help a friend.

The New Hampshire staff's protective stance proved common in campaign field staffs in other states, too, until they got to know the Travelers and what they could do to generate votes. "One thing about people in Arkansas who support a candidate," Patty volunteered, "is they never stop. They will work tirelessly."

She said the people of New Hampshire, too, had expected young college kids to be bused in to work in the campaign "because that's the way all presidential races were run." Bused-in students, mostly from Boston-area colleges, do have an impact, Criner said. Other campaigns had students on every street corner, wearing their candidate's T-shirts. "It was impressive," she said. "I didn't understand— until I learned that these students were bused in, T-shirts purchased and put on them." They would come in for an event but rotate around town to make their presence seem all the greater.

The Clinton campaign bused in young people from the Washington DC area later on, too; but the Arkansas Travelers were the campaign's surprise strength. They were different. "These people get out of cars and vans. They limp and they're fat and they're tall and they're short and they're old and they're public officials," Patty recalled, noting the makeup of the arriving Arkansans.

The New Hampshire people, she said, "were taken aback when they saw they were grown-ups." These Arkansas people had helped Clinton win elections before. They had worked with him and against him in his public life in Arkansas. Or, like Patty, they had literally grown up with him. Mostly, they cared enough about Clinton's candidacy to travel a long distance at their own expense to campaign for him in the cold and snow. It was that fact—and that they really knew their governor personally—that seemed to impress the New Hampshire voters the most.

Terry Shumaker, a key New Hampshire supporter, said he was amazed at how many loyal friends Clinton had, "how much I liked them all and how much they were like us." The Travelers, "quality people who put their lives on hold" to go there and stand up for Clinton, he said, were "pretty effective, pretty impressive."

These were days of limited technology. Communication was by phone or fax or the U.S. mail. The term "snail mail" hadn't been invented yet. Bronfman said they could print a few things from a computer but mostly volunteers would copy and collate information for the Travelers. On-the-road communication to Bronfman in the 1992 primary came by pager. She would get a page and stop to find a landline. "That was our communication," she said. By the general election, Bronfman had a bulky, mobile "bag phone" used primarily to reach people with landlines at headquarters or Traveler destinations.

On a general election trip to North Carolina in 1992, Travelers actually waited for delivery of a "cellular phone." The phone was significant enough to be reported to Sheila by Kirkley Thomas, an Arkansan then working in Washington DC for a Senate committee. The campaign was supposed to have arranged delivery but it wasn't waiting for them at a scheduled stop in Raleigh. Instead, Traveler Laura Bowen Wills, formerly of Little Rock, rented a phone and had it shipped by FedEx to their next stop in Asheville. In addition to Kirkley and Laura, other DC residents on the trip the weekend before the November vote were Arkansas natives Johnna Thomas, Jennifer Rhodes, Eldridge Bowen, and Brynda Pappas. Dona O'Bannon, who attended Georgetown with Bill and Jay Howell, joined them for the trip.

Arranging for another phone, however rare it was to have one, was evidence of another Traveler trait. If they encountered any kind of problem, they just dealt with it and were willing to use their own money to do it.

CITIZEN-TIMES

STEVE DIXON/CITIZEN-TIMES

Members of the "Arkansas Travelers" rolled into Asheville Friday to rally support for Bill Clinton. They are, from left: kneeling, Kirkley Thomas and Eldridge Bowen; standing, Jennifer Rhodes, Johnna Thomas, Laura Bowen, Dona O'Bannon, Brynda Pappas and Jay Howell.

Clinton friends spread their message via van

'Arkansas Travelers' roam country telling why they support candidate

By Clarke Morrison
STAFF WRITER

Eight of presidential hopeful Bill Clinton's friends rolled into Asheville in a van Friday evening to tell why he is the best man to lead the country.

There are about 300 Arkansas Travelers, she said. They break into groups and head out for four day stints in about three states at a time. The eight who arrived in Asheville Friday spent the past two days talking to people in Ra-

These North Carolina Travelers picked up more free media. On many occasions the Travelers got front-page play. (Story by Clarke Morrison and photo by Steve Dixon. Copyright 2000 by Asheville, NC *Citizen-Times*. Reprinted with permission.)

Van travel proved difficult at times. Once, in New Hampshire campaigning for Hillary, Wes Cottrell, a Rogers lawyer, called Sheila to say his van had run out of gas and asked her to come get him. She couldn't. He didn't know where he was. Cottrell ended up walking to find a landmark and then summoned AAA for help.

The van driven in 2008 by Gilbert Cornwell got stuck in the deep New Hampshire snow. He didn't want to call Sheila for help, knowing he would never live it down, but he finally did and all the Travelers pushed the van out of the front yard it was in and onto the road.

Vincent Insalaco got his van stuck in a National Forest in 2008 after following a campaign staffer who was unfamiliar with the area to a deserted location.

In Dallas, during the Hillary campaign, one of the vans got hit. It was drivable but not fit to ride in, so they stacked the Travelers into the remaining vans and went on until another van could be located. Later the same day another van was hit in the parking lot at an event the Travelers were working. Some days it didn't pay to get out of bed, but the Travelers did.

From the days of the earliest Traveler trips, the campaign would provide briefing books about a state, plus talking points. Bronfman would put those and her rules for Travelers into packets that would not be distributed until departing Travelers got to the airport. There were lots of rules, the first of which was that Travelers had to trust Bronfman with credit card and Social Security numbers, so she could book their flights and rooms and get security clearance when necessary.

"The rule was, 'You don't give me your card number, you're not going,'" Sheila said. New Hampshire, the first of the Traveler trips, was a little different because so many people showed up. Other trips were totally booked by Bronfman and her volunteers, working with Steve Davison of Worldwide Travel in Little Rock. Airlines worked well with the Travelers, she said, booking them on the same flights.

They needed to arrive at their destination at the same time, she said, so they could load up the vans and get on their way as soon as they landed. Everyone flew out of Little Rock, Fayetteville, or Memphis, and Davison helped match up their arrivals and departures.

Rooms were booked like a tour group might book them, with Traveler volunteers pairing roommates or assigning them if people had no preference or wanted smoking or nonsmoking roommates. "It took a lot of coordination," Sheila said. The motels, chosen for their affordability, welcomed them on their marquees and would have keys ready for quick check-in. Travelers might not know who their roommate would be nor what van they would be in until they got to the airport.

"All they knew was when to show up at the airport," Bronfman said. That's when they got their tickets, a packet, and a campaign button identifying them as a Traveler.

The practice of providing information on a need-to-know basis developed early on. The Travelers' assignments were fluid, as were the talking points from the campaign. Plans changed rapidly and the leaders had to adapt. Unless they arrived at a locale late at night, Bronfman said they'd have the vans ready to roll immediately.

Morning came early for the Travelers, who sometimes left as early as four a.m. to get to a polling place when it opened or to make a shift change at a manufacturing plant gate. Every van had an assigned leader and two assigned drivers. Those people collectively provided the leadership team for each trip. They met late at night or early in the morning to plan their routes and adapt to new instructions.

A regular order of business was media contact. They carried a simple, fill-in-the-blank news release and a Polaroid camera wherever they went. When they hit a town, they'd find an easily recognizable location or they would stand with local people, for example, on the town square to take a picture, fill in the blanks on the news release and hand-carry the package to the local newspapers.

In 1992, there were more daily and weekly community newspapers and the Travelers got tons of free media everywhere they went. The field staffs in the various states began to see what the Travelers could generate for them.

The Travelers also attracted the attention of reporters and television crews, particularly in New Hampshire, where they would follow the Travelers from door to door, listening to their pitches on behalf of their friend's candidacy. "We were an anomaly," Bronfman said. "We were not from there. We didn't talk like those people." New Hampshirites liked hearing the Travelers' ever-thickening Southern drawls, she said.

In New Hampshire, after long days of retail politicking, the Travelers would go to the town hall meetings where Clinton would be scheduled to speak. Outside, in the cold New Hampshire evenings, they formed a human rope line on both sides of the walkway, shaking hands, saying hello and welcoming the attendees and volunteering to answer questions afterward. Sometimes they'd recognize people they had met while canvassing. Those people were amazed to see that Travelers who had worked all day made the rallies, too.

Early on in New Hampshire, Bronfman found a way to get the Travelers' quick attention when they were dispersed in a crowd. It was, as one Traveler called it, "that blasted whistle." Sheila credited her husband, Richard, with suggesting she use a coach's whistle, which even Richard admits "could be irritating." She gave some van leaders whistles, too, but it was the one Sheila wore on a rope around her neck that grew in infamy. If the Travelers heard the whistle, she said, "they knew to come, that the van was leaving or something had happened." They could hear the whistle's blast even if they were spread out on a town square or in some crowded venue.

"They all make fun of it. They all said they hated it," Bronfman said. But it worked. The whistle was also the source of humor. One time Travelers Donna and Percy Malone bought Sheila a silver whistle from Tiffany's in New York. It didn't have the sound-producing "pea" inside and made no noise. The Malones presented it to an unsuspecting Sheila in front of the Travelers, who got a good laugh when she tried to blow it.

On a trip to Kentucky and Tennessee in 1996, Traveler Peggy Nabors made a late-night trip to a discount store and bought enough plastic whistles to outfit a busload of Travelers. "They all blew whistles when I got on the bus the next morning after what had been a very late night," said Bronfman. Even though the ear-splitting sound didn't feel good, she said, "That was funny."

Sheila still has the infamous whistle, which is part of the exhibit displayed in the Clinton presidential library to honor the Travelers.

"The rule was, when the whistle blew, get back in the van," Bronfman said. "Or we'd leave them." It wasn't an idle threat. The Travelers routinely had tight schedules and needed to get to a subsequent destination. "We couldn't mess up and miss the next event where someone was waiting on us," Sheila explained. So, on several occasions they left a few stragglers to their own devices to get to the next stop.

The Travelers soon learned to get back to the vans on time.

Fred Knight of Little Rock listed among the most difficult challenges for Travelers "long hours, crowded buses and vans, stale air (if you get my drift), no food or, even worse, bad food, that damn whistle and the lady attached to it, and did I mention long hours?" Others had similar comments, but behind them all is admiration for Sheila's ability to get the most from them all.

Sheila gets more respect from her fellow Travelers than she may realize.

Don Bishop of Harrison called her whistle "the clarion call to action." For Dee Pryor of Washington DC, it was a symbol of the spirit of the Travelers, which he described as "hordes of Arkies running around in the snow led by a woman blowing a whistle."

Pryor also said that, under Sheila's command and driving schedule, he learned he could accomplish far more than he thought he was capable of. The experience led him to join President Clinton's advance team. That work was easy, he said, after working for Sheila.

Jeff Mitchell of Fayetteville also talked admiringly of Sheila's example. "Sheila instilled in us the need to do it now, to act in the present because there always was more ahead of us to do. There's not a procrastinating bone in her body," he said, adding that she is "able to lead like nobody else."

She could apparently convince the Travelers to do most anything. When she called Joel Buckner, he'd answer the phone, saying, "I'm not going to go." They'd argue a while, then she'd tell him she'd see him at the airport, reminding him she had his credit card and had booked his flight. Joel would answer that he'd see her there.

Joe Purvis remembers hitting the bed at the end of eighteen-hour days, knowing that the Travelers had done everything they could that day for their friend Bill. The pace was hard but they always felt there were just a few more folks to reach. "It was one of the greatest experiences of my life, and Sheila was the perfect person to ramrod the whole thing."

8.

TRAVELER TECHNIQUES

Personal contact was at the heart of the retail politics that the Arkansas Travelers practiced. It's the way campaigns are done in Arkansas but not, apparently, elsewhere.

"Not one other state did politics like we do in Arkansas," said Mary Anne Salmon, herself an elected state senator and veteran campaigner. Mary Anne noted the Arkansas emphasis on one-on-one contact with voters, directly asking for their votes. Campaigns in other states seemed more focused, she said, on use of media and phone banking.

Rose Crane of Little Rock, who traveled two states in 1992 for Bill and four states in 2008 for Hillary, was the one who described what the Travelers did as "democracy in action." The Travelers were willing "to do whatever it took" to promote both the Clintons' candidacies. Cleverly, Crane and Wanda Northcutt of Stuttgart once stuck their feet in a Fresno fountain to draw attention from a California newspaper photographer. Sure enough, the photo and, more important, a reference to Clinton's campaign, landed in the paper. A laughing Crane had her Clinton campaign sign conveniently displayed on her lap. The Travelers would do just about anything to bring attention to the campaign.

They stopped anywhere they spotted a radio station, went inside, and presented themselves for interviews, which were usually granted. And they played to television cameras when that opportunity arose.

They were usually adorned with a variety of campaign buttons, the most noticeable the ones that identified them as Arkansas Travelers. The buttons changed with elections. In 1992, the

Clinton volunteers dip into Fresno

■ The volunteers for Arkansas Gov. Bill Clinton have become a close-knit group while campaigning for the Democratic front-runner.

By Jim Boren
The Fresno Bee

Two dozen "Arkansas Travelers" descended on Fresno Friday in an effort to persuade Valley voters to support their governor in Tuesday's Democratic primary.

The volunteers for Democratic front-runner Bill Clinton will blanket the state in the last days of the California campaign. In Courthouse Park on Friday afternoon, they didn't let anyone get by without offering them Clinton literature.

ELECTION '92
THE PRESIDENCY

One volunteer was Rose Crane, who has known Clinton since they were in third grade at Ramble Elementary School in Hot Springs, Ark.

"I know Bill Clinton, and I believe in Bill Clinton," she said. "He has the ability to represent all people."

The Arkansas Travelers have become a close-knit group during the campaign and when Crane and Wanda Northcutt, an Arkansas state representative, spotted the fountain in front of Courthouse Park, they both had the same idea.

Pulling off their shoes, they cooled their feet in the fountain.

Faye Rodgers, who runs a jewelry store in Clinton, Ark., continued to hand out literature.

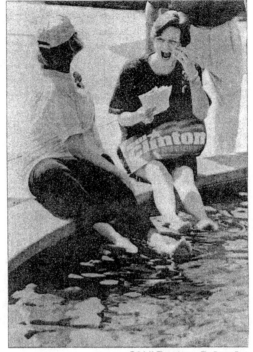

Ralph V. Thronebery — The Fresno Bee

Political dabbling. Rose Crane, left, and Wanda Northcutt take a break from their crusade to cool their feet in the courthouse fountain.

For the past 10 years, she's been Clinton's Van Buren County chairwoman, and she said the nation needs his leadership.

Little Rock lawyer Sam Perroni said Arkansas residents have learned over the years that Clinton cares about them and has worked to improve their state.

"Bill Clinton has been a good friend, and we want to tell the people of California that he is a man we are proud to know and proud to support as the Democratic candidate for president," the travelers say in the literature they hand out.

Sheila Bronfman of Little Rock said the Arkansas Travel-

ers, who participate at their own expense, have been campaigning for Clinton since the New Hampshire primary.

The members change depending on when they can get time off from their jobs.

The travelers flew into Los Angeles on Thursday and drove in rented vans to Bakersfield where they campaigned.

They arrived in Fresno Friday and will campaign today in the Tower district and downtown before heading for Southern California.

Bronfman said they have received a positive reception in the Valley where there is a large concern over the economy and jobs.

In California Rose Crane and Representative Wanda Northcutt stuck their feet in a fountain to gain press attention. (Story by Jim Boren and photo by Ralph V. Thronebery. Copyright by *The Fresno Bee*. Reprinted with permission.)

Travelers wore campaign pins that said, "Ask Me About My Governor," and other buttons that designated them as Arkansas Travelers in New Hampshire and all of the other primary and general election states. For the reelection campaign four years later, their buttons read, "I'm an Arkansas Traveler for President Bill Clinton." In Hillary's campaign, the message was "I'm an Arkansas Traveler, Hillary for President."

Traveler buttons, which were strictly limited, are now collectibles for political junkies. A rare button has brought as much as $1,000 from a collector, according to Phil Ross, editor of *The Arkansas Traveler*, the official newsletter of Clinton political item collectors, and an expert on political memorabilia. All the Traveler buttons, he said, have a value to the right collector.

Polling places were another frequent work site for Travelers on election days in the various states. Travelers tried to persuade voters on the way in to support one or the other Clinton and got feedback from the voters as they exited the polls. Generally, their presence won votes where the hospitable Travelers worked.

At a polling place in downtown Manchester, New Hampshire, Henry Woods, a Hot Springs native who was living in Washington DC, and state Senator Charlie Cole Chaffin of Benton talked with an elderly man who saw their signs and stopped to tell them, "Bill's been a bad boy." On the way out of the polling place, he surprised them. "But not that bad," the old man said with a wink and a laugh. They recorded him as a "yes" vote.

Every Traveler had a set spiel to personalize the conversation with voters he or she individually approached either at the doorways of their homes and businesses or in public places. They all mentioned they were from Arkansas and had paid their own way, a point the Travelers discovered mattered to the people they visited in all states but especially the more distant ones.

The teachers would tell voters they were teachers, focusing on Clinton's education record. The elected officials usually gave their offices. Chaffin, who introduced herself as a state senator, remembers voters being impressed by her office, so she would point across the street to other Travelers and say, "Yes, and that man is the president pro tem of the senate and that man is the speaker of the house of representatives."

Some other Travelers similarly mentioned their professions or businesses. Pharmacist Reid Holiman of Springdale, also a state senator, often visited pharmacies on the road and mentioned how Clinton understood pharmacies' problems.

All of the Travelers tried to answer any questions potential voters asked. Allen Bird, a Little Rock lawyer, reported an extra effort by his wife, Sherry, a marketing director, to answer an odd question about Bill. Some months before, President Bush was quoted as saying he didn't like broccoli. The voter asked Sherry how Clinton felt about Pease, meaning Pease Air Force Base in New Hampshire, scheduled to be closed. Sherry thought the question was about the vegetable. It seemed odd to her, but she said she thought Bill did like peas and went to check with Allen. When she got back, the voter explained what he meant.

Different approaches worked best for different Travelers when they encountered potential voters. Some opened with a brief, straightforward line. "Hi, I'm Donna Kay. I want you to vote for Bill Clinton," said Donna Kay Yeargan of Foreman, whose accent probably tipped off voters that she was from Arkansas. Others fleshed out what they said when a new door opened. "Hello. My name is Jean Hervey. Let me tell you about my personal experience with Bill Clinton. I have known him since the early '70s and this is what he has done for the state of Arkansas. If he can do this for us, think about what he can do for this country if you will just give him a chance," said Hervey, a union representative from Plumerville.

Travelers developed their own ways to counter misconceptions about Arkansas and the Clintons.

Randy and Gail Goodrum, for example, carried a book of Tim Ernst's photographs of Arkansas with them. The photography shows Arkansas as a gorgeous state, rather than a "swamp," as the Bush campaign had depicted Arkansas, she said. David Leopoulos also carried pictures. His were of Arkansas get-togethers on Thanksgiving, Christmas and the Fourth of July with the Clintons and other family friends. "Those pictures said it all," confirming that the Clintons were "regular people," he said.

Although their approaches varied, the Travelers typically told voters their names, hometowns and why they had traveled so far to campaign, then asked for time to talk about the Bill and Hillary Clinton they knew personally. Woody Bassett, a Fayetteville lawyer, said many voters asked him about Bill Clinton's character. "That always opened up the door for me to vouch for his character and tell them, while he wasn't perfect and had made some mistakes, his was overall a life well lived and he truly cared about people," said Bassett. "Most people were friendly and receptive, but of course a few were not."

The best evidence of the latter may have been on a Chicago street when a passenger spat on Rick Watkins, a businessman from Little Rock. The Travelers were doing a "honk and wave" when a yellow cab pulled up. Watkins held his sign up to the passenger door "and got spit on," he said. Watkins smiled, gave them the thumbs up so the car behind would think it was a positive encounter and went on to the next potential voter, just like he said Sheila taught him.

Several Travelers remembered the interest in their Southern accents, particularly when they campaigned in New Hampshire or other Northern states. North Little Rock Mayor Patrick Henry Hays said some seemed less interested in what he was saying about Hillary than in his accent. Another Traveler, Margie Alsbrook, a lawyer from Springdale, admitted she "found it helps if the you dial up the twang quite a bit when you are in the North."

Repeating themselves over and over challenged the Travelers. "I taught myself to smile and show morning energy even when the day was winding down and I was wearing thin," said Dorothy Preslar, who hooked up with the Travelers in New Hampshire in 1992 and traveled out of Washington DC.

The Arkansas Travelers labeled the different techniques they perfected to promote Clinton's candidacy. The basic approaches were "honk and wave," "grin and spin," "knock and drop" or "walk and talk."

"Honk and wave" involved having Travelers stand on street corners or highway overpasses, waving Clinton campaign signs and soliciting passing drivers to honk their car horns. It was an attention-getting device the Travelers frequently used during commuting hours, regardless of weather.

"Grin and spin" was the shorthand description of what Travelers did on town squares, in shopping malls, or on campaign rope lines, where they sought out potential voters. The goal was to smile and talk about what Clinton had done for Arkansas and what the Travelers thought he could do for the country.

Canvassing was nicknamed "knock and drop" or "walk and talk" because the intent was to knock on doors in neighborhoods, visit with those who were home, and leave campaign literature, the Travelers' own campaign card, or videotapes for the occupants.

The Travelers distributed hundreds of thousands of pieces of campaign literature and videotapes over the three campaigns.

Broad distribution of videotapes was a new concept to presidential campaigning. As Dale Evans, the Fayetteville lawyer who was heavily involved in get-out-the-vote efforts in New Hampshire, explained, the videotapes were inexpensive, maybe $1.25 each, and the campaign had free labor—the Arkansas Travelers and a couple of hundred young adults who came in from Washington DC and elsewhere—to carry them to voters in New Hampshire.

"You couldn't put a piece of four-color mail in (a voter's) hands as cheaply," he said, asserting that the videos could snag a few minutes of a voter's time while a mail piece might get only seconds. Plus, he said, the video message was effective, delivered by Bill Clinton directly into the camera. Prospective voters could view the videos in their own homes and hear Clinton one on one. "When he looked you in the eye, you got the sense that he was talking to you," Evans said. "That was one of his magical traits."

For "knock and drop" outings, a van driver, with an even number of passengers, usually twelve or fourteen Travelers, would drop two at a time at the end of long streets in a targeted neighborhood. The team would work opposite sides of the street and be picked up later after the van driver had dropped all the teams on different streets. They worked a grid pattern, Sheila explained, with each team leapfrogging to another street after the van drivers picked them up on a return round.

"You can knock out a huge area if you do it this way," she said, explaining that they worked from maps the campaign field staff provided them. That, too, presented occasional problems since the field staff wasn't necessarily familiar with the states they staffed. Often, Travelers got lost looking for staff-directed destinations.

Van drivers generally worked out where they were going to go and what pattern would be followed. Canvassing in pairs, Bronfman said, created a competition between partners on their respective sides of the street. But it also allowed them to keep an eye on each other for safety's sake. The problem came, she said, when the friendlier Travelers got invited inside for coffee or hot chocolate and a prolonged visit. They couldn't stay in the homes for long because their partners would be out in the cold, worried—or jealous. Fairly often, a Traveler got separated from the group. More often than not, they had lingered too long in a warm New Hampshire home.

The most alarming separation was when a van driver couldn't locate Bill Gaddy, a Little Rock lawyer, after dark in a cold New Hampshire neighborhood. Remember, this was 1992 and they had no personal communication devices to summon help.

Larry Vaught, another Little Rock lawyer, was driving the van loaded with Central Arkansas friends. Joel Buckner and Larry Crane got out of the van with Gaddy to work a three-to-four block area in the suburbs of Nashua. They were to be at their pickup points in two hours. Snow fell unabated for the whole two hours as the Travelers trudged through the neighborhoods. When the van returned, Buckner got in, joining Judy Gaddy, Bill's wife, among others. "They kept circling looking for Bill. ... It was in the low teens and dropping."

"I always go one joke too far," Buckner said. "I told Judy Gaddy there is bad news and good news. Your husband is going to freeze to death and you will be a rich widow." She was not amused. Apparently, the van leader or driver had misplaced the map that showed Gaddy's rendezvous point, where he stood for another hour watching for the van, miserably cold and badly needing a bathroom break. "Just before I was about to water a frozen lawn," Gaddy said, "the van finally rescued me."

State Representative Ernest Cunningham of Helena found himself in a similar situation. He stayed too long in one New Hampshire home and missed the van when it came by to pick him up. He waited, had the same sense of urgency Gaddy experienced before the van returned, and went behind a bush. His van, like Gaddy's, came to the rescue just in time.

J. T. Rose of Rogers recalled being invited into one house in New Hampshire to talk with five or six nuns. They were among the few who invited him inside, Rose said, while the women Travelers he was often paired with got frequent offers of coffee and hot chocolate as they canvassed neighborhoods.

And the Travelers tell a story on Charlie Varner of Fort Smith who stayed overlong in one New Hampshire home. It turned out there were three older sisters living there, charmed enough by Varner to change their commitment from former California Governor Jerry Brown to Bill Clinton.

The Travelers found local Wal-Marts to be good sites to "grin and spin." J. T. Rose, being from Rogers, which is close to Bentonville, home of Wal-Mart, came up with a convenient spiel to persuade Wal-Mart managers to let the Travelers campaign at their stores. Whenever the Travelers were told not to do so, he'd ask to speak to the manager, and then flash his Arkansas driver's license and say he was from Bentonville. "I just talked to Mr. Sam Walton and he said it's OK," Rose would say. If the manager still resisted, Rose would start writing down what he said was Mr. Sam's phone number so the manager could call him up and ask. "I knew the area code and the first three numbers," Rose said. He made up the last four digits but assured the manager that Mr. Sam would be home to answer the phone. One manager after another let the Travelers campaign outside Wal-Mart. Sam Walton, of course, had no idea what the Travelers were doing and probably wouldn't have agreed to let them approach his customers. But Rose's bluff worked.

Sometimes, the Travelers were surprised by what they saw behind the doors they knocked on. Marci Riggs of Little Rock had her biggest surprise at a door in Kentucky. "I knocked on a door and, when it opened, it was a naked man pulling up his pants." Riggs said she covered her eyes and pushed literature toward him. Unfortunately, she was not the only female Traveler to encounter nakedness. Linda Lou Moore, a Paragould Traveler, also had a "buck naked" man answer a door, this one in Texas.

"Not to be deterred," she said, "and not wanting to lose a vote, I kept eye contact." She explained she was an Arkansas Traveler for Hillary and handed him literature. He promised to vote for Hillary.

Ann Henderson Gilbert of Little Rock had a memorable encounter in Texas. "I knocked on a door and waited on the porch. It opened suddenly, and out rushed two huge dogs and a man wielding a running chain saw over his head," she said. "I jumped and said, 'That's a first!' He turned off the motor and said, 'Sorry, I thought you were someone else.'" She stayed just long enough to ask for his vote.

Numerous Travelers noted the number of dogs they encountered at Texas homes. Terry Shumaker, a New Hampshire lawyer who joined the Travelers to campaign for Hillary in Texas, remembered going door-to-door in Longview and "wondering if behind every door and barking dog was someone with a gun who hated Hillary." To his surprise, he said the people there were "very friendly" and many said they intended to vote for her.

Another surprise lurked behind a door when Rush Limbaugh's uncle greeted Randy Laverty's knock on Limbaugh's door in Cape Girardeau, Missouri. He politely told Randy he was at the wrong house.

They had been plainly warned, but the Arkansas Travelers were still surprised by how cold New Hampshire was.

A memo from Sheila cautioned them, "You will be working outdoors in snow, wind, etc. at an average temperature of 10 degrees. You will need to wear insulated, waterproof boots (not water repellant), wool socks, thermal underwear (two pairs at once), ski parkas, sweaters, hats, gloves, earmuffs and layered clothing." She told the cold-natured ones to add even more and advised them to bring sunglasses, moisturizer, and sunblock due to the snow glare and harsh winds. They knew conditions would be tough and the schedules difficult. Sheila's memo plainly warned them that their days would start early and end late and not include regular meal breaks. In other words, these Travelers, who included people from all walks of life, should expect to be cold and wet, hungry and tired.

The Arkansas people went to New Hampshire anyway and most scheduled future trips to campaign. Perhaps the most important instruction to the Travelers was to remember that they would at all times be representing Governor Clinton and the state of Arkansas. They were to wear their buttons identifying themselves as Clinton supporters and as Arkansas Travelers and to introduce themselves as being from Arkansas. "A gracious Arkansas manner with all will reflect proudly on you, our state and, of course, the Clinton for President campaign," Sheila wrote.

As Bronfman was rallying people in Arkansas for the New Hampshire campaign, Henry Woods was doing much the same in Washington DC, recruiting Travelers for Bronfman. Woods, an Arkansan who worked on Capitol Hill for Senators David Pryor and Dale Bumpers, first worked for Clinton in his 1974 congressional race. Active in the Arkansas State Society, a social organization for Arkansans living and working in metropolitan DC, Woods recruited society members and Capitol Hill interns with whom he worked to campaign for Clinton.

A flyer he put out described the planned outing for the weekend before the primary. The schedule had participants leaving Washington in a caravan of vans on Friday evening for Manchester, New Hampshire. After "a nap and continental breakfast," he promised four days of hard work and a return road trip "after the victory party" on primary night. Their activities were to include door-to-door canvassing, phone banking, mall visits, rush-hour intersection rallies, sign waving, crowd packing at Clinton events, poll watching, "and anything else that comes up in the heat of the campaign." Plus, he said each had to pay seventy dollars "for this four-day, no-frills New Hampshire winter wonderland extravaganza." The charge covered the van trip and a room with three others at the Super 8, where Woods said "angels from Arkansas" would host hospitality suites with snacks and drinks "to keep us going." Otherwise, he said, they'd be on a fast-food diet.

"If you are allergic to the harsh cold, this may not be for you," Woods warned. "Think of a Razorback game played in Fayetteville in late afternoon in early December in a high wind and snowstorm. This is New Hampshire every day this time of year." Henry's warning didn't deter transplanted Arkansans from loading up for the caravan to New Hampshire to campaign for a fellow Arkansan.

The Travelers weren't without mishaps during their travels. There were frequent fire alarms in the motels where they stayed, and Traveler drivers sometimes picked up traffic tickets. Only one of the fire alarms proved to be a fire. That came in New Hampshire in 2008, when Travelers were working for Hillary Clinton. Most were out of the hotel and didn't learn until later that there had been a fire.

Donna Malone remembers that her husband, Percy, had first smelled a fire in their New Hampshire hotel. He notified management and the Malones went on to campaign with other Travelers. "It was worse than we thought and guess where we heard that?" she asked. "On the phone from Arkansas." They rushed back, got their clothes out of the room and into their SUV and returned to campaigning.

Mary Anne Salmon, a van leader during that Hillary trip, recalls that Sheila called her to tell her about the fire. "Don't say anything until I tell you to," Bronfman told her. Salmon said her crew just kept working until they finished their canvassing assignment and even worked a rally before heading back to the hotel. There was no need to quit campaigning until the fire marshal would let them back in.

Several Traveler drivers were lead-footed. A few talked their way out of tickets but others paid.

Bill Wiedower, a Little Rock architect, was driving a van in Colorado. Bad weather had delayed the Travelers' arrival, and they spent the first day there trying to catch up. Somewhere between Aspen and Glenwood Springs, a local sheriff's deputy stopped the van, which was covered with campaign signs. The young deputy, estimated by Wiedower to be no more than twenty-one, asked, "Who is Bill Clinton?" "We gave him our best Clinton speech and tried to

TRAVEL TIPS FOR TRAVELERS
PLEASE READ THE FOLLOWING VERY CAREFULLY

In order to make this the most enjoyable time that you have ever had working your buns off and pushing yourselves to complete exhaustion, we have compiled the following list of tips and HARD FAST RULES

1. You will be assigned a van leader and told which travelers will be traveling in which van.

2. Only the van leaders have copies of the schedules. Schedules cast in concrete are a luxury that we DO NOT HAVE. Our schedules can change so many times during a trip that it would be a waste of time and paper to give everyone a copy. BE READY TO GO WITH THE FLOW. Sometimes, you may not understand why you are being asked to do things a certain way -- just bear in mind that it may be due to media considerations or other Campaign directives. Just go with it because it is the best for our President and friend.

3. TIME SCHEDULES -- when we give you a time to leave, that means "checked out" ," ready to go"," sitting in the van", or "sitting in the motel lobby " time. It does NOT mean "I'm thinking about checking out " time or "just getting ready to have breakfast" time. Please cooperate with our time schedules.

4. EATING -- We don't get to eat very often. If breakfast is a necessity, then it is your responsibility to get up early enough to eat and be ready to go at the departure time. We have sporadic (if at all) lunch stops and late, late dinner times. If you must eat frequently , then you will need to carry non- perishable snacks on the van with you. RESTAURANT STOPS - When we stop at truck stops or rest stops, it is for the purpose of working the tables and not for eating or getting coffee. We do not have time for people to get coffee and then stand in long lines to pay for it. Again let me say that if you need to eat frequently, then you will need to carry non-perishable snacks on the van with you.

5. SPEAKING - When a town is reached, the VAN LEADER will assign the spokespersons to deal with the local media connections. The rest of us will hit the town squares, malls, etc. Please remember the following: WE ARE NOT HERE TO TALK ISSUES -- WE ARE HERE TO TALK ABOUT BILL CLINTON AS A FRIEND AND AS OUR GOVERNOR. WE ARE HERE TO HELP ADDRESS THE CHARACTER AND TRUST ISSUES BECAUSE OF OUR FRIENDSHIP WITH THE BILL AND HILLARY. WE ARE ALSO HERE TO TALK ABOUT THE ARKANSAS TRAVELERS ,SO PLEASE:

Let your VAN LEADER deal with guiding people to the substantive issue folks in each van. Please read the back of your Arkansas Traveler card and know and

The Infamous Traveler Rules

understand what it says about who we are, what we are doing, paying our own way, and that Travelers may be are out in other states at the same time we are here . When you are talking about the Travelers, please confine your remarks to the Travelers as a whole and this particular trip. Do not expound on how many trips you have participated in or how much money you have spent or are spending. If someone asks you a question that you cannot answer, please just say "I don't know", ask your VAN LEADER for someone who can answer the question.

6. REPRESENTING ARKANSAS --- Remember that from the moment we arrive at the airport until we land safely back home -- we represent the state of ARKANSAS ,as well as , the Governor and First Lady. With that in mind, Please, please, please : DO NOT COMPLAIN ABOUT FOOD, LODGING OR SERVICE,
DO NOT BE RUDE OR CURT WITH ANY OF THE SERVICE PEOPLE TELEPHONE OPERATORS, ETC **EVERY PERSON WE COME IN CONTACT WITH IS A POTENTIAL CLINTON VOTER.** BE NICE TO REPUBLICANS SUPPORTERS OF OTHER CANDIDATES. THE BEST REPLY TO A REPUBLICAN IS "AT LEAST YOU ARE GOING TO VOTE"

7. I can promise you that your days will be long , you will be extremely tired, you will be in a bad mood at least one time during this trip. I can also promise you that at least one person will get on your nerves (it may well be your van leader.) . If you have a problem please, for the sake of unity and our mission -- take it up with Sheila, or your van leader. I can also promise you that this will be one of the most rewarding times of your life and when victory comes in November, it will be all the sweeter because of your participation in the campaign as an Arkansas Traveler.

THANK YOU FOR YOUR TIME AND EFFORTS ON BEHALF OF GOVERNOR BILL CLINTON AND FIRST LADY HILLARY RODHAM CLINTON.

joke around with him about giving us a speeding ticket while we were on a mission of such importance, but he gave us one anyway," Wiedower said. He said he really didn't mind getting a ticket with "such historic merit."

Dale Evans, a Fayetteville lawyer, was driving a van on a California freeway and crossed traffic to get to an off ramp. He was ticketed for improper lane change and posted the bond but didn't really think he had done anything wrong. When Evans got home, he wrote the scenario down and sent it to the judge, explaining he was unfamiliar with the road and was in the right lane, if only briefly. "I guess name-dropping helped. He sent my money back."

Among the mishaps Travelers still laugh about was when Charlie Varner was at the wheel of a van that kept getting lost. The Travelers found themselves in a lumber yard, with Varner driving between rows of stacked two-by-fours and other lumber, unsure how to get out. "No, Charlie, no," they yelled. Charlie, who had a hearing problem, misunderstood. He thought they said, "Go, Charlie, go." He sped up, circling the wood stacks, and sent those Travelers to the van floor, rolling in laughter.

Varner got them lost again late one night after an event in New Hampshire. They ended up at a highway toll booth. Although he asked for directions, he also wanted to know how late the booth would be open. The booth operator asked why. Varner said he expected to be back several times as he tried to find the way back to the Super 8.

9.

THE ROUGH STRETCH

The Clinton campaign experienced its darkest days in New Hampshire. The candidate was under attack on multiple fronts. Gennifer Flowers, an Arkansas woman who produced an audio tape of a phone call from Clinton, claimed they had a twelve-year affair. There were questions, too, about his military draft status and an infamous "I didn't inhale" quote regarding marijuana use while a student in England.

Dale Evans, working in the New Hampshire headquarters, helped to track probable votes and could stay atop Clinton's changing fortunes. A public labor union in nearby Boston maintained a thirty-five-person phone bank, making daily calls to New Hampshire's likely voters. Volunteers walking neighborhoods similarly reported results from canvassing. All the data was coded and scanned into a computer providing daily tracking for the campaign, Evans said. The software was high-tech for the time. Plus, the campaign was getting affirming poll results from various sources.

Before most of the Travelers arrived, Clinton was holding at eighteen percent in the crowded field of Democrats. He had debuted in single digits in the race, but was steadily gaining ground, according to Evans. Then the Gennifer Flowers story broke. Surprisingly, said Evans, "It didn't change a thing." Clinton's share stayed at eighteen percent and even rose to twenty-two percent as that situation calmed, he said. Soon, however, when questions about Clinton and the draft surfaced, his share "dropped like a rock, down to twelve percent," Evans said.

By then, the Travelers were filtering into New Hampshire in greater numbers. Some arrived on their own; others came when called.

Both Bill and Hillary Clinton wanted their Arkansas friends in New Hampshire, according to Evans. They instructed Bronfman and the others to "get everybody you can."

Jan McQuary remembers being on a cold ski slope passing out campaign literature when Sheila got the news about Gennifer Flowers. The press had heard it from Sheffield Nelson, an Arkansas Republican and longtime foe of Clinton, who was on New Hampshire radio. It was then that the Travelers' mission intensified. "I was scared that people would drop out," Bronfman said. Instead, even more people wanted to be Arkansas Travelers for Clinton, so many they couldn't all fit in Manchester. So Arkansans were also booked into Concord and Nashua motels for the final push. "We were not going to go down without a fight," Sheila said of the Arkansans who flooded New Hampshire for their friend. They didn't want the campaign to end there.

In Little Rock, according to Mary Anne Salmon, who was heading the Arkansas campaign for Clinton, "it felt like rats jumping ship." She was compelled to get to New Hampshire "and set the record straight."

Concerned about people abandoning the campaign, Mitchell Schwartz, the campaign director in New Hampshire, asked Traveler David Leopoulos to help calm the staff. Leopoulos spoke to the assembled staff for about an hour about growing up with Clinton, his middle-class values, how he had lived his life and told them more about all those Travelers who had come, like him, to New Hampshire to support Clinton. He shared "very personal moments" with them, Leopoulos said, so they could really feel Clinton's character. "There were tears all around." The next day he heard there was "a new energy in the staff" statewide.

Patty Criner remembered that night. The New Hampshire co-chairs were also there. "David stood in the middle of the circle and talked about his pal," she said, telling them really personal stories about their friendship. Among them was the fact that it was Clinton who located and called Leopoulos in Italy to tell him his mother had been murdered in her Hot Springs store.

Patty spoke to the staff another time and told them to trust that, in political campaigns, "things get thrown at you that are amplified or exaggerated." Sometimes, there might be a smidgen of truth but other times there is none, she told them. Her example was a long-standing Arkansas myth about Clinton sitting in a tree on the University of Arkansas campus in Fayetteville to protest the Vietnam War. He was studying overseas at Oxford at the time, but the myth persisted. "I told them to hold it together," she said. It helped that all those Arkansas people were standing with him, people who had been with him for most of their lives.

"We were feeling pretty beleaguered," admitted Terry Shumaker, one of Clinton's New Hampshire co-chairs. He and John Broderick, another early backer and co-chair, spent a lot of time "just propping people up," as they wondered themselves if they had misread Clinton and made a mistake supporting him. Shumaker credited Leopoulos and other Travelers with helping the campaign survive. He specifically noted David Matthews's memorable arrival, saying Matthews "planted himself in front of the Dunkin' Donuts … and buttonholed every single person who came in for days."

Alice Chamberlin, another New Hampshire supporter, recalls spending a lot of her time dealing with the larger character issues, calling supporters over and over to make sure they did not lose confidence or bail from the campaign. Only one or two people did, she said. The Arkansas Travelers were "a true and effective counter to a lot of the media at the time," she said. They easily related to New Hampshire voters and were not afraid of talking about the character questions. "Frankly, I am not sure Bill would have been the Comeback Kid without the work of the Travelers," she said. "They were able to make a big impact in a small state." Shumaker said much the same, praising the Travelers' "mostly unheralded efforts" that helped counter bad press reports.

David Leopoulos did hundreds of interviews with local and national media for the campaign. He was personally upset with the coverage and went to New Hampshire to counter the impressions being left of his childhood friend. "I learned that the press is not honest at all. They manipulated and omitted important character information every time I did an interview," he said. "They wanted to project Bill as a spoiled rich kid who was handed everything, which was the total opposite of who my friend was and is."

Shumaker remembers being called in with other co-chairs for a meeting with Clinton. These were Clinton's "New Hampshire people," and the candidate wanted to meet with them alone. "This isn't going very well, is it?" Clinton said then, according to Shumaker. Down to fourth or fifth in the polls, he went around the room asking each of the co-chairs what they thought he should be doing. "That was unheard of," said Shumaker, a veteran of many presidential elections. That hasn't happened before or since in either party's presidential campaigns, he said.

John Broderick, another co-chair, was first to answer, asking why Clinton was doing so many press conferences. The candidate was being asked the same questions over and over, denying and explaining too many of the same things, said Broderick. "Why don't we go to the mall and talk to real people?" Broderick asked.

When Shumaker got his turn, he told Clinton that it was traditional to have candidates introduced by prominent local politicians but, he added, "people think we're in this because we're going to get something out of it." Also, he said, the New Hampshire people had only known Clinton for six months. Shumaker suggested he have David Matthews, his Arkansas friend, introduce him. Matthews wasn't a political figure there and would be effective, Shumaker said, because he believed in Clinton.

Soon after the meeting, Clinton did go to the Mall of New Hampshire, just outside of Manchester, to talk to people and Matthews began introducing the governor at all his speaking engagements.

The presidential campaign really needed the political experience the Arkansas people brought, explained Craig Smith. Smith was the Arkansan in Clinton's national headquarters figuring out where to put the campaign's resources on a day-to-day basis. "The Travelers were one of my tools. I had the staff, the budget, campaign materials, candidate time, and the Travelers," Smith said. "These were people we could drop in like paratroopers to supplement our campaign efforts. That's what it started as. Then it morphed into something else that was more critical and most important."

When the allegations came out about Clinton's womanizing and the letter released about his avoidance of the draft, Smith said potential supporters in New Hampshire started to have questions and doubts. The Arkansas Travelers provided what a paid staff couldn't: personal validation. "Here all of a sudden we'd have fifty people show up in towns and say, 'I've known Bill Clinton for 20 years. I went to college with him. I went to high school with him. Let me tell you about who this guy really is and what he's really done.'" That sort of validation proved to be the Travelers' true value.

No Traveler may have been more visible than David Matthews. Initially, Clinton didn't even know Matthews was there. The former state representative took assignments from Bronfman to speak up for Clinton. When he didn't have an assignment, he approached random voters on the street. What was supposed to be a one-week trip turned into three after Clinton asked him to stay until the primary. David traveled with Clinton and introduced him for most of his remaining speeches there.

Matthews, who had been a major legislative supporter of Clinton's, talked about Clinton's record in Arkansas. But he also addressed head-on the Flowers allegations. "I truly, genuinely, 100 percent believed in my heart of hearts at that time that Gennifer Flowers was a complete fiction, that it was all a lie," Matthews said. He was disappointed when Clinton later admitted he had an "inappropriate relationship" with Flowers. "But, at the time, in 1992, I believed that that was all bunk," he said.

"And so, I mockingly talked about that, in introducing him the very first time, and he's standing over in the wings." Matthews asked the crowd if they believed her claim, then ridiculed her evidence, a tape recording of a conversation with Clinton. "Listen to the tape! … The phone rings, she answers it, 'Hello.' And the voice on the other end says, 'Hello, Gennifer, this is Bill Clinton.' And she replies, 'Oh, hi, Bill.' If they had been having an affair for twelve years, he wouldn't need to say, 'Hello, Gennifer. This is Bill Clinton.' I guess I'll call my wife tonight. I haven't seen her in about two weeks and when she answers the phone, I'm going to say, '…Hello, Mary Beth. This is David Matthews.'"

The crowd laughed with Matthews, who segued to a story about "the Bill Clinton that I know." The story was about a seven-year-old boy from Matthews's hometown who had been a cancer patient in Little Rock at Arkansas Children's Hospital. The boy was given a brief furlough and his mother took him to visit the nearby Arkansas State Capitol. Governor Clinton encountered the bald-headed child in his office lobby, introduced himself, then stopped a meeting in his office to bring the boy in to have his photo made sitting in the governor's chair. "That's not particularly noteworthy," said Matthews, who continued the story.

About four months later, young Aaron Pile was back in the Capitol on another hospital furlough. Clinton, who was talking to a group of legislators, saw the boy, excused himself, walked across the rotunda, stuck out his hand and said, "Hello, Aaron. I'm glad to see you here again." That still wasn't the end of the story. On election night in 1990, Clinton is in a serious general election race against

Republican Sheffield Nelson. Aaron Pile is back in the hospital and they're trying to get him to go to sleep. He won't.

"I want to stay up so I can see if my friend Bill wins the election," Aaron told the nurse. "Well, that nurse told someone, who told someone, who told someone else," Matthews said, "and the next day, a courier hand-delivered a note to the bedside of Aaron Pile that said, 'Thanks for pulling for me, pal. I want you to know I'm pulling for you. Your friend, Bill.'" David noted that Pile grew up to be a firefighter and a policeman in Lowell and a recent recipient of a community service award.

Just days before the primary, retired Colonel Eugene Holmes of Fayetteville released a letter Clinton had written twenty-two years earlier to the R.O.T.C. commander at the University of Arkansas, where Clinton was scheduled to enroll. Holmes alleged Clinton had deceived him to dodge service in the Vietnam War. "I will never forget the brilliance—the brilliance—of James Carville," said Matthews, referring to the Clinton campaign advisor's reaction to the situation. "He says, 'You don't need to run from this letter. ... You've got to make this letter your friend. ... That is a story of an anguished man who loves his country, who wants to do right by his country and can't stand what his country is doing.'" Matthews said Carville was "absolutely right" about the long letter Clinton wrote, explaining his opposition to the war to the colonel who saved him from the draft.

The situation was "touch and go," Matthews said, as the primary neared. Then Clinton gave "the best political speech ever," Matthews said. He was in a Dover gymnasium and spoke from the heart. "This election is not about me. This election is about you. ... I'll tell you what the real character issue is, who really cares about you," Clinton told the Dover crowd. He ended with a promise not to forget who gave him a second chance and said he'd be there for New Hampshire "'til the last dog dies." That phrase turned up again during the roll call vote for Clinton's nomination at the Democratic National

Convention. As the New Hampshire delegation cast its votes, the delegates declared they'd support Clinton "'til the last dog dies."

Eight years later, President Clinton returned to Dover and asked Matthews to introduce him for the anniversary speech. The president was late getting to the gymnasium where 5,000 people gathered. First George Stephanopolous, then Matthews spoke to keep the crowd there. When he had run out of anything substantive to say, Matthews told them, "You know the only thing us folks in Arkansas have got against you people in New Hampshire is that, although he's our favorite son, we kind of think he likes you better than us." The least they could do, he said, was learn to call the Hogs. He then spent twenty minutes teaching them the "Wooooo, Pig, Sooie" cheer for the Arkansas Razorbacks. When the president did arrive, the crowd surprised him with the Hog call.

"After eight years and almost exactly nine days to go, the last dog is still barking," Clinton told the Dover crowd. "Don't forget that even though I won't be president, I'll always be with you until the last dog dies."

It was not so certain in February 1992 that candidate Clinton would have anything to celebrate at all. The situation in New Hampshire had gotten ugly. The national campaign staff, led by David Wilhelm, was spooked.

Once an hour, Wilhelm would drop by to ask Craig Smith what he was hearing out there. "He'd ask how were we holding up?" Smith said. Wilhelm spent a whole day doing that as the news worsened.

Clinton's numbers did hold up pretty well after Gennifer Flowers's allegations broke, Smith said; but they started to move down when the draft issue erupted. "It was almost like everybody said, 'We'll give you one for free.' When the second one came, everybody said, 'OK. That's it.' It was too much." That's why, Smith said, what Arkansans did in New Hampshire was so important. Besides the Travelers on the ground, 150 Arkansans put their names and phone numbers in a full-page ad in the *New Hampshire Union Leader*, inviting collect calls to them about Clinton. "They didn't get that many calls," he said. But their willingness to publish their private phone numbers made a difference. It all caused doubting New Hampshire voters to think Clinton might be OK after all.

Veterans from Arkansas led by Hershel Gober also wielded considerable influence in New Hampshire, Smith said. Their job was to counter damage caused by the letter released about Clinton's draft status during the Vietnam War. With his prospects plummeting, Bill Clinton personally asked Gober, director of the Arkansas Department of Veteran Affairs, to come and bring veterans to help with the draft issue. Gober got the call just before midnight from Clinton, who said he was "being torn up over the draft issue," Gober said. He asked Gober to go first to the Little Rock headquarters to meet with campaign staff.

Gober cut a radio commercial for Clinton that related how Gober had been ambushed in Vietnam. "Now they're ambushing my friend Bill Clinton in New Hampshire," it continued. The ad ran widely in New Hampshire. Gober and a small crew of Vietnam combat veterans actually flew from Arkansas with the Clintons to New Hampshire. They immediately began working the American Legion halls and Veterans of Foreign Wars posts across the state.

"I knew how to use the vets," said Gober, whose contingent was made up of U.S. Army and Navy retirees from around Arkansas. All had been in command posts in veterans' organizations and could readily relate to New Hampshire's veterans. Gober's team members included Jimmy Red Jones, also a former Arkansas state auditor as well as adjutant general of the Arkansas National Guard, Grady Brown, Kirby Johnson, John Haney, Claude Carpenter, Charles Ragsdale, John Steer, Othar Smith, and Bill Murphy.

Most had been enlisted men. A couple of them were generals. Gober was a retired major. All were combat vets speaking up for

Clinton, who had successfully escaped the draft during the war in Vietnam. What veterans wanted to know, Gober said, was what Clinton would do to protect veterans in the future, particularly regarding their health care. Clinton had been "a great governor for veterans," said Gober. In 1992, not all veterans could use the Veterans Administration hospitals but there was talk of letting Medicaid patients into them, according to Gober. Clinton took the stance that no nonveteran would be admitted until all veterans had access, Gober said.

When he told that to veterans at a town hall in French Town, Gober said, "the event went wild." The local veterans' leaders told them to go call ten veterans "and tell them this and have them call ten more" to turn out votes for Clinton. Gober and his team of Arkansas veterans would travel to other states both in the primary and general election campaigns. In the general election, Gober advised Clinton to go before the American Legion National Convention in Chicago, against advice from some of his campaign staff. His speech there addressing the draft issue head on, Gober said, "was the defining moment in his campaign as it pertained to veterans' issues."

Gober would later follow Clinton to Washington DC. He served as deputy secretary of Veterans Affairs and led delegations to Vietnam, Laos, and Cambodia to negotiate more searches for U.S. troops who were missing in action. He served as the acting secretary in the final months of the Clinton administration. President Clinton at one point offered to make Gober the ambassador to Vietnam, but Gober declined in order to work on Clinton's 1996 reelection. More recently, Secretary of State Hillary Clinton asked if Gober was still interested in the ambassadorship. Gober told her he was too old.

While all the accusations were flying in New Hampshire, Clinton got sick, suffering a cough and bad cold. Plus, he had to go back to Arkansas on business. Some of his New Hampshire supporters reportedly got concerned that he wasn't fighting back. David Matthews, who was working in the headquarters that day making phone calls, had heard the complaints.

"In walks James Carville," he said. Matthews introduced himself and told him of the supporters' concern. "He snapped at me and said, 'We can't get our message out. The press is controlling what goes out.' I said, 'I understand you've got a bunch of campaign money but you're not going to need it past this primary, if you don't spend some of it.'" Matthews added, "Let Bill Clinton do what Bill Clinton does best." He suggested getting Clinton in front of a crowd of supportive people, giving a speech, and filming it for an ad.

Carville turned on his heel and didn't say a word. Matthews told Sheila that he'd "ripped his britches" with Carville. About a half hour later, Carville comes back and tells Matthews, "I just want you to know that I heard what you said." Matthews didn't know what to make of the comment. The next night, he was summoned to a big meeting in Manchester and drove through "horizontal snow" to get there. "What do I walk into?" Matthews saw Clinton standing in front of a huge flag, speaking to a supportive crowd that was cheering him on. "And they are filming it."

When they let Clinton be Clinton, Matthews said, his rally started.

Traveler J. T. Rose similarly recalled that, when Clinton was sick, the staff confined him to a hotel. The fretting staff couldn't decide what to do, trying to manage the candidate. Rose also remembered Matthews's admonishment to let Clinton be Clinton. That meant getting him out of isolation and back among people, Rose said. "What he was, was stir-crazy."

The campaign subsequently scheduled Clinton to campaign in a mall, where people lined up to meet him. The Travelers were there, too, and worked the crowd with him. Peter Jennings, the ABC News anchor at the time, was there. "He really is a remarkable campaigner, isn't he?" Jennings remarked. The way Clinton fed off the crowd was another reflection of Clinton's lifelong "need to be adored,"

Matthews said. Removing him from the people was "like cutting out the thing that gave him energy."

During those difficult days in New Hampshire, when the national press expected Clinton to quit, Matthews was with the Clintons as a throng of media followed them to the state capitol in Concord. "There is a mob. ... Bill has got Hillary on one arm and I've got her on the other," Matthews said. They make their way through the mob, with reporters yelling questions and bumping into them with boom mikes and cameras. They finally get into a room and, while Bill leaves to make a talk, Hillary and Matthews are alone. "Hillary is exhausted and I will never forget what she says. ... She let out a big sigh and she said, 'You know, David, if I didn't really think we could change the world, it wouldn't be worth it.'"

"Governor, you are one tough son of a bitch," New Hampshire co-chair Shumaker told Clinton late in the primary campaign. "Any other candidate would have been dead, buried and forgotten by now." Instead, the New Hampshire people were gravitating back to Clinton, who came in second with twenty-six percent of the primary vote.

"We came back better than we had anticipated," said Traveler Dale Evans. "A lot of campaigns can't come back."

He believes the Travelers' charm, their Southern accents, and their personal testimonials for Clinton helped swing the numbers back to Clinton.

"You can't give it all to the Travelers in New Hampshire, but they had great influence," said Patty Criner.

10.
THE COMEBACK KID

"New Hampshire tonight has made Bill Clinton the Comeback Kid," Clinton famously declared on primary election night.

The packed house at the Merrimac Inn in Dover included an emotional bunch of Arkansas Travelers, who had traveled to the state to bail their friend out of trouble. A grateful Clinton first thanked Hillary, without whom he "wouldn't be fit to be here," and numerous New Hampshire people, including his state co-chairs. Then he turned to the visiting Travelers.

"I want to thank my dear friends from Arkansas who have been up here for so long," Clinton said. He singled out U.S. Senator David Pryor (D-AR) and his wife, Barbara. "I first met David and Barbara Pryor twenty-six years ago and I don't know who is more surprised about this night—me or them."

"I have proved one thing," Clinton said that night, "I can take a punch."

As the results came in, it became clear Clinton would finish strong, said James Jones. "We felt like we had accomplished what we came to do," he said. "I was as excited as I was the night here in Little Rock when he won the presidency."

The Travelers felt, as many people have said since, that they really had made the difference in how the primary ended. Clinton didn't win. But his second-place finish drew more attention than former Senator Paul Tsongas's victory that night. Without the Travelers, Jones said, Clinton's campaign "would never have made it out of New Hampshire."

Richard Bronfman said he almost felt sorry for Tsongas. He had won, but the media only wanted to talk to Bill. It was the same media, he said, that had written Clinton off.

The press awaits the "Comeback Kid" election night in 1992 in Merrimack, New Hampshire.

Percy Malone, an Arkadelphia pharmacist, had gone to New Hampshire, he said, simply because "my friend was in trouble."

When Clinton traveled around Arkansas in 1991 to see if there was home state support for his running in the middle of his gubernatorial term, a lot of these friends said not to do it. "I was telling him that he should wait," said Malone, fearful then of President George H. W. Bush's popularity.

"Everyone told him to wait, but nobody hesitated to get out and work for him," added Gregg Reep, then mayor of Warren. Clinton got in the race, with many of his friends expecting him just to make a good first showing in the Democratic primary. That, one Traveler after another said, would have set him up for a bid when a popular president wasn't on the Republican ticket.

As the campaign soured in New Hampshire, that prospect changed. A major loss not only would have ended the 1992 bid, it could have dashed Clinton's future chances. Malone was certain

New Hampshire was Clinton's "last chance." His second-place finish gave Clinton new momentum and resurrected the national campaign strategy set long before the New Hampshire experience.

The night before the vote, he directly thanked the Arkansas Travelers for their help and told a Manchester audience, "This Arkansas army can win this election for me." It was the last rally before the vote. He also thanked Senator David Pryor, who had introduced him that night.

"I have the friends of my lifetime here in this room tonight, people who have been my friends for more than thirty-five years, friends who have come up here to stand by me and work to the very end of this campaign," Clinton said in his rally speech.

"I have taken no lick. But I have seen people in New Hampshire licked and hurt and beaten and deprived. And it is wrong and we can do better."

On election night, he repeated the theme.

"Someday, when the history of this campaign is written, they may say, 'Well, you know Clinton took a lot of hits in this campaign.' And I want you to know something and I want you to never forget this. The hits that I took in this election are nothing compared to the hits that the people in this state and this country are taking every day of their lives." He went on to single out economically stressed people he had met in New Hampshire and their everyday challenges to survive. "Those are the hits I care about," he said. Later, he would further hone that message, delivered first in the eleventh hour of his New Hampshire campaign, for other states.

"Here's what we knew we needed to do," said Craig Smith, whose national campaign responsibilities had shifted early on from finance to Super Tuesday and the South.

"We knew we needed to beat expectations in New Hampshire. We didn't necessarily have to win but we had to do better than anybody thought we could. Then we had to sweep the South, which

A jubilant Clinton greets supporters in New Hampshire, 1992.

started out with Georgia on Tuesday." Next up was South Carolina the following Saturday and then Super Tuesday, when there would be primary elections in Florida, Louisiana, Massachusetts, Mississippi, Oklahoma, Rhode Island, Tennessee, and Texas. Additionally, there were caucuses that day in Delaware, Hawaii, and Missouri. The next week would bring a critical Illinois vote. "We knew if we didn't get basically a sweep out of the South, we weren't going anywhere."

Smith said the campaign was short on staff and simply didn't have as much money as everybody else in the race. "We come from a state that doesn't have a tradition of raising a lot of political money. We had to get by the best we can." In some states, the campaign had no staff. In others, the staff was maybe one or two people.

"We needed to supplement our efforts in those places with people willing to go in and show the flag and raise the profile of our candidate," he said. "That's where the Travelers came in."

Bill and Hillary Clinton address the excited crowd.

These were people who had spent their lives in politics in Arkansas, he said. They knew how to meet people and they knew Bill Clinton.

Sending vanloads of Travelers into a state, according to Smith, was "almost like a campaign staff in a can." They could be dropped into a town "and suddenly you'd be covering every neighborhood. ... They knew how to do this."

Georgia was the first of the Southern states to hold a primary. Clinton was a Southern governor and the expected favorite. "If the candidate of the South lost in the South, it was pretty much done," according to Smith. "The next week was Super Tuesday and we had to have a win before Super Tuesday," he said.

Clinton had placed only second in New Hampshire and needed to win not only Georgia but also South Carolina, which was to vote on Saturday between the Georgia election and Super Tuesday, said Smith.

Arkansas Travelers, fresh from the experience in New Hampshire, were dispatched to Georgia. More than three dozen made that trip, spending nine days there before the vote. Mary Anne Salmon, H. T. Moore, and Donna Kay Matteson led the group all over the state of Georgia.

The campaign had survived the draft and Gennifer Flowers issues in New Hampshire and, with success in Georgia, proved Clinton could win.

"Then the issue became, can we win anyplace but the South?" he said. The proving ground was Illinois, a key northern state and another major destination for the Arkansas Travelers.

"We knew we had to win there," Smith said. The campaign was confident it could win downstate Illinois, which was almost closer to Little Rock than Chicago, Smith said. He asked the Travelers to concentrate on the urban voters because that's where their support was most needed.

At the same time, the campaign was targeting Michigan and New York, hoping to show Clinton could win in the East.

Bill Clinton could not have been president without the Travelers, Smith said flatly. "If we had finished in worse shape than we did in New Hampshire, the campaign would have ended."

The Travelers made a huge difference in the South. If Clinton had lost there, he would never have won the nomination, Smith said. "The same was true about the Illinois win."

The Travelers did a lot in "do or die" places, Smith said. "We needed them."

Clinton's national staff learned something from sending Travelers to places where candidates couldn't go. If the Travelers were treated like celebrities in those places, Smith said, think how the candidates would be received out on the road.

He credited the Travelers' celebrity with helping shape the decision to put Clinton and Al Gore, his vice presidential running mate, on bus tours through different states. The tours produced huge crowds and thunderous welcomes for the candidates and their wives.

"Showing up in small towns," Smith said, "shows respect for the decisions these people made to stay in those small towns."

Arkansans inherently understood that fact. Their home-state campaigns always include small-town events like Bradley County's Pink Tomato Festival in Warren, the Hope Watermelon Fest, or the Gillette Coon Supper.

In 1992, Smith said the campaign put the Travelers in states that Clinton should be winning "and where we needed some validation" or in states that were close "and we needed a boost to get us over the top."

Use of the Travelers increased in the general election, although no single trip ever came close to the 137-person showing the Travelers made in New Hampshire in the primary.

In 1996, when Clinton was seeking reelection, the two primary needs the campaign originally had for the Arkansas Travelers were covered.

"We didn't need the validation," Smith said. "Everybody had their opinion about Bill Clinton."

Also, by that time, he said, "We had all the money we needed so we didn't need to supplement the staff." The Travelers, who did make three reelection trips, were nonetheless welcome additions, he said.

By the time of Hillary Clinton's bid for the presidency in 2008, Smith was living in Florida, working as a professional campaign consultant. He didn't get involved in her campaign until after she had lost key caucus states, including Iowa.

She had promised not to campaign in Florida after that state scheduled its primary at an unsanctioned time. Smith said he ran a "rogue campaign" for her in Florida with no help at all from the national campaign. "We won anyway," said Smith, who helped in Texas, too, where Clinton also won the primary.

"Texas was do or die for us," he said. "My first instinct was to get the Travelers. They were close and we needed them down there." While the campaign had almost unlimited funds and plenty of staff, he said public confidence in Hillary Clinton had been shaken. "We needed people down there who could say, 'Let me tell you, I know Hillary Clinton,'" Smith said.

11.

ROCKY RELATIONS

The relationship of the Arkansas Travelers to the campaign field staffs, in both Bill and Hillary Clinton's presidential races, was rocky at times. In fact, those clashes are what many Travelers recall as among their most difficult experiences.

Often, they felt they "were fighting against the field staff," Sheila Bronfman said. The national staff in Little Rock, in Bill Clinton's campaigns, was supportive as were the local people in any given state. It was the out-of-town field staff, usually young, politically involved people, who presented the problem.

"All they see is a bunch of old people, forty or fifty, coming in, taking up their time." Trying to see the situation from their perspective, Bronfman said, "They don't know what to do with us."

An occasional staffer recognized the Travelers' worth and helped line out schedules for them, she acknowledged. Most of the time, there were battles over scheduling.

The Arkansas Travelers became widely known as the Friends of Bill, or FOBs. FOB campaign buttons proliferated during the campaign, not just for the Travelers but also for other Clinton supporters. David Matthews said the term "did not start out as a badge of honor." It was a "derisive term" used by the paid staff in New Hampshire who, he said, didn't like the Arkansas people. Someone heard the paid people talking disparagingly about one of the Travelers and saying that was "just another one of those FOBs." It was an early sign of friction between the field staff and the Travelers.

Dale Evans acknowledged that the Travelers could "get in the way." That's why Mitchell Schwartz, the campaign director, sent Evans to "herd them a little bit … and try to keep them from coming into headquarters all the time." Schwartz "didn't want to be mean to them" because these were friends of Bill Clinton, Evans said. But the Travelers, many of whom had strong personalities, could sometimes be "overwhelming to deal with."

"There was a fear by some of the staff that you couldn't offend these people. If you said anything that made them mad, they knew Bill Clinton personally and you could be devastated by it." Nor did the Travelers always take instruction from the campaign.

When Clinton's numbers were locked in the twenty-two percent range, Evans said the campaign strategy was to pull as many voters out as possible. If the percentage held, Clinton would win New Hampshire, they figured.

However, after the rough spell over Gennifer Flowers, the draft, and the "I didn't inhale" quote, the strategy shifted. The campaign wanted only known Clinton voters to be sought out in get-out-the-vote efforts.

The campaign printed lists for canvassers that targeted Clinton supporters only. But, Evans acknowledged, "You send people out and they do what they do." The Arkansas Travelers ignored those marching orders and continued their door-to-door push, trying to swing prospective voters over from other candidates and claiming success when they tried.

The Travelers learned to "do what we do," Bronfman said. They took their cue from a New Hampshire conflict in 1992. The field staff was starting to block some Traveler activities and giving them "busywork," Bronfman said. "I was not taking kindly to it." She was particularly perturbed that they were upset with David Matthews. "They had been treating David badly," she said. "They called him a washed-up former legislator. And we were just so ticked."

It happened that both Bill and Hillary were coming to speak to the headquarters staff and their New Hampshire supporters that night. The staff specifically counseled Bronfman and Ann Henderson not to bother Bill or Hillary about their dispute. "They said, 'Don't talk to Hillary,'" Bronfman recalled. "So I wrote her a note. I didn't talk to her. I wrote her a note."

Sheila stood next to Hillary at the meeting under the watchful eye of the staff members. "They were just about to have a fit because they saw me pass her the note." What Sheila wrote was that the staff wasn't letting the Travelers do what they knew how to do.

Hillary clenched her teeth. When the meeting was over, "she whirled on me." Sheila thought she had stepped over the line. What Hillary said, rather adamantly, was, "Y'all know how to do this. You've gotten him elected five times in Arkansas. You've been doing this for years. You go and do what you know how to do and you tell anyone who has a problem with it to call me—that I said so."

Bronfman thanked her and said, "That's all I needed to know." She promptly started working directly with the people from New Hampshire who were supporting Clinton to line out where the Travelers should be and how they could be best utilized.

The New Hampshire campaign staff didn't bother the Travelers after that. Bronfman suspects Hillary Clinton had some words with the staff privately.

Also, she noted, Matthews became "such a hit" in New Hampshire that the staff tried to control him, instructing Matthews on one occasion specifically to introduce Clinton as the "governor of Arkansas and the next president of the United States." Instead, Matthews wound up the introduction calling Clinton "my friend, Bill," and stared down the campaign staffers as he did so.

Keeping peace between these politically seasoned Travelers and the campaign's field staff, often made up of young people who thought they knew more than these Arkansans, was a challenge to the national campaign office, too. Craig Smith, who worked with the Travelers from Little Rock, heard about it from both sides. "Sheila would pick up the phone and say, 'We're here and they haven't gotten us a schedule. They don't know what they're doing.'"

"Hell, I knew that," said Smith. He would hire someone from Pennsylvania to run the Illinois campaign and a week later send him or her to Colorado, a place the operative had never been before. When Bronfman and the Travelers complained that the field staff didn't know anything about a state, they were correct.

"Then I'd hear from the staff," said Smith. "'These people just showed up and they expect all this. I have a staff of four people to run a whole state. They want detailed schedules for six teams to go out across the state. They want media appearances arranged. ... How am I supposed to arrange all that?'" Every field staffer was concerned that the Travelers had Bill Clinton's ear, or Hillary's. "All the people on the ground knew they were all his friends and they were all going to see him," said Smith, noting that the campaign always tried to have the Travelers at some Clinton event. Consequently, the staff tried to be diplomatic with the Travelers, less diplomatic with Smith.

"You know Sheila. She's going to call and tell you what's not right." In turn, Smith would call the state director and explain what she was unhappy about. "They said they'd try to fix it."

In time, some of the problems eased. Since the campaign would move the same field team from one state to another, those staffers got accustomed to working with the Travelers, Smith said. The staff began to request the Travelers' help. An example he noted was the field staff's request for Traveler help in western Kansas late in the general election. The campaign staff was focused on Kansas City, so the Travelers were dispatched on a route that included stops at small towns. More than fifty Travelers made three forays into Kansas in October 1992. When the 1992 campaign was done, Smith said, Clinton's staff "felt like the Travelers were really critical."

The night before the New Hampshire vote, after Clinton's last rally, more than 100 Travelers and staff members gathered with

New Hampshire supporters. Schwartz was following Bill and Hillary Clinton through the shoulder-to-shoulder crowd as they thanked and hugged their longtime supporters from home.

"I think if it hadn't been for the people of Arkansas, this would have been one of the worst weeks of my life," the governor told a reporter from *The Morning News* in Springdale. Instead, Hillary Clinton said it was "a great week" for them.

Schwartz by then was saying the Arkansas Travelers were "an absolute, incredible godsend." He called them the campaign's "truth squad," answering attacks on Clinton. New Hampshire voters may not know where Arkansas is, but they know it is "far away," he said. When Arkansas people "come up here and talk to people, pay their own way and speak from their hearts," Schwartz said, "it means a ton."

Relations between the Travelers and Hillary Clinton's campaign were really strained. Her candidacy came sixteen years after the Travelers had made such a difference in New Hampshire and other primary states. There was a whole new crop of young staff people working for her, most with little knowledge of Bill Clinton's run for the presidency, much less the Travelers' role. Hillary had requested their help, so the staff tried to accommodate them. "But they truly did not understand what our group of politically experienced Travelers could do," said Sheila.

12.

GEORGIA AND BEYOND

Bill Clinton's campaign sent the Travelers in large and small numbers to at least ten more states before their respective primary elections. They traveled alone, in pairs and in bunches, numbering as many as sixty-five on a six-day trip to Illinois.

Their first assignment after New Hampshire was Georgia, where Travelers spent nine days crossing the state in vans or in the private cars of those who drove from Arkansas.

This Georgia trip, according to Harry Truman "H. T." Moore, was a little bit of an afterthought. He was visiting with Clinton in Little Rock in the middle of a legislative session, he said, when Clinton asked what he was doing the following Thursday.

"When I said 'nothing,' he said, 'You're going to Georgia.'"

Moore said Sheila was busily preparing for a Traveler trip to Illinois, a key Super Tuesday state, when the campaign decided to add Georgia to the Travelers' itinerary. Georgia was to vote the week before Super Tuesday. Clinton's strong showing there would help propel him into the Super Tuesday contests.

The quick turnaround to get to Georgia wasn't a problem. The campaign had materials about Georgia, including talking points ready for distribution to the Travelers as they gathered for the trip.

The Travelers received notes about Clinton's support spreading around the country, how Tsongas had lost in his own backyard in the Maine caucuses, a *Houston Chronicle* poll that showed Clinton with a strong forty percent of the vote and news that Clinton TV ads had hit the airwaves on stations across Georgia.

The Travelers reported good days and bad ones on that Georgia outing. One day, Moore said, was filled with successful campaigning in banks and other businesses and making connections with military people in Warner Robins. The next day went downhill, he said, when the campaign staff in Atlanta wanted to focus on Atlanta, not the smaller communities Travelers had discovered to be fertile ground for them.

"We were on our own. No one knew we were coming," he said of that second day. They couldn't get the newspaper in Rome to talk to them and ended the day depressed. The only light moment was an encounter on the highway with a Cadillac-driving Elvis impersonator. "That day had been absolutely awful," H. T. said.

The Travelers capped it with dinner out. Since they had cars, they went to different places to eat and then regrouped at a rock 'n' roll dive. Tom B. Smith, a Traveler from Wynne, went with one group to a restaurant in a converted abbey. Leaving the beautiful abbey and going to Johnny B. Goode's, Tom told H. T., was like "leaving heaven and going right to hell."

Linda Lou Moore, H. T.'s wife, was among thirty-seven others on that trip. Tommye Wells and her daughter, Beverly, of Sheridan had to drive to Atlanta and pick the Moores up at the airport. Other Travelers similarly teamed up to make multiple stops, mostly in smaller towns on Atlanta's outskirts.

Linda Lou said the Travelers were successful because they went "where others wouldn't go or couldn't go" to find votes. She said the win in Georgia's primary set Clinton up for a Super Tuesday showing that virtually sealed the nomination.

Importantly, Clinton picked up Georgia Governor Zell Miller's endorsement, H. T. noted. Miller helped to turn out a crowd for a big rally with Clinton at Stone Mountain. The Travelers met him there and worked the crowd.

Later, when H. T. visited in Little Rock with Richard Threlkeld of CBS News, Threlkeld told H. T. that the other candidates had overlooked Georgia and Clinton got a boost there. Threlkeld later corresponded with H. T., telling him that he and the other Travelers deserved the accolades they would get during the inaugural.

H. T. offered a colorful tale of small-town politics from the trip. In Warner Robins, a man called the Big Possum controlled the black vote in that county. "Our hosts said we won't know until the Possum walks who will get their vote," Moore said. The Possum "walked"

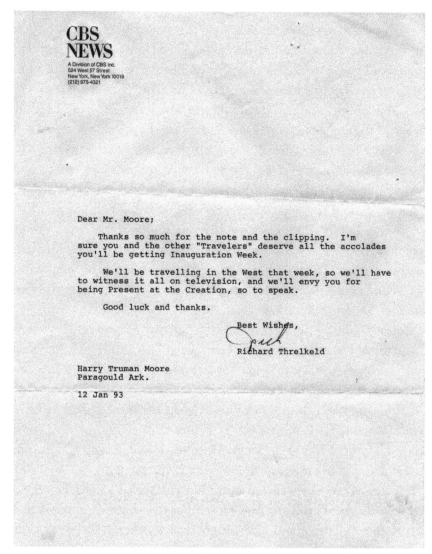

CBS NEWS
A Division of CBS Inc.
524 West 57 Street
New York, New York 10019
(212) 975-4321

Dear Mr. Moore;

Thanks so much for the note and the clipping. I'm sure you and the other "Travelers" deserve all the accolades you'll be getting Inauguration Week.

We'll be travelling in the West that week, so we'll have to witness it all on television, and we'll envy you for being Present at the Creation, so to speak.

Good luck and thanks.

Best Wishes,

Richard Threlkeld

Harry Truman Moore
Paragould Ark.

12 Jan 93

This letter from Richard Threlkeld, CBS News correspondent, acknowledges the well-deserved accolades that the Travelers would receive during inauguration week.

about 6:30 a.m. on election morning. When the vote came in for the county, Clinton got seventy-three percent. Clinton won the Georgia primary with fifty-seven percent of the vote.

Next up was South Carolina the following Saturday and then Super Tuesday on March 10th, when there would be primary elections in eight states and caucuses in three more. While Craig Smith, directing field operations from Little Rock, concentrated non-Traveler resources elsewhere, the Travelers' Super Tuesday focus was on Texas and Florida. Clinton won both, Texas with more than sixty-five percent of the vote and Florida with better than fifty percent. Six more Super Tuesday states also gave Clinton victories, as did South Carolina the weekend before.

Thirty Travelers spent two days in Texas before Super Tuesday, while seven traveled to Florida the first week of March. The latter were the group of veterans led around the country by Hershel Gober, one of the early Travelers. In Texas, Donna Kay Matteson of Foreman and Emily Chick of Texarkana led groups to work one east Texas town after another on Saturday, leaflet churches on Sunday, and meet up with Governor Clinton on Sunday for a rally in Tyler. Donna Kay reported that he was glad to see friendly faces working the crowd.

While the Travelers were in Texarkana, in the wee hours of the morning, fire alarms and sirens awakened them, Mary Schroeder of Texarkana recalled. When they were gathered in the motel lobby, Mary realized the day's schedule was still upstairs and sent Donna Kay back to get it in spite of the fire alarms.

Several trips by Arkansas Travelers were set up quickly to address problems in states where Clinton needed a boost. These individuals or teams of Travelers were appropriately called SWAT teams. They could travel at a moment's notice, booking quick flights to answer calls from the states for campaign help. Several traveled to primary election states. Others campaigned in the general election.

The Travelers dispatched a small crew of four to Maryland before its March 3rd primary. Henry Woods led the team of Clark Ray, Jennifer Harris, and Paula Thomasson. It was a last-minute get-out-the-vote effort with lots of visibility. The Travelers were doing what they do best: "honk and wave," "grin and spin," and "knock and drop." Clinton ran second to former U.S. Senator Paul Tsongas in Maryland's primary, getting just under thirty-six percent of the vote.

Woods later led the same four-person crew to New York for its April 7th primary. They traveled all night from Washington to spend three days there.

Woods reported back to Bronfman, saying, "When the Clinton campaign coordinator met us, he told us that, among other things, we would be greeting commuters at the central intersection in Rochester. That intersection is the corner of Clinton and Main." He told his fellow Arkansas Travelers, "God wanted us to win this election. Look where he put the center of town!" New York went for Clinton in its winner-take-all primary. Clinton got just shy of forty-one percent of the vote.

Vic Snyder, a state senator from Little Rock and a future U.S. congressman, made a one-man SWAT trip to his native Oregon just before that state's May primary. There for eight days, he went canvassing alone in different towns, drawing free media when the campaign headquarters called the local press to tell them an Arkansas lawmaker was going door-to-door for Bill Clinton.

The Travelers name and claim "Comeback Hill" outside Super 8 Motel in Manchester, New Hampshire, on February 19, 1992. (See Photo Index for Names.)

The Traveler vans were always packed. Shown are Nick Thompson, Peggy McClain, Woody Bassett, Ann Henderson, Joel Buckner, Ronnie Bumpass, Bob Aspell, Nancy Monroe, Mauria Aspell, Rocky Wilmuth, and others in the back and front rows. February 1992.

Dressed up for victory. Front row, left to right, are James Jones, David Folsom, Ann Henry, Morriss Henry, Ann Pride. Back row, left to right, Woody Futrell, Mary Anne Salmon, Peggy Tucker, Maria Haley, and Del Boyette. New Hampshire, February 1992.

At the famous pig roast in Meredith, New Hampshire, January 19,1992. All reported it as the coldest they had ever been. Notice the icicles. Back row, left to right are Ted McNulty, Wayne Gruber, Lewis Frazer, Gregg Reep, Jay Bradford, Bruce Gruber, Mary Beth Frazer. Front row, left to right, are Jan McQuary, Sid Johnson, Anne Bradford Mourning, Dale Evans, and Sheila Galbraith Bronfman.

Bill and Hillary Clinton listen as David Matthews fires up the Clinton faithful in Manchester, New Hampshire, February 1992.

Georgia primary Travelers after a good day on the road. From left to right are Tom Marshall, Mack Dyer, Mary Schroeder, Bill Schroeder, Mary Anne Salmon, Diane Boyt Woods, Donna Kay Matteson Yeargan, Beverly Wells, Linda Lou Moore, Tommye Wells, Harry Truman Moore, and Weldon Chesser.

Working the cattle barns in Perry County, Georgia, are Tommye Wells, Linda Lou Moore, and Beverly Wells.

Bill and Hillary are green with glee, primary night in Chicago, March 17, 1992.

The Travelers get a first-hand view of "new technology" as Clinton changes ties under the watchful eye of Dee Dee Myers in preparation for multiple national interviews that will air the next morning.

"Honk and wave" in Cape Girardeau, Missouri, carrying the banner that traveled all over the United States. From left to right are Bobette Manees, Mary Newberry, Jim O'Brien, Dan Stidham, David Bailin, Jerry Woods, and Sue White.

The Travelers spent the day with Tipper Gore in Cape Girardeau, Missouri, going door to door, doing interviews, and preparing for a big rally. (See Photo Index for Names.)

President Carter offers Southern hospitality at his home in Plains, Georgia, the Sunday before the general election. Front row, left to right, are Roosevelt Coleman, Herby Branscum, Milana Dennis, Richard Bronfman, Sheila Bronfman, President Carter, Eleanor Coleman, and Kerry McKenney. On the back row are Barbara Hartwick, Sam Perroni, and Vic Fleming.

Carrying the banner again at the West Georgia State Homecoming Parade. Left to right are Cliff Hoofman, Roosevelt Coleman, Milana Dennis, Eleanor Coleman, Barbara Hartwick, Sheila Bronfman, Herby Branscum, H. T. Moore, Shelby Moore, Lisa Ferrell, Richard Bronfman, Weldon Chesser, Sydney Probst, Vic Fleming, Paula Storeygard, Dorothy Preslar, and Sam Perroni,

A trip to Kansas for this hard-working and dedicated group was mixed in with a Halloween campaign event. Back row, from left to right, are Richard Hutchinson, Mary Beth Frazer, Rene de Turenne, Jim Keef, Delberta Keef, Waldo Fowler, Tom Marshall, Joe Purvis, and Randy Laverty. Front row, from left to right, are Berta Seitz, Sue White, Ben Thomasson, Nelwyn Davis, Pat Youngdahl, Wes Edwards, and Sallie Graves.

Sue White and Wes Edwards celebrate Halloween with Kansas Democratic locals having some fun with costumes.

(Both top and bottom photos.) The Arkansas Travelers were special guests at the exclusive Macy's Party at the Democratic National Convention in New York. The Clintons came to thank them and celebrate as Ohio put him "over the top." They then made the historic walk escorting the party's nominee to the floor of Madison Square Garden. This was one of the most incredible, exciting, and rewarding Traveler experiences.

At the election night Traveler party in Little Rock, Randy Goodrum (center), who co-wrote "Stand By Your Van," leads the Travelers in song with help from his back-up singers Harry Truman Moore (left) and Joe Purvis (right).

President-elect Clinton at the staff "thank you" party. His name tags say "No Staff Worked Harder," "I Can't Talk," "You Did a Great Job," and "No Staffer Worked Harder."

On the way to Louisville, Kentucky, in 1996, the Travelers were diverted to Chattanooga to work a rally with Tipper Gore. It was on this leg of the journey that lives were saved by Larry Bryant, their excellent bus driver, when a major accident occurred on the freeway. (See Photo Index for Names.)

A minor accident actually occurred with the restroom on the bus which led to the "Back of the Bus Gang" holding their noses. Front row left to right: Don Bishop, Mayor Gregg Reep, and David Hodges. Second row: Lorene Leder, Berniece Duffey, Shirley Montgomery, and Sue White. Third row: Susan Jones, Marian Hodges, Lila Riggs, and Tommye Wells. Back row: Senator Kevin Smith and Marci Riggs.

"Hope and Beyond" to Louisiana in 1996 was the last trip for Bill Clinton's Arkansas Travelers. (See Photo Index for Names.)

Hillary Clinton celebrated her birthday in 2007 in Ames, Iowa with her Arkansas Traveler friends after they worked an event with her. (See Photo Index for Names.)

Senator Hillary Clinton, President Clinton, Chelsea Clinton, and the Travelers pose after a rally in Manchester, New Hampshire in 2008. (See Photo Index for Names.)

"Honk and wave" in snowy New Hampshire. From left to right are Candace Jeffress, David Bailin, Ann Harbison, and Grady Bailin.

"Though their rooms were on fire, they just kicked it even higher and the Travelers kept rolling along." They didn't miss a beat when their hotel burned in Nashua, New Hampshire.

The Travelers are in good spirits after the fire as they move to a new hotel. Front row, from left to right, are Linda Ellington, Diane Lyons, Sue Smith, Dr. Morriss Henry, Ann Henry, and Brenda Gullet. Back row, from left to right, are Beth Nyhus, Wes Cottrell, Gale Byrd Hinson, Robert Hinson, and Dr. Bob Gullett.

Sergio De Leon (center), a native Arkansan living in Texas, and his family opened their home to host all 70 of the Arkansas Travelers for dinner and to watch Hillary Clinton's debate after a long day of campaigning. Sergio worked side by side with the group providing invaluable information and assistance.

Sue Smith and Fred Knight "honk and wave" the day before the primary in the sleet and wind in Texas (2008).

Chelsea Clinton with Margaret Whillock and Ann McCoy at a star-studded Dallas fundraiser for Hillary Clinton that the Travelers were asked to attend. Rob Reiner is in the background.

13.

PROVING GROUND

Pivotal to Bill Clinton's 1992 nomination, Illinois was also among the more memorable locales the Arkansas Travelers worked.

Travelers arrived in March a few days out from the state's March 17th primary election. They headquartered in Oak Park, a conservative, largely Republican suburb of Chicago.

The Travelers also worked neighborhoods on Chicago's south side and elevated train stops in the city and attended minority churches while there.

Tsongas, the former U.S. senator from Massachusetts, and Clinton were "head to head" going into that primary, recalled Bill Trice, a Little Rock lawyer and one of sixty-five Travelers who went on that six-day Chicago-area trip. "It was a watershed moment," said Trice, who knew Clinton well because his son, Will, and Chelsea Clinton were close friends and attended school together.

Mary Anne Salmon of Little Rock was also on the trip. As they had done in Clinton's previous Arkansas campaigns and in New Hampshire and Georgia just weeks before, the Travelers relied on Arkansas-style retail politics to promote Clinton.

"Everywhere we went we asked for votes and talked about our governor and it worked," she remembered. Illinois primary voters gave Clinton more than fifty-one percent of the vote. Salmon, who had previously worked for the governor's office, later entered politics herself and won repeated election to the Arkansas House of Representatives and the Arkansas Senate.

The Travelers encountered a less welcoming environment in the conservative Oak Park neighborhood than elsewhere. They did find a surprise source of Clinton supporters when they worked the commuter stops for the "L" trains, where they ran into many transplants from Arkansas happy to see them.

Mark Stodola, a prosecutor then and now mayor of Little Rock, said the Travelers caught riders getting off the trains. It made an impression, he said, "because no one had tried that kind of tactic" there. The unflappable Chicago commuters were stunned to see folks standing in the cold handing out campaign material and trying to talk to them about Bill Clinton.

In Chicago, the Travelers ventured into some rough neighborhoods. They went to a minority church that weekend. Salmon remembers seeing a lot of burned-out buildings as they tried to locate the church. "It was scary on the way," she said. "But the church was so welcoming." The congregation held a reception for the Travelers, as did several of the churches they attended on their travels. Bill Trice spoke to the congregation, prompting Stodola to say he didn't realize his lawyer friend had such an evangelical flair.

As always, Travelers tried to leave the people they talked to with the answers they wanted to hear about Bill Clinton. Occasionally, they went too far. A tale told almost universally by Travelers, including Bill and Donna Linder, is about an encounter between Charlie Varner of Fort Smith and a voter in snowy Chicago who wanted to know what Clinton was going to do about the ozone. Charlie's answer? "Bill will fix it."

Charlie climbed back in his van and told fellow Travelers what the woman had asked. When he told them how he answered, the Travelers adopted "Bill will fix it" as a ready response for a variety of situations. It was almost as popular as their mantra, "Bill would do it for us," used when they encountered new difficulties.

As had been the case in New Hampshire, snow and cold weather made door-to-door canvassing difficult, but most of the Travelers had come equipped this time with heavy coats and boots. Still, it was a challenge, said Ann Pride, who remembers a conversation with a mail carrier she encountered on a Chicago street. Pride, now the federal governmental affairs director for Entergy Corporation in Washington DC, was a lobbyist for the company in Arkansas in 1992. "The wind in Chicago was brutal in March, and there was still snow and ice on the ground," she said, emphasizing that the Travelers were going door-to-door at houses that each had a number of steps leading to the front door. "The postman on the route asked what we had done to make the organizers mad. He said only new postmen like himself got assigned that route," said Pride.

Like all of the canvassing Travelers, she said she was schlepping a bag full of heavy videotapes door-to-door, which made the steps that much more challenging. "It took a ton of Advil to get over that day's route and the St. Patrick's Day Parade march the next."

As they had in small towns, Travelers turned out early to march in a Chicago neighborhood's St. Patrick's Day parade, wearing special green Clinton T-shirts and carrying the Traveler banner they wagged all across the country. Being a Traveler was "very taxing physically," Bronfman said. People had to be in decent shape to work the long days and carry bags of literature and videotapes.

The Travelers had another reason for those pain relievers Ann Pride mentioned. After several long days of fighting strong winds, climbing steep steps, avoiding the neighborhood dogs, and working to exhaustion, the Travelers unwound at an Irish pub in Chicago, O'Sullivan's, on the night before the election.

Traveler Rick Watkins bought the bar for the evening, paying $1,000 for all the Travelers could eat and drink. It was a bad deal for the bar, according to all the Travelers; but Watkins tipped the manager well. "We needed fellowship," Rick said.

The party couldn't have come at a better time for them. The Travelers were feeling the groundswell of support for Clinton's nomination in Illinois and were reinvigorated by the late-night gathering—though slowed a lot the morning after when they had to work the polls.

Jan McQuary, the Little Rock kindergarten teacher, danced with Skip Holland, a lobbyist, before she famously danced on the bar during the revelry that night with Lee Douglass, who was Arkansas insurance commissioner. Sheila was up there, too, with State Senator Jay Bradford. The Travelers were letting off steam—and a lot of it. Mark Stodola said he "got a new understanding" of his friend the kindergarten teacher when he saw her dancing on the bar.

They had worked hard in Chicago and were ready to party. Kimball Stroud, one of the younger Travelers, introduced them all to "lemon drops." She convinced everyone to have a group shot and demonstrated the technique, which involves taking a shot of vodka followed by a bite of lemon wedge dipped in sugar. Jeff Mitchell was also among the revelers. His most vivid memory of the night is of a row of flaming Dr Pepper shots lined up along the long bar in front of the Travelers. Mitchell and Dee Pryor ordered those (a mix of amaretto, rum, and beer). "A well-skilled bartender can make them all flame up at the same time. It's just beautiful," Jeff said.

The Chicago bar wasn't far from where the Travelers were staying; but it was too far to walk, especially in the condition many were in. At the end of the night, only one fifteen-passenger van remained at the bar with something like twenty-two or twenty-three mostly inebriated Travelers needing rides back to the hotel.

While they waited for the van, Bill Trice danced around the street lamps, doing his best Gene Kelly impression. The remaining Travelers stacked themselves into the van for the ride back to the hotel. Stacy Sells, a Little Rock public relations executive, was the designated driver. Before they even took off, a policeman stopped them. Sells, about eight months pregnant at the time, assured the officer she had not been drinking. He still made her get out of the van. She was every bit as pregnant as she had said. He helped her climb back in and dubiously let her take her out-of-control passengers to the hotel.

The Travelers had considerable difficulty getting out of bed the next day. Jerry Bookout, a state senator from Jonesboro, and Skip

Holland, a lobbyist from Little Rock, refused to answer the phone. "Finally, there was just dead silence," said Mary Anne Salmon, who had called to rouse the duo. "They had jerked the phone out of the wall." Someone banged on their door until they got up, and off they all went to work the polls. Only the pregnant Sells was allowed to sleep in. The Travelers were working the polls and had to be out really early. Sheila and Ron Hope were working one polling place and took turns, one talking to the incoming voters and the other lying down on a park bench. Bar-dancer Jan leaned against a wall to get through the day.

The Chicago trip was memorable for Jeff for more than the flaming shots. It was Jeff Mitchell's first Traveler trip. The law school student, who sold some stock to finance his trip, expected a couple of people from his hometown of Paragould would be there but knew no one else. Mitchell fortuitously sat down on the plane by Ron Hope, a Little Rock lawyer. Hope would later hire Mitchell to work in his law firm.

By night, it was time to celebrate again. The results were coming in and Clinton was a clear winner. The campaign chose the Palmer House Hotel for Clinton to make his acceptance speech, recalled Bill Trice of Little Rock. Clinton was at the podium and green and white confetti rained down on him, Trice said. "It was a gorgeous setting."

Clinton let the Travelers participate in special ways. They got to see how the whole campaign system worked, Trice said. He specifically remembers watching Clinton upstairs after the speech, changing shirts and ties to do interviews by satellite with local press from the states that were coming up. "Then it was a new tactic, and now it is old hat," said Trice.

By then, the Secret Service was being far more protective of Clinton. Bronfman and Ann Henderson had noticed agents getting rifles out of a car and staking out rooftops before the parade a few days earlier. Security was tight that night at the hotel, too, causing the Travelers to realize Clinton needed the protection.

Bobby Roberts, who heads the Central Arkansas Library System in Little Rock, was not thinking about that when the Secret Service stopped the group in the Palmer House. They were wearing their Traveler buttons, which were supposed to give them access and Clinton himself had asked to see the group. Roberts tried to convince the Secret Service of that and actually got into an altercation with them until his fellow Travelers stepped in to calm the situation. Even then the Travelers were scared Roberts might end up in custody. However, Bobby prevailed and all the Travelers got to see Clinton that night.

What did Clinton say to them? He put his arm around Rick Watkins and said, "I understand you had a very good time in the bar." Obviously, the Traveler promise that what happens on a trip, stays on a trip, did not work that night.

Senator Jerry Bookout plods door to door through the snow before the Illinois primary.

Showing the Traveler Irish Spirit in a Chicago St. Pat's Parade, 1992.

Enjoying the hospitality of Rick Watkins, who bought out the bar in Chicago, March 16, 1992. Clockwise from far left: Jim McAdams, Bob Razer, Jimmie Hays, John Selig, Bobby Roberts, and Dick Norton.

Shown celebrating are Kimball Stroud, Rick Watkins ("the man of the hour"), and Jennifer Harris.

Mild-mannered kindergarten teacher Jan McQuary dances with Skip Holland, before she left the floor to dance on the bar with Insurance Commissioner Lee Douglass.

The D.C. crowd joins in the celebration. Around the table are Paula Thomasson Scott, Dee Pryor, Jennifer Harris, Henry Woods, Kimball Stroud, Clark Ray, and Jeff Mitchell.

Getting ready for election night results. Left to right are Bill Trice, Mark Stodola, Sheila Bronfman, Lee Douglass, Jan McQuary, Skip Holland, and Ann Pride.

The "Bubbas for Bill" group at the Palmer House in Chicago, election night, March 17, 1992. Left to right are Tom Marshall, Mack Dyer, Charlie Varner, Bill Schneider, and Bill Linder.

14.

CELEBRATION AND SUCCESS

When the Arkansas Travelers reached California, Clinton's nomination was pretty much secure. They still had plenty of campaigning to do, but they also found time for more "fellowship."

The trip included a significant stop at the UCLA campus, where the Travelers met up with Clinton. Rose Crane said the Travelers spotted "some smarty-britches boys" maneuvering to hold up a giant-size marijuana cigarette. The crafty Travelers threaded themselves into the crowd in front of them and quietly unfurled the Travelers' long banner. It went undetected until Sam Perroni, the tallest of the Travelers, and Faye Rodgers from Clinton, another tall Traveler, held the banner up to block the view of what the students were doing. One of the boys standing behind Crane asked, "How did you all do that?" She said, "We are older than you are and we have all done it before."

In Bakersfield, the Raisin Council sent the Travelers away with a gift of raisins. The only problem was that there were twenty-six Travelers in the group and each got ten pounds of raisins. "So we had 260 pounds of raisins to try and do something with," said Rose. They sent some home. Some they ate. There were raisins everywhere in those crowded vans.

The Travelers' most memorable California stop was a visit to Gail and Randy Goodrum's home, where they recorded the infamous crusade song, "Stand By Your Van." The Goodrums wrote the parody to Tammy Wynette's "Stand By Your Man."

The Travelers filled hours of van time singing the song, especially on those long stretches between towns across the Midwestern states. Even today, they can launch into lyrics that are forever imprinted in their brains:

Sometimes it hurts to work for Clinton
But just the same we know we should
The campaign always needs us
And yet they never feed us
Even Hillary's cookies are sounding good!

Stand by your van
Even though your feet are freezing
Sheila says we're leaving
And we roll 'em at 4 a.m.

Bill's biggest fans
We're not afraid of torture
We'll get him all the votes we can
While we stand by our vans

We all got lost in South Chicago,
Manchester thought we all talked strange;
But we are always fearless
Because we're never beerless
Fresno will never be the same—
Without the Travelers!

Stand by your van
Though freeway traffic stalls us
We go where duty calls us
And knock on doors for Billy

Stand by your van
In mountains, snow, or desert
We'll get him all the votes we can,
And we'll stand by our vans!!

This group recorded "Stand By Your Van" while campaigning in California. (See Photo Index for Names.)

Bill Clinton plays the sax with entertainer Kenny G at the Biltmore Hotel on election night, June 2, 1992.

The crusade song detailed what the Travelers experienced as they traveled by van in different states. "Lyrics came quickly," Gail said. They could have written fifty verses. Henry Woods led the choir in their den that night as Goodrum, who had his own recording studio on the property, taped the song on a boom box. He couldn't get a microphone from his studio into his house where dozens of Travelers were packed.

The Travelers ended their California trip at the Biltmore Hotel in Los Angeles at an election-night party celebrating Clinton's win in the primary. Entertainer Kenny G performed and coaxed a willing Clinton onstage to play the sax. Clinton's 47.5 percent win essentially secured the nomination. The next stop would be the National Democratic Convention in New York.

Later, Randy Goodrum wrote, or co-wrote, two other serious pieces of music for the campaign. "Circle Of Friends," which Goodrum

1992 Primary Election   102 Days on the Road • 12 States

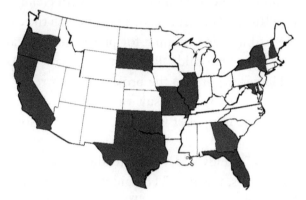

Florida Straw poll

Two groups. Dec. 1-16. Dec. 9-16 (7-16 days) 10 people.

NH   Numerous trips. Travelers were in and out of the state
until the primary. Patti Criner and Dale Evans went Sept.
of 1991- Feb. 20, 1992. Sheila Bronfman took the first
group January 8-20, 1992 (13 days), and second group
Jan. 17-20 (3 days). Third group started with Bronfman
and Larry Crane February 3-19 (17 days). Fourth group
Feb. 7-19 (12 days). There were others in and out and
the biggest group came starting on February 13-19
(6 days). 137 people total.

SD   February 1-9 (9 day) 2 people

MO   February 22 (1 day) 3 people

GA   February 25 to March 4 (9 days) 38 people

MD   February 28 to March 2 (4 days) 4 people

TX   March 7-8 (2 days) 30 people

OK   March 8-9 (2 days) 11 people

FL   March 1-4 (4 days) 7 people

IL   March 13-18 (6 days) 65 people

NY   April 4-8 (5 days) 4 people

OR   May 10-18 (8 days) 1 person

CA   May 28 to June 3 (6 days) 26 people

co-wrote with Arthur Helmsley, was sung at the close of the Democratic National Convention when Clinton was nominated for president. Goodrum said he had wanted to write with Helmsley, who wrote "Cry Me A River." Goodrum called him early in the campaign and told him he had a friend running for president and wanted to write a song for him. "He said, 'President of what?'" Goodrum laughed. Once Helmsley got into the project, he was really into it. Goodrum's "Reunion" was the result of a request from Hillary Clinton. It didn't come until after Clinton's election in November.

"Circle Of Friends," Randy said, "was intended to bring everybody, not just political cronies, together." He said he respects the office of president and wanted to convey that "We're all in this together, as opposed to 'All hail the king.'" Randy remembers sitting high in the stands of the convention hall in New York as the spectacular show came to a close. He was watching his high school pal, nominated for president, being embraced by a throng of people on stage. Balloons and confetti fell from the rafters. He listened to the huge, hopeful crowd sing "Circle Of Friends" as the celebration came to a close. "We're looking across the entire arena of people and they were locking arms. Total strangers. That's when you feel it," he said. What did he feel? "There's not a word," he said softly. "When you see something like that affect so many people, you just can't explain it. It's overwhelming. 'Overwhelming' is the word, I guess."

The lyrics to "Circle Of Friends" are:

Let's form a circle of friends
One that begins … and never ends
You know our future depends
On making this unfriendly world
A circle of friends

There's way too many people out there hurting
Doesn't anybody care about the pain
How can we pretend it doesn't matter
We can't close our eyes and make it go away

Let's form a circle of friends
Bring everyone in ... and get together again
We know our future depends
On making this unfriendly world
A circle of friends

My hand in your hand
Her hand in his
Can't you feel how strong the circle is

Let's form a circle of friends
One that begins ... and never ends
You know our future depends
On making this unfriendly world
A circle of friends

Let's form a circle of friends
Bring everyone in ... and get together again
We know our future depends
On changing this unfriendly world
And making this unfriendly word
A circle of friends

Excited Travelers arrived on a chartered jet in New York for the Democratic National Convention in mid-July. Travelers were all anxious to experience the Big Apple, witness their friend's nomination, and launch the general election campaign.

There was still work ahead. Hillary Clinton had come up with the idea to use the Travelers and other Arkansans as "ambassadors" to the other states at the convention. She called to ask Sheila if she would coordinate the Travelers and the other Arkansans who might want to participate. "Of course, I said 'yes,' and I thought it was a great idea," Sheila said.

Many Travelers were assigned as "Arkansas Ambassadors." Their role was to attend delegation caucuses of the states to which they were assigned, get to know the delegates better, persuade any who weren't committed to Clinton to vote for him, and, perhaps most importantly, lay the groundwork for the November campaign. Frequently, the Travelers who were ambassadors were working delegations of states they had personally visited during the primaries. They were supposed to be lining up future visits as well, continuing to build a bond with voters from all around America.

"You can make as much out of this program as you are willing to put in," advised Bronfman and Skip Rutherford, as they instructed the Arkansans who had agreed to work as Arkansas Ambassadors.

The program proved successful and helped to give delegates personal knowledge about Clinton and to fire them up for the fall campaign. A briefing memo for the participating Ambassadors explained the goal: "While most of the delegates are supporting Clinton for president, it is essential that they go home feeling even more inspired and that those delegates who did not come to New York with Clinton as their choice leave New York with great and positive feelings."

Each Arkansas Ambassador was assigned to serve as the personal ambassador for a specific state or states. Larger delegations were assigned multiple ambassadors. They were all to attend morning meetings of the respective state delegations to get to know the delegates, let them get to know people from Arkansas who have known the governor for many years, and answer their questions about Bill

Clinton. Each was also to speak to the delegation at a Wednesday meeting, emphasizing their personal relationships with Clinton.

The Arkansas delegation sat front and center in the convention hall, with New Hampshire to one side of them. Both delegations were constantly shown on national television, made celebrities among the rest of the delegates. Some Arkansans were singled out for roles in the convention itself.

Jan McQuary, who had traveled for Clinton as early as the Florida straw poll, was among delegates called to the convention stage one night of the convention. She was there as an Arkansas teacher on a night when the party was highlighting the occupations of delegates. McQuary said it was "a goose-bump moment for a girl from Tillar, Arkansas, to be on that stage." She and the other Travelers knew how much hard work was ahead, but they reveled in the excitement of the convention and the many parties. "For that week, we Arkansas Travelers were going to enjoy ourselves," she said. "Sheila and the others had worked so hard to make it a fun time for all of us."

David Matthews had several special moments during the convention. Clinton had asked Matthews to be on stage when he accepted the nomination. Up there on stage, Hillary came to him, embraced David, and said, "I think there was a time that you and I were the only ones that really thought he could do this."

Mostly, the Travelers attended parties in New York. Some were involved as delegates and had a round of caucuses and platform meetings to attend. But others were free to enjoy any and all of the breakfasts, lunches, receptions, and dinners to which they were invited. Corporate friends hosted multiple parties, like the one that Entergy threw at the Waldorf-Astoria.

But nothing any of them did that week quite topped the gathering they had in a basement restaurant, the Cellar Grill, in Macy's

Department Store. They were exclusive guests invited to watch the convention roll call with Bill and Hillary and Chelsea Clinton. They all knew where the count was going as one state, then another cast its delegate votes. Virginia Kelley, Bill's mother, cast Arkansas's votes for her son. New Hampshire delegates said they would be with Clinton "'til the last dog dies.'" When Ohio cast its votes, the tally hit the magic number. Clinton was the nominee.

The Travelers and the Clintons celebrated as Ohio put Bill over the top, then began their historic march from Macy's to Madison Square Garden where exuberant Democrats awaited their nominee.

Only a handful of Travelers knew they were going to escort the Clintons to the convention hall. Sheila, Gail, and Ann had carefully distributed red buttons with "**CLINTON FOR PRESIDENT**" spelled out in dark navy blue to those who would promise to be at Macy's that night. The campaign pins were to be their access badges, although Sheila would be at the door to confirm the identity of each for the Secret Service. The Travelers pretty well knew the Clintons would at least stop by that night. But there was a much bigger plan for them, and it was hardly spontaneous.

"Every bit of that was staged," David Matthews said. Harry Thomason, the Hollywood producer, had called him about a month before saying, "I don't know much about politics, but I know an awful lot about TV." Thomason had this idea to have Clinton make an early appearance at the convention the night of the roll call. Nominees had traditionally made their first convention showing the night of their acceptance speeches. Thomason's idea didn't stop there. He wanted David's help to persuade state party officials to let Virginia Kelley cast the Arkansas votes for her son, and he needed for David to locate a place and a group for the roll call watch party.

Matthews knew the group that was right for the job and found the site in Macy's basement. Getting Democratic politicians to take a backseat to Clinton's mother was a little tougher, but Matthews got it done. There was one more snag. Bill and Hillary Clinton weren't convinced that this was the right thing to do. So Thomason got David and his wife, Mary Beth, to stand in for Bill and Hillary in a simulation of the walk out of Macy's, down Seventh Avenue and into the bowels of Madison Square Garden. Thomason's crew filmed the whole thing for Bill and Hillary Clinton to let them see what the walk would look like to TV viewers.

The Clintons were convinced and the plans were locked down. When it happened, Travelers in the convention hall were screaming as they watched their friends on a huge screen that broadcast the images to delegates, who chanted, "We want Bill. We want Bill" the whole time. Back home in Arkansas, family and friends were watching, too, on their TV sets, spotting people they knew in the crowd. When Bill entered the hall, he went directly to the Arkansas delegation. He hugged his mother, then reached over to shake Jimmie Lou Fisher's hand and those of many of the Arkansas delegates. While the jubilation continued inside, the Traveler escorts found themselves outside the hall and disconnected from the ongoing event. Their moment was over.

Still to come were the showing of that Thomason-produced film about "The Man from Hope," the acceptance speeches by Gore and by Clinton, and that closing song, "Circle Of Friends."

15.

THE FALL CAMPAIGN

For the Arkansas Travelers, the general election campaign for Bill Clinton boiled down largely to same song, second verse.

They had different challenges and different experiences in the fall campaign, but their mission was unchanged and they relied on the same strategies that helped bring Clinton success in the primaries.

If anything, they ramped up their canvassing, particularly in small-town America where they were having undisputed influence. In September, Traveler teams would strike out for South Carolina, South Dakota, Nebraska, Illinois, Missouri, and Pennsylvania. These groups ranged from as few as one to as many as twenty. They traveled as little as a day or as many as five. Travelers found doors to knock on and local media outlets to hit in all those states.

A good example of the kind of publicity the Travelers often attracted was on the front page of the *Ipswich Tribune* in South Dakota. Thirteen Travelers, a full vanload, "stand by their van" in the photo, holding Clinton-Gore campaign signs.

The cutline reads in part: "You didn't need to go to the Fiddle Contest in Yankton this past weekend to hear the Arkansas Traveler (a fiddle tune). ... The group, calling themselves the Arkansas Travelers, visited more than 40 South Dakota towns last week. The Travelers, who act as ambassadors for the Clinton/Gore campaign, travel the country at their own expense to spread the word about Clinton's record as governor of Arkansas."

That kind of attention was money in the bank for the Clinton campaign, which didn't have to buy advertising to reach the *Ipswich Tribune* readers with a positive message. Travelers repeatedly got such stories as they crossed the country. When the local reporters weren't covering Traveler events, Travelers tracked them down at newspaper offices and radio stations to volunteer interviews.

South Dakota was one of the Travelers' early general election trips in 1992. In all, twenty Travelers made their way through South Dakota and Nebraska over a five-day span in late September. State Representative Myra Jones of Little Rock was a native South Dakotan, and State Representative Wanda Northcutt of Stuttgart had visited there often with Jones. The pair had made a SWAT trip by themselves to South Dakota during the primary election.

For the general election, they planned a tightly scheduled trip to cover the entire state with two vans going high and two vans going low across the state. They left from the same place and met up on the other side of South Dakota. Sheila and Myra led one pair of vans, Wanda the other.

The Travelers met with elected officials and campaigned at rodeos, Indian reservations, football games, and even casinos in Deadwood, South Dakota, where they claim they didn't gamble. One vanload did take time away from campaigning to dress in early twentieth-century attire for a photo.

George Kopp, of Washington DC, offered a story on Ed Fry from their South Dakota trip. The pair were supposed to meet up with the rest of the Travelers in Minneapolis, but their flight from DC was delayed. They rented a car. Ed drove, George slept. "I fell asleep about one a.m. and awakened as we were surrounded by state police," Kopp said. The car was clocked at 105 mph as it crossed the border into South Dakota. The officer in charge, a Clinton supporter, said he'd give them a break but ticketed them for going 95 mph in a 55 mph zone. "Some break," said Kopp. "We didn't pay it."

On an American Indian reservation, Lib Carlisle was asked to talk at a football game. He knew people wouldn't want to hear a political speech at a game, so Carlisle introduced himself as being from

After crowding into <u>ONE</u> taxi, these Travelers posed to record a special moment in history in Deadwood, South Dakota, 1992. They worked hard and played hard and became lifelong friends. Shown here back row from left to right are J. T. Rose, Ed Fry, Ted McNulty, George Kopp, and Mike "Baby Face" Malone. Middle row left to right are Judy Robertson, Richard "Bootlegger" Bronfman, Sheila Bronfman, and Lib "Bagman" Carlisle. Front row left to right are Myra "Flapper" Jones and Ann "Barefoot Babe" Gilbert.

Arkansas and taught them to call the Hogs. Then he said, simply, "Vote Clinton" and ended his talk. It was one of several occasions when Travelers taught strangers the University of Arkansas Razorback cheer.

Matt O'Neil of the Clinton-Gore campaign staff in South Dakota wrote Sheila Bronfman, the Travelers' leader, a thank-you note after the trip. This was long before some others on campaign field staffs realized the value of the Travelers. But O'Neil had seen their work in another state. "I cannot tell you how grateful I am that the Arkansas Travelers, under your leadership, were willing to come to South Dakota. They were just magnificent once again and I am convinced that the Travelers' efforts could very well represent our margin of victory in November," he wrote. There was no way, he added, that the campaign could have purchased the media that the Travelers attracted "just by being themselves."

That's what they did best, not only in South Dakota but also in Nebraska, where that same group of Travelers slipped across the border, or in South Carolina, where another crew of six Travelers spent three days.

Sam Perroni, a Little Rock criminal-defense lawyer, had a solo assignment to work his home state of Illinois during the general election campaign.

"It was like stepping back in time," said Perroni, who grew up playing high school basketball in many of the cities he visited on Clinton's behalf. "Just driving into those towns brought back memories," the 6'7" tall Perroni said. He traveled ten to fifteen places before finishing in Bloomington.

Perroni's Illinois travels began in Springfield and were strategically planned to take him through parts of the state that historically voted Republican and where he had played basketball.

Perroni also recalled going to Lincoln, Illinois, where Abraham Lincoln spent fourteen years of his young life, and hearing Clinton compared to Abe Lincoln. Wherever he went, Perroni said he met with local politicians who would take him over to the radio station and newspaper. Or he'd find them on his own and try to get them to do a human interest story about Clinton. "I used to have about an inch-thick stack of articles that were generated from that Illinois trip." Headlines like "Walking Tall for Clinton," "Clinton Traveler pays visit," "Arkansas Traveler touts Clinton," and "Travelers pound pavement here for Clinton" followed Perroni on his five-day trip.

Travelers also managed two three-day runs through Pennsylvania. Rick Watkins and Ron Hope took one SWAT trip in September. Rick went back with Don Beavers of North Little Rock, then a railroad labor lobbyist in Arkansas, on another trip in October. On both occasions, Pennsylvania Lieutenant Governor Mark Singel escorted the Travelers from town to town for interviews and speaking engagements.

The people there wanted to know what Bill Clinton could do for them. Watkins, Hope, and Beavers were more than willing to tell them about the governor's twelve-year record in Arkansas, including improvements in education, economic development, and health. Watkins emphasized Clinton's experience and said he could carry the reforms to Washington. Hope maintained there was "no better man to run the country." And Beavers worked one-on-one with labor leaders to convince them to support Clinton. All the while, the men were picking up free media.

The Travelers met with the editorial boards of local newspapers, did interviews on radio, and met with local Democrats at committee meetings that drew thirty to eighty people. They recounted stories of Clinton's success in Arkansas, citing improvements in education, economic development and health care. They were "easy" interviews, Hope said. In one memorable media exchange, Watkins said Clinton was "one hell of a governor." The remark, he regrets, made the headline.

These Travelers wore coats and ties rather than the Travelers' usual rough-weather garb and were chauffeured by a state police officer in a minivan for what Sheila Bronfman called "cushy" but productive trips.

Watkins and Beavers were in Pennsylvania during the days before and after one of Clinton's debates with President George H. W. Bush and H. Ross Perot. Watkins remembered being at a Pittsburgh college, where he and Beavers did media interviews after the debate. As the candidates were debating, the Travelers received updated talking points from the War Room at Clinton's national headquarters in Little Rock, preparing them to react to the debates for news reporters.

Something Watkins learned early on was how to change his "shtick" for the crowd. Introduced at an event as a Traveler "who saw Bill Clinton this morning," Watkins responded, "Yeah. On the *Today* show." That wasn't what the crowd wanted to hear, Singel told him, leading Watkins to emphasize his personal connections with his governor in later speeches.

Missouri, a critical swing state next door to Arkansas, drew Travelers on three different general election trips. Sheila Bronfman took a large bunch of troops there in late September for three days, including a rally with Tipper Gore. Randy Laverty led another group to the state and Virginia Laverty yet another. Both of those trips were in October. In all, forty-eight Travelers crossed Arkansas's northern border to talk to their neighbors about Bill Clinton.

On one of the Missouri trips, David Bailin, an artist and professor at the University of Central Arkansas and at Hendrix College, balked at taking communion in an evangelical Missouri church in 1992. Bailin is Jewish. Sheila flashed a "Bill would do it for us" sign at the Little Rock man. David shook his head and said, "I don't think so." He remained seated without incident, but Sheila kept the sign handy for such situations.

On a run along the Texas border to Oklahoma, Jo Parker and J. J. and Amie Lee Galloway failed to make connections with a larger group of Travelers. A TV station from Sherman came to interview them, expecting more. The reporter was a Clinton supporter, Parker said, who had his cameraman film them talking to people in the Wal-Mart parking lot. "The idea was it would look like more were there. Guess it worked as he gave us good feedback."

In Oklahoma, the Travelers were instructed to attract as much attention as they could for Clinton. They drove their highly decorated van through Main Streets, waving at people. They really didn't have time to stop on the trip, which was to cover 700 miles in two days. If the town was large enough to have a Wal-Mart, they'd leaflet customers. One man followed them through a town and back out on the highway. To his disappointment, Parker said, "We finally had to stop and tell him Bill Clinton was not in the van."

The next week, two more crews went to two states each. One of those trips was to Kentucky and Tennessee by a thirteen-member crew for six days. The other trip was a two-person trip to Washington and Oregon.

Among the Kentucky stops was the Breckenridge County Courthouse in Hardinsburg. The Travelers met with Democratic supporters and schoolchildren and showed a videotaped interview with Clinton, then answered questions about the Clinton-Gore ticket. Seventh- and eighth-grade gifted and talented students were in the audience. Prior to their visit to the courthouse, the students had voted in a mock election that Clinton won with eight votes to President Bush's five and Ross Perot's four. The other five class members were undecided. After meeting with the Travelers, the students voted again and gave Clinton an overwhelming majority, according to the report in the local newspaper. This time the Travelers got free media with local kids' names in the copy.

In Kentucky, the Travelers were all designated as "Kentucky Colonels." The distinction is like the "Arkansas Traveler," a signed certificate given by Arkansas governors to people who will spread good will for the state.

It wasn't even mid-October. The Travelers had over a dozen general election trips behind them and more to go.

Happy times on the "Clinton carousel" while campaigning in Faulkton County, South Dakota, before reading to children from the library on September 18, 1992. Shown here from left to right are Bob Baxter, Rep. Wanda Northcutt, Russ Meeks, Weldon Chesser, Joel Buckner, Mary Ellen Lackey, Gloria Calhoun, Rick Eoff, and Ron Oliver.

Riding in a local South Dakota parade are left to right Ed Fry, Myra Jones, Ann Henderson, Ted McNulty, J. T. Rose, George Kopp, Mike Malone, Sheila Bronfman, Judy Robertson, and Lib Carlisle.

The vans crossed the state of South Dakota in 1992 working every town along the way. Two vans went high and two went low. This one went across the top of the state. Shown here front row from left to right are Rick Eoff, Rep. Wanda Northcutt, Gloria Calhoun, Mary Ellen Lackey, Rose Crane, and Weldon Chesser. Back row from left to right are Russ Meeks, Joel Buckner, Ron Oliver, Bob Baxter, and local supporter.

Each van carried this sign for motivation. When they got tired or cranky, the group would pull it out for a laugh. Shown from left to right are J. T. Rose, Lib Carlisle, and Charlie Varner in Kentucky, October 1992.

162

Arkansas Travelers Destinations

1992 General Election   **91 Days on the Road • 27 States**

NY Ambassadors
　　　　July 13-16 (3 days) 107 people

PA　　September 9-11 (3 days) 3 people,
　　　　Oct. 14-16 (3 days)3 people

SC　　September 11-13 (3 days) 6 people

SD/NE　September 16-20 (5 days) 20 people

IL　　September 23-27 (5 days) 1 person

MO　　September 25-27 (3 days), Oct. 10-12 (3 days),
　　　　Oct. 24 (1 day) 48 people

LA　　October 2 (1 day) 1 person

OK　　October 3 (1 day) 10 people

WA/OR　October 7-11 (5 days) 2 people

KY/TN　October 7-12 (6 days) 13 people

CO　　October 7-11 (5 days) 14 people

AZ　　October 15-18 (4 days) 1 person

AL　　October 16-18 (3 days) 5 people

IA/NE　October 14-20 (5 days) 33 people

KS　　October 17 (1 day), Oct. 30-Nov. 2 (4 days) 56 people

TX　　October 20-25 (5 days) 17 people

MN/WI　October 21-25 (5 days) 37 people

ME　　Fall of 1992 (3 days) 1 person

MI/IN/IL/WI
　　　　Fall of 1992 Mitch Miller Tour (5 days) 2 people

NC　　October 29–November 1 (4 days) 8 people

GA　　October 29-November 2 (5 days) 39 people

16.

DAYS TO GO

With only half of October and a couple of days in November left before the general election, the Travelers made the most of them. SWAT teams rolled out to a few more states and larger crews headed in every direction. Time was slipping away with the November vote looming.

Harry Truman Moore and Weldon Chesser of Paragould took a SWAT trip to Washington and Oregon. It was a five-day, fully packed swing through eleven cities and towns, large and small. H. T. spent two hours in one city meeting with gifted and talented classes that were studying the American political process. He and Weldon passed out leaflets in downtown Winslow, Washington, with a reporter following them. The response was so positive that the reporter accused H. T. and Weldon of having "baited" the street to make their effort look so successful.

"I don't hunt, fish, smoke or drink. Least I don't drink much. What I do, I talk about my friend Bill Clinton," Chesser told Marla Williams, a *Seattle Times* reporter. Chesser was scouring a small Washington town for a barbershop, not to get a haircut but to engage the clientele in campaign talk. "Talk gets repeated in barbershops and beauty salons and that's what I want," he told the reporter. On another occasion, a voter in a pub explained to the reporter that although she was a Republican, she was going to vote for Bill Clinton because two people from Arkansas had come all the way to the State of Washington to work for Clinton.

One of the most unusual requests to the two Travelers came when they were asked to ride in the Eastern Washington University homecoming parade. Williams wrote, in the lengthy article, "Members of a remarkable network of longtime supporters, Arkansas Travelers and other Friends of Bill's may be helping Clinton's political career more than all the highly paid, professional campaign strategists put together. Not only do they high-tail it to Clinton's aid in a crisis, but they stump for him tirelessly, spending time in small towns typically passed over." Travelers had been from Winslow to Olympia, Vancouver to Spokane, stopping everywhere from a shipyard to a university's alumni house, she wrote.

"Nobody collects friends like Clinton, or puts them to better use." She could not have capsuled the story any more accurately if she had traveled the country with them. That's as much a testament to how skilled the Travelers became in working with news reporters as it is her reporting skill.

Colorado proved challenging to the Travelers, whose plane got diverted en route because of a tornado between Little Rock and Dallas, the site of their connecting flight. The plane was sent to Oklahoma City until late that night before returning to Dallas. The weary Travelers couldn't even get a room in Dallas for the unscheduled overnight there. The airport was closed and the hotels were all booked. Thanks to Traveler Rick Eoff, a small-business owner from Little Rock, and his connections, they finally bedded down in a motel forty-five minutes away from Dallas but only for about two hours. They had to be back for a 6:30 a.m. flight to Denver. Gail Goodrum, who was leading the trip, said they didn't have their luggage, so no toothbrushes, no change of clothes. They just managed.

Later on the trip the group stayed in a Colorado luxury spa resort while Travelers in Kentucky at the same time found themselves booked into a three-story walkup motel in the town's red-light district. A campaign field staffer, who didn't know the town, had secured the location.

Behind schedule from the moment they hit the ground, the Travelers in Colorado were already two hours late for their first appointment. Coloradans had cooked for them. "You can't insult your local people," Goodrum said. They had to get there and were pushing the speed limit. The cop who pulled them over leaned in and looked at them and said he'd been following them for two miles. The van driver, Bill Wiedower, couldn't see him for the luggage they had hastily stowed in the back. Gail, the van leader, apologized profusely, taking the blame herself and gave the officer the van registration. When he came back to the van, he said it was the wrong registration. She had switched the registration between two vans, something that happened more than once to the Travelers.

"Oh, I'm so silly. This is such a big mistake. Look what I did," she said, trying to talk her way out of the situation. He went to his car, came back and said, "I've got good news and bad news. The good news is I'm not going to impound this van, and I'm not going to take you to the police station. ... The bad news is that your driver is getting a really big ticket." It was a "really, really big ticket," she said, that the offending Travelers chipped in to pay.

Colorado Democrats welcomed the Travelers, thrilled to see Clinton supporters in a mostly Republican state. A handwritten note from Bell Goddard, "Grand Ma" of Grand Ma's Restaurant in Palisade, Colorado, reported to the Clinton family that "a very excited group" stopped at the restaurant in Mesa County, a known Republican stronghold. Republicans visiting the eatery said they would still vote for George Bush, she wrote; but they agreed "these people were doing one hell of a job" for Clinton. Grand Ma also sent the Clintons some of the same homemade jam she had given the visiting Travelers.

Colorado leans Republican and the numbers of Democrats in the small towns there were few but grateful to see Clinton's supporters show up. "They'd bring potato salad and chicken and everything, wanting us to eat," Gail said. As hungry as they were, the Travelers could eat only sparingly and dash away to the next stop on their schedule. So grateful were these Colorado Democrats that one woman went to Gail with tears rolling down her face. "She said,

'We're so glad you came. We never met the president.' I said, 'Well, I'm not the president' and she said, 'But you know him.'" That "real person-to-person stuff," Gail said, "is what kept the Travelers going."

The Travelers received lots of correspondence thanking them for their visit to Colorado. "Thank Heaven he will be in the White House next January," wrote Samantha Dunham of Pueblo. Linda Cacchione of Sedalia appreciated their "bringing a piece of Arkansas here. The Democrats in her county "were still talking about what a great group of people you are."

Yet another Traveler SWAT team went with a group that passed through Pennsylvania. It was called the "Mitch Miller Tour" and was led by the band leader, who was accompanied by Dr. Ruth Westheimer, the sex counselor. The *Morning Call* in Allentown reported on their visit, which included stops in Michigan, Indiana, Illinois, and Wisconsin. Idavonne Rosa, a nurse and social worker from Melbourne, and Frank Whitbeck, an insurance executive from Little Rock, both Travelers, went along with Al Gore's parents and the two aging celebrities. They met with about twenty retired Teamsters at the Lehigh County, Pennsylvania, Senior Citizens Center.

Gore's parents tried to charm the crowd into voting for the Clinton-Gore ticket. They'd been at it nonstop for a month. "Albert and I decided that we would stay in the eye of the political hurricane as long as it was blowing, up until the day of the election," Mrs. Gore said. Miller led the crowd in a sing-along and Dr. Ruth emceed. A survivor of Nazi Germany, she said it's important to participate in democracy. Idavonne and Frank reported to Sheila that it was harder work than they had expected, but an incredible experience. The trip, they said, was "just a blast."

Gilbert Cornwell, a North Little Rock businessman and Clinton's cousin, made a late one-person SWAT trip to Arizona, traveling the state for four days. Once again, free media was the order of the day. The Arizona field staff wrote a memo to the Clinton head-quarters detailing Cornwell's trip. He had gotten coverage from three radio stations, two large Phoenix news stations, and a Tucson TV station. "We were excited to secure a spot on KFYI (in Phoenix) since they have been very pro-Bush. All three spots went GREAT!" the staff reported. Cornwell also worked an Arizona State Fair booth to talk to people and planned a campaign walk. After receiving the memo, Sheila forwarded it to Skip with the note, "The Travelers Strike Again!"

Five Travelers went to Alabama for three days. They covered the area with several Alabama politicians, following a schedule set by the local campaign. Dr. Richard Bronfman called the Alabama trip the "Cadillac" of Traveler trips. Not only was the trip well coordinated within the state, requiring only that the Travelers show up, he said the visiting Travelers were carried around in recreational vehicles and well fed.

As frequently happened with SWAT teams, Richard and the others were called on a Tuesday to be in Alabama that weekend. Whoever could go on short notice went. It was easier then to fly, he said, so they got tickets and headed to Alabama. Also on that trip were Ron Oliver, a businessman; Sam Boyce, a Newport attorney; Tom Parker, head of the Arkansas Petroleum Council; and Martha Dixon, an African American seamstress and dressmaker. Oliver and Boyce traded off, speaking at the various events, while the others generally worked the crowds. They all provided that tangible connection with the candidate.

"I could tell from the reaction from the crowd, they were interested in hearing somebody that knew Clinton," said Oliver. During the primary, people were clamoring for information about Clinton. By the general election, he was a better-known commodity. Travelers, because they knew him personally, were still treated like celebrities, which amused Richard Bronfman. "If you knew Bill, you were a celebrity to a lot of people." Oliver recalled being asked by a youngster for an autograph. "It took me a few minutes to realize he thought I was Bill Clinton," Oliver said, laughing.

Iowa presented at least one van a lot of laughs when they weren't actually campaigning. It's the sort of activity that was supposed to "stay in the van."

The van made a quick stop at a Kum and Go convenience store and Carl Whillock, a retired executive from Little Rock, went inside. The proper Southern gentleman came back out, climbed in the van, and revealed his purchase: a brown paper-wrapped copy of *Penthouse*. The Paula Jones stories, accusing Bill Clinton of more misconduct, had hit the news. Whillock proceeded to read—and embellish—the graphic account for his van mates, sending Tom Prince, a Little Rock attorney and future mayor of Little Rock, and others in the van into convulsions.

Debra Buckner of North Little Rock was in that same van and recounts another story, "We were exhausted. Sheila's back hurt. Ted McNulty was driving and got lost. We drove into this small town and they were having a parade. We got in the middle of the parade and there was a split second when we wondered what to do and then we just decided, 'heck, let's go for it.' So Ted hit the gas pedal and we were in the parade. All the people were wondering, 'Who are these people and how did they get into this parade?' We just waved and drove on."

"Sheila would always insist on promptness and being in the van at the appointed time," Margaret Whillock said, "and anyone late would be left behind." After a reception, Margaret recalled, "Everyone in our van was seated and ready to go, except Sheila, who was doing a radio interview. Almost in unison, we all said, 'Let's go!'" Ted McNulty started the van. They left Sheila, or so it appeared.

"We went to the local liquor store as we had had a very long day," Margaret said. "In the meantime the Democratic ladies in this small town called the state police to stop us and send us back to pick up

Shelia without knowing that we had already gone back and picked her up. The police came after us, with lights flashing. Sheila assured him that she indeed was in the van."

Then they all got out and took photos with the officer, posing as if he'd arrested them. "We were laughing until we realized people in passing cars were probably wondering why the Clinton for President van passengers were in trouble with the law."

Campaigning in Newton, Kansas, a group of Travelers were met on the town square by about twenty Mennonite families. Joe Purvis said the Mennonites fixed each of the Travelers a boxed lunch, and their children pitched in to buy the Travelers canned drinks. He called the encounter "the living embodiment" of Christian spirit.

A sweet tooth could have cost Sue White a real tooth, but for the cool thinking of Rene de Turenne in Kansas. They had gotten Tootsie Pops at a convenience store en route to a Wichita event. Just as White brought hers to her mouth, the van made an abrupt stop. The sucker broke Sue's tooth almost to the gum. Sue was about to panic but Rene called ahead to Democratic headquarters for help. "When we arrived at the headquarters, there was a big party for the other Travelers and a young lady dentist for me," Sue said. The Wichita dentist, a Democratic Party volunteer, took Sue to a dental office and reattached the tooth.

The Travelers were in Russell, Kansas, Senator Bob Dole's hometown, on Halloween night in 1992. They saw a couple, the wife dressed as George Bush and the husband as Barbara Bush, complete with pearls. "It was odd," Joe Purvis said, "standing next to 'Barbara' at the urinal." That wasn't the only oddity. The next morning, the Travelers worshipped at Dole's home church, where they heard a pro-Clinton sermon.

Texas Governor Ann Richards wrote the Travelers, thanking them for the "tireless efforts" in the Texas campaign. "While we did not quite win Texas for Bill Clinton, we did manage to force George Bush and the Republicans to expend vital resources here allowing Bill Clinton to win the states he needed. Your contribution made a big difference."

She concluded, "Thanks to all of your hard work, we have a new beginning in Texas and the nation. Congratulations on a job well done." Seventeen Travelers went to Texas in late October led by Rick Eoff of Little Rock.

At the beginning of a reception for the local Democratic Party at a Wisconsin event, the chairman said, "I always wanted to meet a Southern boy with two names, and I want to meet Joe Dan." Peggy Nabors was there when he obliged. Joe Dan Yee, a Traveler of Asian background, stood up.

Their first night in Wisconsin, Randy Laverty and Don Richardson slipped off with a Traveler van just before midnight. They found a beer joint not far from the hotel and walked in wearing Clinton regalia. "Every eye was on us," Laverty said. Don ordered a Bud Light but the quick-thinking Laverty asked what beer the bar regulars were drinking. It was Leininkugel, the waitress said. "That's what we'll have," said Laverty. After they got the beers and were sipping, Laverty said one of the locals announced to the bar, "They must be OK. They're drinking 'Leinies.'" Randy and Don campaigned for Clinton in the bar until it closed. They asked about a carry-out order but the bartender couldn't sell beer to go. Instead, he said they should check the steps behind the bar as they left. A full case of Leinies was waiting, compliments of the chef.

On another stop, Randy was with other Travelers at a Democratic reception in Ironwood, Michigan. Next door was a wedding reception for the local sheriff's son and his bride. According to Randy, he wound up dancing with the bride at the Traveler reception after "someone" kidnapped her and brought her there. The unhappy groom and his friends retrieved her, but Randy reports none of the Travelers had stitches the next morning.

Mayor Herb Bergson of Superior, Wisconsin, wrote Traveler Mike Malone after the election, thanking him for the Travelers' stop there. "It is clear that the work that the Arkansas Travelers did may have very well made a difference in this presidential election, and if so, the whole future of the United States as we know it."

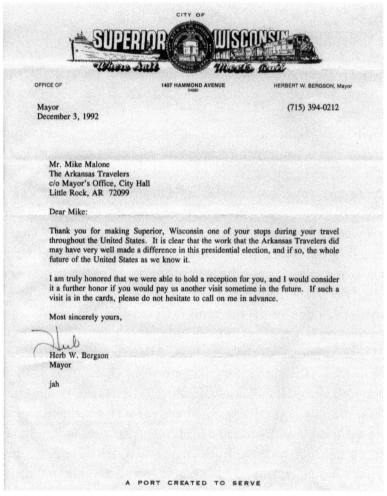

Mayor   (715) 394-0212
December 3, 1992

Mr. Mike Malone
The Arkansas Travelers
c/o Mayor's Office, City Hall
Little Rock, AR 72099

Dear Mike:

Thank you for making Superior, Wisconsin one of your stops during your travel throughout the United States. It is clear that the work that the Arkansas Travelers did may have very well made a difference in this presidential election, and if so, the whole future of the United States as we know it.

I am truly honored that we were able to hold a reception for you, and I would consider it a further honor if you would pay us another visit sometime in the future. If such a visit is in the cards, please do not hesitate to call on me in advance.

Most sincerely yours,

Herb W. Bergson
Mayor

jah

A big "thank you" from Mayor Herb Bergson of Superior, Wisconsin. He noted that the Travelers had "made a difference."

172

Harry Truman Moore and Weldon Chesser campaign at the Eastern Washington State University homecoming parade in Cheney, Washington, as part of a six-day "SWAT" trip in 1992.

Tom Parker, Ron Oliver, Jean Hervey, an Alabama supporter, Richard Bronfman, and Sam Boyce travel in style as they give stump speeches all over the state of Alabama three weeks before the election. This was a "SWAT" team trip.

October 27, 1992

Arkansas Travelers
Rick Eoff
▓▓▓▓▓▓▓▓▓▓
Little Rock, AR   72211

Dear Rick:

Isn't it a great thought? One week from today, Bill Clinton
will be elected as our next President!

It's people like you who helped it to happen. I very much
enjoyed getting to meet and visit with the Arkansas
Travelers. I had to give you all a welcome hug. Thank you for
bringing a piece of Arkansas here and for sharing your
viewpoints with us. The Democrats in Douglas County, Colorado
are still talking about what a great group of people you are!

We are working hard to help Clinton be the winner in
Colorado. Our country needs the kind of leadership we see
reflected in Bill Clinton --- and in the people who have
supported his candidacy right from the start. It's a great
time to be an American.

Bill and Maggie Larsen (formerly of Ft. Smith) send their
regards. Thank you for taking the time and making the effort
to come to Castle Rock. We all hope you will come through
again one day soon.

With warmest wishes,

Linda

Linda Cacchione

Sedalia, CO   80135

The Travelers frequently received letters from people they visited.

In 1992, an Iowa sheriff was called to chase down the van, which had left behind
Sheila Bronfman, who was delayed while talking to a reporter. The Travelers waited
for no one, not even the leader.

Senator Cliff Hoofman, Gail Goodrum, Russ Meeks, Nancy Balton, and Richard
Hutchinson work the Jefferson Jackson Dinner in Iowa before Hillary Clinton
speaks in October 1992.

State of Texas
Office of the Governor
Austin, Texas 78711

ANN W. RICHARDS
GOVERNOR

November 12, 1992

The Arkansas Travelers

Little Rock, AR 72209

Dear Rick and the Travelers:

I am writing to express my personal thanks and gratitude for your tireless efforts put forth on the Unity '92 campaign. While we did not quite win Texas for Bill Clinton, we did manage to force George Bush and the Republicans to expend vital resources here allowing Bill Clinton to win the states he needed. Your contribution made a big difference.

Now that the election is over I hope that you will take a well deserved rest and spend some time with friends and family. Thanks to all of your hard work, we have a new beginning in Texas and the nation.

Congratulations on a job well done.

Sincerely,

Ann Richards
Governor

Texas Governor Ann Richards congratulated the Travelers.

A Polaroid camera was used to take a picture and left with a "canned" press release for local newspapers. The Travelers generated a lot of free publicity. This is a group of Travelers in Texas in 1992.

Women from Washington County, Arkansas, travel to Fort Scott, Kansas, to celebrate the Year of the Woman in October 1992. Showing off their t-shirts are, from left to right, Phoebe Harris, Virginia Spencer, Othelia Paul, Millie Nelms, Jill Smith, and Katy Nelson.

A lot of time was spent in airports. The Minnesota/Wisconsin Group takes off in October 1992. (See Photo Index for Names.)

Randy Laverty campaigns at a wedding reception and dances with the bride on the Minnesota/Wisconsin trip in 1992.

The 1992 Wisconsin group prepares to walk the neighborhood. Shown from left to right are Pat Morrow, James Rawls, Don Beavers, Ronnie Williams, Wooten Epes, Sue White, Lauren Bowen Wills, Rick Lorence, Peggy Nabors, and Nelwyn Davis.

17.

REALIZING THE DREAM

Georgia, where the Travelers were particularly effective in the primary, was a must destination for the general election. Once there, the Travelers' presence mattered more than anyone might have imagined.

The Travelers had gone back to Georgia to work right up to election eve, planning to devote the last three days of October and the first two of November doing what they do. The timing proved fortuitous. Supporters of President Bush filled the airwaves with negative ads depicting Arkansas as some kind of a swamp with a vulture looking out over a dark and barren landscape. The ugly image was supposed to convey that Clinton had poorly governed Arkansas. The Arkansas Travelers, who really knew the state and its governor, were there to fight back.

The Travelers' intervention "carried the day," Sheila Bronfman said. They disputed the ad's content and answered accusations that Arkansas didn't celebrate the Martin Luther King holiday or have education reform. Among the Travelers on their march through Georgia were Myra Jones, a state lawmaker who had written the state's law on celebration of King's birthday, and Eleanor Coleman, an African American educator. Coleman could verify her friend Jones wrote the King law and, as a teacher, could also answer questions about Arkansas education. Along, too, was Herby Branscum, chairman of the Democratic Party of Arkansas.

When the need arose to refute the claims in that Bush ad, Sheila said, "We had all the right people with us." The Travelers were in Atlanta and had just arrived at Jimmy Carter's presidential library for a rare break from campaigning. They were to have had a whole hour for a quick tour of the library, but Sheila got a call over the loudspeaker that quickly changed their plans. Atlanta Mayor Andrew Young was on the phone, asking the Travelers to come do an emergency press conference with him. Besides Young, Georgia Governor Zell Miller and U.S. Representative John Lewis (D-GA), would be there. This was the day before the general election, and the press conference—featuring Travelers Jones and Coleman—was reported statewide.

"It was huge," Sheila said, explaining that the rest of the Travelers provided a backdrop for all the clicking cameras. "We put it all together in the van," she said. The Travelers responded quickly, going over what they had to do to counter the ugly Bush ad as they made their way to the press conference. Again, Travelers were thinking on their feet, or seats, as it were.

As always, Bronfman said, "No one said, 'I can't do that.'" They just stepped up to the challenge. "Their dedication to a cause was just amazing to me," she said of the Travelers.

That dedication prompted Eleanor and Roosevelt Coleman of Little Rock to use money they had saved to celebrate their anniversary to make the Georgia trip. "What I wanted was to go and campaign for Bill Clinton," she said. Roosevelt worked for state government while his wife taught. This had to be an anniversary trip for the record books, considering the role Eleanor played in the Travelers' rebuttal of that ad. "I was from Arkansas and so I knew what was true." They didn't really know the other Travelers well, although they had met Sheila. "I knew her but I didn't know she was that bossy," Eleanor said. Most people know candidates from afar, she said, but they knew Bill "up close" and that made a difference.

This trip to Georgia started out like all the other Traveler trips. The only element that made it different was its closeness to the vote. The Travelers had a schedule with slated stops that included churches and town squares—all their usual haunts.

There was another difference in Georgia. All across the state, the Travelers had police escorts, thanks to the relationships the small town people had with their local police. Officers from different departments "handed off" the Traveler cavalcade as it crossed jurisdictions.

At one point, Bronfman said an escorting policeman was leading the van "at a leisurely pace." She said they were running late to the next appointment and needed to be going at least the speed limit. She had her van driver pull up beside the police vehicle, stuck her hand out and rolled it in a circular motion to speed up the escort. "My van got a laugh out of that."

On another occasion, Traveler vans were in a caravan behind a police escort with its lights on. As they passed, cars were pulling over and stopping on the side of the road, apparently mistaking the vans as a funeral procession.

"I think they think Mom died," volunteered Herby Branscum, one of the Travelers in a heavily decorated van bearing Clinton signs and the Traveler banner. The Travelers waved to the stopped cars as they went by them.

The bulletin for First Missionary Baptist Church in Thomasville, Georgia, announced the Travelers' presence on Sunday. So did the minister, from the pulpit. "WELCOME—CLINTON-GORE DELE-GATION!!!!!!!!!!!!!!!!!!!!!!!!!!," the church bulletin screamed, reminding congregants to go to the polls on Tuesday. Sam Perroni of Little Rock was one of the white Travelers who had never attended a black church. "The preachers were great," he said. Perroni spoke at a church in Georgia and reminded them that Bill Clinton was about hope, hope for their children, and hope for the future."

H. T. Moore of Paragould also spoke at a black church in Georgia, using for his sermon the convention song Randy Goodrum co-wrote. "You are part of our circle of friends now and we want you to invite other people to be part of our circle of friends," H. T. said.

Waving to the crowd in yet another parade. Some rode and some walked while handing out candy. Dorothy Preslar, Sydney Probst, Paula Storeygard, and Weldon Chesser ride with the locals in October 1992.

Georgia Travelers pose with local officials during a full day of campaigning. (See Photo Index for Names.)

Eleanor Coleman is interviewed as Travelers Barbara Hartwick, Sam Perroni, Milana Dennis, and others work at a Habitat for Humanity project in Georgia in October 1992.

The town of Woodstock, Georgia, welcomed the Arkansas Travelers for a day of campaigning in October 1992. (See Photo Index for Names.)

H. T. Moore and the Travelers are welcomed in Bartow County in October 1992. Messages like this appeared all over the country.

The Gordon County Court House welcomes Arkansas Travelers to town. (See Photo Index for Names.)

It was there, too, that Richard Bronfman, who is Jewish, drew a line as the church prepared to pass communion. "I have done a lot of things for Bill Clinton but I won't do this," he said. Sheila and Gail, sitting on either side of him, took care of the situation. One took the wafer, the other the wine so as not to be noticed by the usher passing the elements. It was a great slight of hand. Remember, the same scenario had happened before in Missouri to Traveler David Bailin.

After church, as the vans neared Plains, Georgia, Travelers were scrambling to try to see former President Jimmy Carter. Herby Branscum had Chip Carter, the president's son, on the phone and finally worked out the details. The former president came walking down a driveway, wearing a polo shirt. He had wood chips on his shoulder from a kitchen-remodeling project he was doing. He flashed a broad smile and took time to visit and pose for photographs with the waiting Travelers.

The Travelers were getting more complex briefing papers by then and their objective in Georgia was plainly spelled out: thirteen electoral votes. Clinton got them all after what proved to be a close popular vote. Independent Ross Perot pulled about thirteen percent of the votes, leaving Clinton and Bush neck and neck. Clinton won by fewer than 14,000 votes out of the more than 2,321,000 cast. It was a sliver of a difference, the kind the Travelers had made time and again.

Finally, it was election night. Returns were coming in from around the country. Expectations were high. President Bush hadn't proved to be nearly as popular as Skip Rutherford had warned Bill Clinton he would be more than a year earlier.

Those thirteen hard-won electoral votes from Georgia combined with 357 more to secure Bill Clinton's election. He was home in Little Rock to celebrate, back at the Old State House, where he had announced his candidacy, surrounded again by his Arkansas army.

The Arkansas Travelers were home, too. Most were at the Travelers' private party in the old Bale Chevrolet Building. Travelers were inside and outside the Old State House and in nearby hotels and in the streets of Little Rock. Some were home with their families watching their long journey for and with Clinton play out on national television. Even those who had gone to Georgia made it home in time for the raucous celebration in the Arkansas capital.

The Traveler who had known Clinton his whole life long, Joe Purvis, was there, his eight-year-old daughter, Elizabeth, on his shoulders in the crushing crowd. High school pal Randy Goodrum was there, right below the stage, with wife, Gail, both shivering in the cold because the Secret Service had unexpectedly guided them to this place of honor before they could grab their coats. Everyone was on "Clinton time," awaiting the future president's public appearance.

Sheila and Richard Bronfman, Skip Rutherford, and Mary Anne Salmon were all there, as were so many of the Travelers. They listened as President-elect Clinton said, "Time after time, when this campaign was about to be counted out, The Arkansas Travelers exploded out of this state, around the country, to tell people the truth about what we had done here together; how we had pulled together, what we believed in, and what we could do as a nation." It was Bill Clinton's victory party and theirs, too.

In August of 1992, Sheila found herself making arrangements to get the Travelers to Washington DC for the 1993 inauguration. Sheila so believed that Bill Clinton would be elected president, she signed a contract and booked Washington's Sheraton Carlton Hotel not knowing for certain that she and the Travelers would be celebrating a win with their friend Bill.

"All of these people just believed. There was never a doubt," she said. When she put out the call for early reservations, Travelers responded quickly, snagging the available rooms at the Sheraton Carlton, buying airline tickets. They'd gotten quite used to letting Sheila charge their credit cards. Individually, collectively, they were out hundreds and thousands of dollars of their own money over the year, all of it invested in getting Clinton elected. They sure wanted to be there to see it happen.

"It ended up beautifully," Sheila said. The Travelers were treated like royalty at the hotel and pretty much everywhere else in the capital city. Restaurants were catering to Southern taste buds. Everyone seemed to be practicing their drawls, imitating the Arkansans who packed into DC for the parties, the parade, the fancy balls, and, of course, the inauguration itself. Once again, the Travelers donned their winter gear to stand in the cold, this time amid a sea of other Americans to watch their friend take the oath of office.

All their effort had been directed toward that moment when Bill Clinton would be sworn in as president, the first ever from Arkansas. These really were his friends of a lifetime. When he hurt, they felt his pain. And, when he reached the political pinnacle that had been his dream, they shared his joy.

Charlie Varner, described by another as the "quintessential Traveler," had sent a holiday greeting to his fellow Travelers in December. "As you know the Travelers need new credit cards and food stamps for the trip to DC. I hope the Carlton don't board up and take bankruptcy before we get to try their facilities." His note joked about Bill and Hillary being "homeless and unemployed" when they left the governor's mansion and said not to tell Sheila that he just finished reading his Kentucky travel packet. Varner promised he'd try to help the Clintons "worry about the ozone hole, Socks the cat and the 29 fireplaces in the White House."

The note collapses into a few lines the nature of all these trips the Travelers' made, their closeness with Bill and Hillary, their shared history, and their fondness for each other. "You are a special group of people," wrote Varner, who said he wouldn't swap his Traveler trips for anything. Few, if any, of them would.

One of the Travelers' own, David Pryor Jr., or "Dee," put together the Absolutely Unofficial Blue Jeans Bash for them, the Clinton

M E M O R A N D U M

Date: December 17, 1992

Phone

TO: Arkansas Traveler and Friends

FROM: Charlie Varner, Ft. Smith, AR. 72901

RE: "Merry Christmas and Happy New Year"

I discovered I could send a few words for the same price as a card. And as you know the Travelers need new credit cards and food stamps for the trip to D.C. I hope the Carlton don't board up and take bankruptcy before we get to try their facilities.

Sure was a good party Saturday before Bill & Hillary got homeless and unemployed. Sheila and crew did a super job and I know all appreciated it very much.

Don't tell Sheila but I have just finished reading my Kentucky travel packet. ha The air plane driver would not keep wheels up long enough to absord all the material. She must have forgotten Bill Clinton is the one that keeps three novels going and reads all the newspaper and keeps up with world affairs. I try to help the Clintons worry about the ozone hole, socks the cat and the 29 fireplaces in the White House. I am glad Hillary does not have a dog to drag her off the helicopter every Sunday.

In spite of it all I think all the Travelers had a big year and made lots of good friends. I would not swap my trips for anything.

I look forward to seeing you all in D.C. next month and hope each and all have a Merry Christmas and a Happy New Year between now and then. You are a special group of people.

Best Regards

cv

Charlie Varner was a beloved Traveler with a great sense of humor. He gave all the Travelers great insights as they prepared to head to Washington for the inauguration.

campaign staff, and other Arkansans who couldn't afford the high-dollar tickets to an official inaugural ball. Held in the ornate National Building Museum, this was a low-cost event featuring rock 'n' roll music and barbeque for the blue jeans-wearing crowd. The relaxed apparel and the down-home food and music were, as Dee said, a "flat-out rejection" of the black-tie, privileged ideals associated with the departing Republican political elite.

Pulling the event off was Dee's most satisfying experience as a Traveler, partly because so many people, including his father, U.S. Senator David Pryor, said it wouldn't work. David Sr., a Traveler himself, should have known better. Dee is an Arkansas Traveler and nothing can keep Travelers from completing a mission.

Whatever their part was in Bill Clinton's election, the Travelers had persevered through challenging situations, worked harder than many thought they could and had fun doing it. They were due some more fellowship and found it at the Blue Jeans Bash.

(Above) Sheila Galbraith Bronfman and Gail Goodrum, the co-leader of the Arkansas Travelers, preside over a breakfast for the Travelers at the 1993 inauguration.

(Left) Sheila Galbraith Bronfman, alias "Attila the Hen," is the leader of the Arkansas Travelers. The sweatshirt speaks for itself.

191

(Above) President Bill Clinton and First Lady Hillary Rodham Clinton wave to Travelers in the stands during the Inaugural Parade in January 1993.

(Right) Virginia Clinton Kelley celebrates with the Travelers at the "Blue Jeans Bash" during the inaugural.

18.

REELECTION

Americans knew President Bill Clinton well, "warts and all," by the 1996 reelection campaign. Work the Travelers did was directed more toward getting out the vote and energizing the electorate. Most Americans knew whether they would or would not support the president's reelection. The Travelers, like the campaign, focused on helping voters remember what President Clinton had accomplished in the first term.

The Travelers made only three trips. For the primary, they went to Iowa, the state Clinton had ignored in 1992. They also made two bus trips during the general election campaign, one to Kentucky and Tennessee and the other to Louisiana. Both were marked by peril, although of different sorts.

The first stop was Iowa, where the nation's first caucuses are held. The reason Clinton skipped them the first time around was U.S. Senator Tom Harkin. Harkin was Iowa's favorite son and Clinton's time could be better spent elsewhere. Iowans supported the Clinton-Gore ticket, however, in the general election.

For the Arkansas Travelers, the 1996 trips were reunions of a sort, bringing back together people who had bounced their way across America in packed vans where they could do nothing but get to know each other extremely well. The bond never broke. Theirs were shared experiences, the sort that aren't easily forgotten.

There were new Travelers, of course; but the veterans embraced them, as evidenced by a newsletter edited by Traveler Tyler Thompson of Little Rock to chronicle their trip through Iowa.

They were back on the road to get the Iowans' attention and did all those things they did in 1992: canvassing neighborhoods, flagging

1996 Re-Election   **12 Days on the Road • 4 States**

IA	February 9-13/96 (5 day) 46 people
KY/TN	October 26-29 (4 days) 42 people
LA	November 1-3 (3 days) 45 people

down commuters, approaching mall shoppers, and visiting Main Streets. It had all become second nature to the Travelers.

The 1996 newsletter revealed some of the camaraderie they had shared four years earlier on those long van rides, interrupted by stops in one town after another. Then, the motto was "what happens in the van, stays in the van." In 1996, they were sharing what happened in the vans in a printed newsletter.

"Was Iowa great or what?" asked the lead article. "We had five days of no sleep, little food, freezing temperatures and a very gusty wind. Okay, so it wasn't paradise, but we each came home feeling like it was." Why? It could have been because they were helping Bill, make that President Clinton. Or the support they found in Iowa. "Or maybe, it was that we had been traveling with 45 wonderful people where friendships were formed, reformed or

194

strengthened." The count was slightly off. Forty-six Travelers made the five-day trip. (Note: Text from the newsletter is included in Appendix B.)

Marci and Lila Riggs, sisters who traveled together to Iowa, Tyler Thompson, Harry Light, and Sheila Bell contributed reports from the different vans. They included some details of the work the van families had done, but the articles also poked fun at individuals, none more perhaps than Sheila Bronfman, who was back to lead the Travelers again, whistle in hand and in full control.

New Travelers were warned about Sheila's van, how her crew never got to eat or stop for a bathroom, how she mercilessly blew that blasted whistle, and how they really might be left stranded somewhere if they were ever late getting back to the van.

The oldest of the Travelers when she traveled in 1996 was eighty-year-old Elmo Wolfe, a retiree from Fordyce, who easily kept up with the rest of the Travelers, most of whom were roughly half of Miss Elmo's age during the 1996 campaign.

"Her stamina was incredible," Bronfman said. "She never missed a beat. Not one." Sheila's niece, Mandy Childress, then a nineteen-year-old Hendrix College student, provided the contrast. "The line was, Mandy slept, Miss Elmo didn't," Sheila said. Mandy slept every time she got back in the van, but Miss Elmo "would be telling stories and passing out brownies and snacks she had baked and brought from home."

Sixteen years later, when many of the same Travelers were back on the road for Hillary Clinton, they had added small step stools to help them get in and out of the vans, something Miss Elmo didn't have, or apparently need, during Bill Clinton's campaigns.

As they had in 1992, when their friend Bill was running for election, the Travelers were scheduled from time to time to meet up with him. This time, he was "Mr. President" and the task was more formidable for the Travelers and for others trying to see Clinton.

One of those important intersections of the Travelers with the president was to be in Des Moines at Northern Iowa Area Community College. No sitting president had ever been there.

Traveler Ron Oliver acknowledged that some of them, many of whom had been with or near this president for four years, "had become jaded" about that sort of thing. As they approached Des Moines, drivers were complaining about having sore arms from fighting strong winds that buffeted their heated vans around.

When they came upon the crowd of people lined up outside, bundled up against that same harsh wind for the chance to see a president—this president, their friend—the Travelers went to work. They got out of the vans and talked with those people about Clinton, spreading the Traveler gospel.

Some of those Iowans had been standing in the cold and wind for four hours just for the opportunity to be in the same room with Clinton. Not all got the chance. The crowd was so large, part of the group had to go into an alternative space to watch him on TV. Randy Laverty and some of the other Travelers stayed with those who were separated from the main event and tried to entertain them as everyone waited for Clinton.

What happened next would make Laverty a target for the Traveler newsletter. He was wearing a ball cap and a shiny baseball jacket that day. Someone in the crowd mistook the Arkansas state legislator as some kind of athlete. Randy played the part as youngsters approached him for his autograph. After developing writer's cramp, he signed one without the "y." He became "Randy LaVert" that night and in the Traveler newsletter.

Lila Riggs wrote that none other than their own Randy Laverty had stolen the show from President Clinton. "The funniest moment of this already funny episode is when a young boy approached Randy with his pad and pencil ready and asked him, 'So, what team do you play for?'" Travelers hung close by, watching, as LaVert signed one autograph after another.

A significant difference for the Travelers in 1996 was related to security. The easy access they had to Bill Clinton early in his first bid for the presidency, including late-night chat sessions after campaigning, was no longer possible with President Clinton. The Travelers learned, as the president himself did, that the Secret Service isn't kidding around. The Travelers still met up with Clinton from time to time, as they did in Iowa. The encounters were just more restrained.

There was another change for Travelers in 1996. They had traveled almost exclusively in rented vans four years earlier. This time Sheila chartered buses for two trips. Instead of flying to a destination, they left from Little Rock. The first bus trip was to Kentucky and Tennessee and the second and last trip to Louisiana.

Larry Bryant of Benton, owner of Cherokee Coach, was the driver of the forty-seven-passenger bus chartered by the Travelers. He had never been a part of a campaign trip before and was enjoying the experience. He especially marveled at the discipline of the Travelers, all brought about by Sheila and her whistle.

The bus was full of doctors and lawyers and other professionals; yet, when Sheila commanded, they all popped out of their seats, scurried down the hallway and out the bus door. Sheila was clocking them, demanding they get out of and back into the bus quickly. It didn't matter who they were. Larry said, "Before they were done, they could clear the bus in three minutes flat. I've never seen that kind of discipline with professional people in my life."

The trip was to be a long loop out of Arkansas, across Kentucky and back home through Tennessee. There were forty-two Travelers aboard for the four-day campaign trip.

In Kentucky, there was another incident involving tardy Travelers. Two got back to the bus late and found themselves being shunned by everyone else. Gregg Reep, then mayor of Warren, and state Senator

Kevin Smith of Helena had been dispatched to campaign in a local municipal office and didn't come back, Sheila said. That's when the idea of shunning them came up. When the pair finally got on the bus, none of the Travelers spoke to them, instead looking out the windows and keeping straight faces. "Gregg goes, 'Is nobody going to talk to us anymore?'" Sheila said the busload of people waited a full minute or longer before they erupted in laughter.

It was different taking a bus down residential streets, but Larry made it work on both bus trips, Sheila said. The Travelers worked long days, climbing in and out of the bus to campaign and seek out media contacts. One day, they had canvassed neighborhoods in Bowling Green, gone to church and worked an afternoon barbeque at the Kentucky governor's mansion in Frankfort. They were en route that evening to Louisville, when Sheila got a call from the campaign asking the Travelers to divert to Chattanooga for a rally with Tipper Gore.

The Travelers took a vote because diverting would cost them the money they had put down on hotel rooms in Louisville and they'd have to travel through the night. The Travelers chose to sacrifice the money and sleep and go on to Chattanooga.

It was late in the night, Bryant was driving the speed limit, or maybe a little bit more, on I-75. Sheila remembers Travelers were singing, talking, playing cards and walking the aisles.

Large trucks and small cars were zipping past the bus. As he rounded a curve, Bryant saw vehicles stopped on both sides of the road, pointed every which way. He threaded the fast-moving bus between the tight rows, trying everything he could to slow it down. Up ahead, a major truck accident had blocked the usual traffic lanes. There was nowhere for the bus to go.

"I never did tell anyone this, but I had already made up my mind that we were going to crash," said Bryant. "I was looking for the lesser of the evils." He thought he might have to take another vehicle out.

It was all happening fast and Bryant was out of options. He turned on the turn signal and honked the bus horn twice, trying to signal the driver of a small car to the left of the bus. The driver understood and gave the bus room. Another vehicle up ahead made an avoidance move. The bus came to a stop.

"I can see it like it was yesterday," said Levi Phillips of Berryville. He heard the brakes "chunking," Levi said. Lights on the adjacent cars "were going past like crazy" as Larry steered the bus down the center of traffic. Levi said, "Larry prevented an accident that could have happened on either side of the bus."

A relieved Bryant, who had imagined awful scenarios as he pumped the bus brakes on the slick highway, shook the other driver's hand and hugged him out in the middle of the highway. He was grateful for that last-second chance to avoid a collision. A veteran driver and airplane pilot, Bryant said it was the closest he has ever come to such an accident, which might have put the bus in the pileup with the two trucks.

"You want me to remember all those things I've spent the past sixteen years trying to forget," said Bryant, explaining that the pavement had been wet, possibly from fuel leaking from one of the trucks.

When the bus finally stopped on that dark Tennessee highway, everyone on board breathed a sigh of relief. "We all sat quietly contemplating life and then somebody said what a great headline it would have made for Bill if a busload of Travelers had been killed," Sheila said. That kicked off a round of dark humor, but the Travelers bored of it and realized there were a lot of people stuck out there on the highway. All that backed-up traffic had to stay put for about two hours while a hazardous materials team cleaned up the spill.

"Someone said, 'Let's get some stuff and go talk to them,'" Sheila recalled. Everyone got out of the bus "and up and down the highway we went, passing out literature." Fred Knight of Little Rock said the truck drivers sitting in their stalled rigs "loved us." Elaine Johnson, who is from Hope, said everyone wanted to talk to her about the president.

It was a good distraction for the unnerved Travelers. "I think everyone on that bus clipped a coupon at that time," said Levi. "Larry was a damn good bus driver."

That same bus provided the Travelers with a lot of laughs, too. Shirley Montgomery of Conway was one of the privileged Travelers who ended up riding in the back of the bus on the Kentucky-Tennessee trip. They called themselves the "back of the bus gang." The problem was that the restroom wasn't working and they lived in odiferous conditions throughout the trip. Montgomery had "Back of the Bus" T-shirts made for them later.

With maybe two hours of sleep after the near crash, the crew was up and ready to work the rally with Tipper Gore in Chattanooga, Shirley said. "Sheila planted us on the street and said, 'Travelers don't move.' The woman in charge of the Chattanooga rally came over and said, 'Travelers follow us.' We just looked at her and shook our heads. Sheila walked up, blew that whistle. We jumped and started marching."

The Arkansas Travelers seldom felt threatened as they campaigned for the Clintons. The exception came that year in Bastrop, Louisiana, where Travelers were on another bus trip late in the president's reelection campaign.

The Travelers had paid $3 each to get into a county fair in what proved to be "a very unfriendly town," Bronfman said. "It was the only place we've ever been kicked out of."

A voice came on the loudspeaker asking the "Clinton people," who were dispersed through the fair crowd, "to please leave," Sheila said.

They later found out that the town was in the middle of Ku Klux Klan territory and "very Republican, very conservative, very religious," Bronfman said.

She sent several scouts out into the crowd looking for the Travelers, blew her whistle, and had Larry tap the bus horn trying to get the Travelers' attention.

"We had to leave. It was time to leave and they were pushing us out. There was going to be an incident if we didn't get out," she said.

"I had strong suspicions that we might be shot out of the event," said Nan Snow, a Hot Springs businesswoman. "I don't think the road we took there had ever been traveled by a bus and I'm not sure if some of those folks had ever considered a Democrat for any elected office, much less Bill for president."

So the Travelers loaded the bus and got out, leaving two stragglers. Charley Penix, a Little Rock architect, and Kerry McKenney, of Washington DC, who were happily campaigning, unaware of the bad vibes. The pair discovered they were there alone and the bus was gone. They knew the rules about being left and began searching for a way out. They found a local campaign person who had discreetly waited to bring them to the Traveler bus after their "nerve-wracking experience."

The next town was "altogether different, very friendly," Sheila said. A relieved Charley and Kerry rejoined the group there.

The Travelers visited two churches in Monroe, Louisiana. One was a friendly minority church, where Travelers were welcomed with open arms. The other was a white evangelical church. State Senator Cliff Hoofman of North Little Rock had overslept and been left behind and had found his way to this church, the Travelers' second scheduled stop. He met the arriving Travelers and warned them not to enter looking like they were with a campaign.

The Travelers didn't campaign in any church but did wear their buttons. Cliff had visited with the minister and gotten the distinct impression that the Travelers were unexpected and not particularly welcome. They went to worship and the minister introduced them as "Senator Wolfman from Arkansas and his friends." As Cliff recalls, "When we got back on the bus, everyone starting chanting, 'Wolf, Wolf, Wolf.'" To this day, there are Travelers who call him "Wolfie."

The difference in the political environment between 1992 and 1996, Joe Purvis said, was huge. In 1996, the only white support

Clinton drew were "rock hard Democrats" and college professors. "I felt like it was 1961 and we were Freedom Riders. ... That church had a very cold atmosphere."

On that uncomfortable trip, Don Bishop recalls another uncomfortable event. He had to share a room and a bed one night with Joe Purvis, who outweighs him by about 100 pounds. They had asked for two rooms but only one was available with one double bed. When Joe lay on the bed, he took up most of the surface and made it sag, Bishop said. "For the whole night, I clawed at the edge of my side of the bed trying not to roll down into that pit with him," Don said. "We made a pact that we'd never tell anyone that we slept together in the same bed, so don't spread it around."

Travelers for President Clinton depart for Iowa in February 1996, with the youngest Traveler, Mandy Childress, 19, and the oldest Traveler, Elmo Wolfe, 80, holding the Traveler sign. The joke was that Mandy slept, and Miss Elmo didn't. She outworked everyone. (See Photo Index for Names.)

BILL CLINTON

February 16, 1996

Ms. Sheila Bronfman

Little Rock, Arkansas 72207

Dear Sheila:

Hillary and I want to thank you and the rest of the Arkansas Travelers for heading to Iowa on behalf of my campaign. The Travelers made a big difference in my 1992 campaign, and I'm glad to know I can depend on you to do the same this year.

It means a great deal to me to have fellow Arkansans like you working for my re-election. With your help, we'll win in November.

Sincerely,

Bill Clinton

P.O. BOX 19300 WASHINGTON, D.C. 20036-9300
Paid for by the Clinton/Gore '96 Primary Committee, Inc. Contributions to Clinton/Gore '96 are not Tax Deductible

Letter from President Clinton

President Clinton greets Travelers backstage at Drake University in Iowa, 1996. Left to right are Nettie Gibson, Peggy Nabors, Judy Robertson, Levi Phillips, Sue White, Lila Riggs, Sheila Bell, Weldon Chesser, Mary Anne Salmon, President Bill Clinton, Randy Laverty, Mandy Childress, Pat Morrow, Lorene Leder, Tyler Thompson, Joann Martin, Idavonne Rosa, and Sheila Bronfman.

Vic Snyder, future Arkansas congressman on the right, relaxes while celebrating the birthday of Lila Riggs with Mayor Harry Light in Iowa, 1996.

The Travelers worked caucuses all over the state and celebrated that night with Senator Chris Dodd (D-CT). (See Photo Index for Names.)

Get me to the church on time. The Travelers made a point of always attending church and getting their spirits lifted while on the road. This group is on the 1996 Kentucky/Tennessee trip. (See Photo Index for Names.)

19.

PURSUING HILLARY'S PRESIDENCY

"I'm in."

With two words posted to her Web site in January 2007, Hillary Clinton ended the speculation. The U.S. senator from New York would be a candidate for the Democratic nomination for president in 2008. "And I'm in to win," she added in a subsequent statement.

Hillary had long been considered the frontrunner, should she enter the race, and the news of her candidacy buoyed her supporters around the country.

In Arkansas, she had a ready-made support system. The Arkansas Travelers, who had helped Bill Clinton be elected president, quickly rallied to help Hillary. They wanted the rest of America to know "The Hillary We Know" and set out to reintroduce her as their friend, a wife and mother, and to remind voters of Hillary's many accomplishments in Arkansas and elsewhere.

Her campaign proved to be far and away the most frustrating of the Travelers' campaign efforts, mostly because the nomination ultimately went to Barack Obama, not Hillary. The Travelers just weren't able to do for her what they believed they had done for Bill Clinton by helping him be nominated and win election twice.

Hillary did win New Hampshire, a state in which Bill had finished in second place. That early win, which rejuvenated her campaign, happened with a lot of help from the Arkansas Travelers, as had the New Hampshire rally of the "Comeback Kid." Eighty-one Travelers campaigned there for a week.

Her win in New Hampshire came on the heels of a disappointing second-place finish in Iowa, where thirty-five Travelers campaigned

Arkansas Travelers Destinations

2007-2008 Primary   **31 Days on the Road • 4 States**

IA	October 24-28, 2007 (5 days) 35 people
NH	December 27, 2007 to January 9, 2008 (15 days) 2 people
NH	January 2-9 (7 days) 81 people
AR	January 31 to February 3 (4 days) 58 people
TX	February 28 to March 5 (7 days) 70 people

for Hillary. The surprising Iowa win by Obama upended preelection expectations nationwide for Hillary. The developments in Iowa seriously concerned the Arkansas Travelers. They knew from Iowa on that there was a problem with her campaign. The problem was not with her. "She worked herself to death," said Sheila Bronfman.

In contrast to Bill Clinton's first New Hampshire campaign, Hillary had at the end of 2007 a campaign staff of at least eighty people in place in New Hampshire, with local campaign offices open in sixteen communities. They had access to lots of young volunteers anxious to participate and plenty of money for campaigns in all the states.

The campaign staff was confident, too confident. Their candidate was, after all, the former first lady and a formidable, respected U.S. senator. And she was widely expected to win New Hampshire's first-in-the-nation primary and march to the nomination. That was until Obama caught fire in Iowa.

The battle-seasoned Arkansas Travelers weren't deterred from putting their best efforts into her campaign in Iowa, New Hampshire, Arkansas, and Texas before Hillary withdrew from the race.

After experiencing the Iowa caucus, Berta Seitz decided only primaries should be held. The caucuses, she said, limit participation because participants must be present throughout and willing to defend their choices publicly. Sheila made the Travelers do a practice drill so they would be comfortable with what they saw at the caucus, but neither the drill nor the real event persuaded Berta that primaries aren't better.

Eileen Soffer, a Traveler from California who is the Bronfmans' cousin and made all four trips for Hillary, related personally in Iowa to a single mother of four teenage daughters. One of four daughters of a single mom herself, Eileen heard the woman's concerns about being unemployed and on disability and worried about her girls getting pregnant. For every issue the woman cared about, Hillary and the Democrats were in her corner, Eileen said. Yet the mother was terrified of voting in the public caucuses where her family and church members would see. It would be the general election before the Iowa mother "might feel empowered enough to vote her heart, not what is expected by her neighbors," Eileen said.

The best moment of Hillary's campaign for the Travelers, besides her wins in New Hampshire and elsewhere, was the opportunity for them to celebrate her birthday with her. At an event at Iowa State University in Ames, they had birthday cake for her backstage, recalled Fred Knight.

Iowa was Lisa Powell's first Traveler trip. The Batesville woman hadn't met Hillary but soon would. "When Hillary came backstage, I was just wide-eyed." At the party, Hillary was speaking to everyone there, naturally calling the names of all the Arkansas people she had known for decades. "Her people were amazed," Sheila said. That's why the Travelers were there.

Typically, Hillary personalized the interaction. "Levi, did the state police let you out of Arkansas?" she said, as she hugged Levi Phillips. The bond between Hillary and the Travelers should have clued the campaign staff into the Travelers' potential as campaigners, but the staff didn't quite get it.

The Travelers had some interesting challenges in the campaign for Hillary, much of it from media-inspired images of her. As Soffer put it, Hillary was very different from the image portrayed in the media. The Travelers gave another view. "I think that was powerful."

When Hillary showed some emotion on camera in a New Hampshire coffeehouse, Travelers were there, Vincent Insalaco among them. "She broke down and all of sudden, it was international news." The media reaction underscored for him how Hillary had become so much larger than life that people forgot she is human.

Americans knew her as first lady, as the woman who had done a controversial health care plan and for standing by Bill Clinton after he had been unfaithful to their marriage. "They didn't know her as the woman with the great laugh and the hilarious sense of humor. They didn't know the mother who drove her kid to ballet in her old Oldsmobile. They didn't know the daughter who took care of her mother," Sheila said.

Traveler Craig Douglass of Little Rock, long a friend of Hillary's, designed a piece of campaign literature about "The Hillary We Know," presenting her more personal side. It portrayed her not only as a hands-on mom and a daughter devoted to an aging mother but as an intelligent and fun person. Wherever the Travelers campaigned, they carried the four-color brochure, which was different from any of her other campaign literature.

The Hillary
We Know

Arkansas citizens sharing
stories and information
about Hillary Clinton – our
friend, our partner and our
Arkansas First Lady.

The Travelers told the story of "the Hillary we know."

The Hillary We Know

For 33 years, we've known Hillary Clinton – the advocate, teacher, lawyer, wife, mother and friend. And we know Hillary, the Arkansas First Lady, who has not only fought the good fight for life-improving issues, but won those fights through insight, intelligence, a sense of humor matched with a sense of caring and the experience and persistence it takes to fight and win!

Through the years we have watched and admired Hillary as her life's journey has progressed. Her 1975 marriage in Fayetteville, Arkansas, to Bill. The birth of Chelsea in 1980. Sunday services at Little Rock's First United Methodist Church. The afternoon carpools to school and dance class. And her gracious hosting of bridal luncheons, wedding and baby showers and organization events at the Governor's Mansion. These are all experiences that have shaped our lives and hers.

Hillary has laughed with us, cried with us, joined with us and led us. She has always been a true friend to us. She was here in Arkansas, and still is.

Join us in supporting Hillary. Learn more about her and then share with others the Hillary you know.

When Hillary's national campaign staff didn't want the Travelers to put out the piece, they raised the money themselves and did it anyway. The Travelers showed the same initiative that had served them so well in Bill's campaigns.

Both Bill and Hillary Clinton let the Travelers know directly they appreciated their presence in Iowa. A note from President Clinton to Sheila Bronfman in October 2007 reacted to the Travelers' visit there: "I read the article about the old, but 'new and improved' Travelers going to Iowa to help Hillary—It will sure help. Thanks, Bill."

Hillary, after seeing the Travelers in Ames, wrote to thank them for traveling to Iowa to talk with potential caucus-goers. "I understand that you and your fellow Arkansas Travelers covered over 5,000 miles and visited over twenty-eight counties. Amazing!" she told Sheila.

"As I travel across the country, the support of old friends like you means so much to me. Together, we will make history, secure a better future for our children and restore our nation's reputation abroad. I look forward to seeing you again on the campaign trail. Ever onward!"

The national media "was not particularly good to her" during her White House years, said Fred Knight. Their brochure and what the Travelers had to say about Hillary countered some of those perceptions.

Many of Hillary's campaign staff had been in grade school when the Travelers made their mark on Bill Clinton's campaign. They had no idea how much the Travelers could do to reverse perceptions.

In Bill's campaigns, the Travelers "could spin on a dime," Sheila said. In Hillary's campaign, they wasted a lot of time, "because we were trying to do what the campaign wanted." The Travelers got more independent as the campaign moved on.

"We wrote back that we were in trouble, but nobody really listened," Bronfman said. They saw Obama gaining momentum in Iowa and were worried for Hillary. "We loved Hillary and would do anything for her," Sheila said. So they scheduled Traveler trips to New Hampshire, hoping for a turnaround.

Mary Anne Salmon told President Clinton about some of the Travelers' frustration. She felt that he, too, was getting more and more frustrated at how Hillary's campaign was going.

The field staff did not coordinate well with the Travelers. An example was when the Travelers saw a local cooperative office in Iowa. The van screeched to a halt so Bob Lyford, attorney for Arkansas electric cooperatives, could go talk to employees and customers inside. The staff, knowing which Travelers would be in the state, could have anticipated that opportunity and more, Sheila explained. She always provided staff with advance details on which Travelers would be making a trip, so such matches were possible.

Hillary asked the Travelers to campaign for her, emphasized Marci Riggs of Little Rock, who took a strong leadership role with the 2008 Travelers. "We all thought we would personalize her like they had done with Bill." Many new people wanted to volunteer as Travelers for Hillary. And she did want them there. The field staff in New Hampshire didn't see the need.

The Travelers actually geared up in 2007, when Hillary called Sheila to recruit the Travelers' help. "She asked me if I thought it would work." Sheila said it would. "Everybody thought they knew her. ... But they didn't know Hillary." At least not like the Travelers did. Elaine Johnson from Hope had told people years before, "Wait until Hillary runs. She was the smart one."

Marci Riggs and Tim Giattina, a Clinton School of Public Service student, went to New Hampshire the day after Christmas in 2007 and stayed for fifteen days, advancing a five-day trip for eighty-one more Travelers, who came right after New Year's and stayed through the January 8th primary. The primary was moved up much earlier than in past years and came just days after the Iowa caucuses.

OFFICE OF
WILLIAM JEFFERSON CLINTON

10/21/07

[handwritten note]

Dear Sheila —

I read the article about the old, but "new and improved," Travelers going to Iowa to help Hillary. It will sure help.

Thanks,

Bill

A handwritten note from President Clinton in 2007 reads: "Dear Sheila, I read the article about the old, but "new and improved," Travelers going to Iowa to help Hillary. It will sure help. Thanks, Bill."

216

HILLARY RODHAM CLINTON

November 7, 2007

Sheila Bronfman

Little Rock, AR 72207

Dear Sheila:

It was wonderful seeing you in Ames! Thank you for traveling to Iowa to talk with potential caucus-goers about my record in Arkansas and for your dedication to my campaign. I understand that you and your fellow Arkansas Travelers covered over 5,000 miles and visited over 28 counties. Amazing!

As I travel across the country, the support of old friends like you means so much to me. Together, we will make history, secure a better future for our children, and restore our nation's reputation abroad. I look forward to seeing you again on the campaign trail. Ever onward!

With appreciation and warm regards, I am

Sincerely yours,

Hillary

Hillary Rodham Clinton

Thanks so much for all your help

4420 NORTH FAIRFAX DRIVE, ARLINGTON, VA 22203-1611   TEL (703) 469-2008   FAX (703) 962-8600
www.HillaryClinton.com
Contributions to Hillary Clinton for President Exploratory Committee are not deductible for federal income tax purposes.
Paid for by Hillary Clinton for President Exploratory Committee.

The Travelers were excited to receive this letter from Hillary acknowledging their work in Iowa in 2007.

Giattina and Sarah Argue, another Clinton School student, were among the youngest Travelers in 2008. Both are politically involved and found the campaign to be a learning experience. As Argue, who is from Little Rock, said, "I know the divisive nature of politics." Seeing the Travelers' mission showed her that politics "could be so unifying." Not being with the campaign, the Travelers' voices were compelling, Sarah said, because their independence lent authenticity to their words. Tim, too, understood the impact they were having and saw voters being energized where they traveled in New Hampshire.

The Travelers turned to old friends made in New Hampshire for help in getting where they needed to be for Hillary. While the local people still loved the Travelers, the field staff treated them as a burden. "They made life miserable on more than one occasion," Sheila said.

Travelers encountered another challenge in New Hampshire of a different sort—fire in their hotel. It didn't faze take-charge Sheila.

They were staying in Nashua, New Hampshire. Tim had stayed back at the motel on Sheila's orders that fateful morning. He had worked night and day and needed sleep. The Travelers were gone for the day by 7:15 a.m. The fire alarm went off not ten minutes later. When the alarm sounded, Tim thought, "I have heard this before, and I'm not getting up." A knock on his door rousted him. From the lobby, he could see the fire and smoke in one wing of the motel.

Giattina worried, "Sheila will probably be mad at me. ... I'm standing here watching the motel burn. Our hotel is burning to the ground." Four or five fire trucks were there by the time he called Sheila.

The hotel didn't burn to the ground but sustained a lot of damage, especially from smoke. The fire destroyed one Traveler's room and its contents and damaged others. Sheila kept Tim's news to herself, telling only other van leaders. Instead, she coordinated everything from her phone, getting the Travelers booked into another hotel and arranging to have their smoke-damaged clothing cleaned overnight. Meanwhile, the Travelers were walking neighborhoods and carrying out their normal campaign duties.

"There wasn't anything we could do about it," Sheila said, so she kept the Travelers on their scheduled rounds while she negotiated with the hotel staff and cleaners.

By 2008, she had a cell phone and was able to make the necessary arrangements from the van. She also had all of the Travelers' credit card numbers and could charge their new rooms quickly. When the Travelers finished the day and went back to the scorched hotel, most were just learning what had happened.

Some knew what was up but didn't tell the others. Jeff Mitchell and Robert Rhodes, both of Fayetteville, liked being in Sheila's lead van and sat near enough to overhear her making arrangements. Another Traveler heard the news by phone from Arkansas, where it had been reported. But most of the Travelers were clueless until they returned to the hotel.

There wasn't time enough to tag all their clothes; so, when the clothes came back from the cleaners, Travelers had to go through them to identify what was theirs, grab it and get back to campaign work from their new hotel.

Jim McClelland, a civil engineer from Little Rock, lost all his belongings—his computer and clothing—in the hotel fire. Hillary joked with him later about the fire. She said, "I told them to light a fire under you, but this is too much," he recalled. McClelland missed most of the next day's campaigning while Nancy Richards-Stower, a New Hampshire friend of the Travelers, took him shopping for replacement clothes.

A verse was added by state Senator Jimmy Jeffress of Crossett to the Travelers' theme song for Hillary to reflect the experience. Yes, by then, they had written lyrics for Hillary's campaign. Don Bishop and his van mates in Iowa wrote the parody of "The Caisson Song":

Over hill, over dale, as we hit the campaign trail,
And the TRAVELERS keep rolling along.
In and out, hear us shout, round the town without a pout,
And the TRAVELERS keep rolling along.

Then it's Hi! Hi! Hee as we work for Hillary, shout out your
number loud and strong.
Where e're we go, they will always know, that the TRAVELERS
keep rolling along!

Even though, we don't know, where we've been or where we'll go,
And the TRAVELERS keep rolling along.
Rain or shine, sleet or snow, just don't let that whistle blow,
And the TRAVELERS keep rolling along.
  (CHORUS)

Though our rooms were on fire, we just kicked it even higher.
And the TRAVELERS keep rolling along.
  (CHORUS)

You and me, got to pee, but we're working can't you see?
And the TRAVELERS keep rolling along.
Make that call, tell them all, that our Hillary's best of all,
And the TRAVELERS keep rolling along.
  (CHORUS)

Town by town, state by state, up and down the interstate,
And the TRAVELERS keep rolling along.
We can't wait for the date; we won't rest until '08,
And the TRAVELERS keep rolling along.
  (CHORUS)

New Hampshire was so cold, Faye Rodgers of Clinton said, that the Travelers were canvassing neighborhoods in six-degree weather. A man opened his door to her and he said in his Northern brogue, "Lady, you must be crazy to be out in this weather." Then he commented on her accent. "I think that I got a vote when I said, 'I don't have an accent but I think you do.'"

Yet another accent was a source of fun for Shelby Moore of Batesville. In New Hampshire, his wife, Beatrice, was continually asked to pronounce "Hillary" with her French accent. Residents did double takes at their doors, he said, when Beatrice said she was from Arkansas, asking them to vote for her friend, "Hee-lary." She got their attention long enough to do her spiel.

Another Traveler had a narrow escape in New Hampshire in 2008. Vincent Insalaco's van was in the hinterlands and being led by some "directionally challenged" kid through deep snow. "We kept going up and up, getting more lost by the mile, when we finally stopped and someone realized we were on the edge of a cliff and about to go over," he said. Vince said his passengers responded to the crisis by bailing out of the van and leaving him all alone "to back that sucker down," escaping disaster in a remote national forest.

Again in 2008, Arkansas Travelers noticed the wide public interest in all kinds of issues. A pink-haired waitress and a busboy wearing an earring in a diner might be stereotyped in some communities by their appearance. Yet, when these two were interviewed on TV, "their answers blew me away because they were so sophisticated and intelligent," said Sherry Joyce. To her, those two demonstrated how seriously New Hampshire voters take their responsibility. She also remembers a home where the parents of premature twins had posted a sign announcing the birth but asking campaigners to leave their literature. Even the parents of tiny newborns still wanted campaign literature and set out a box to collect it.

Their acts couldn't match the renegade van of lobster-eaters in Bill's campaign; but two Travelers, Maryaleese Schreiber and Fran Flener, admit to a rebellious moment or two in Concord. Like all Travelers, they had been abiding by Sheila's instructions, staying on task, when they spotted some shirts in a store window. One held their signs while the other ran into the dress shop to buy one. They worried Sheila might spot them and hid their purchases behind their backs until they could stash their loot in a van. "I guess you're going to know this now, Sheila," Maryaleese said. Most likely, there are a few more renegade moments Sheila has yet to hear about.

The pair mostly stayed in line, as they did when they encountered two high school boys from Charlottesville, Virginia, on a history-class field trip to observe the New Hampshire primaries of both parties. The students weren't there for any candidate, just interviewing people to understand the process. They were impressed so many people from Arkansas cared enough about the future of the U.S. to come all that way. The boys in turn impressed the two Travelers with what they had learned about the candidates and the process.

In 2008, the Travelers' work contributed to Hillary Clinton's "marvelous upset" of Obama, said Terry Shumaker, one of her New Hampshire supporters. Pollsters were saying she'd lose to Obama by double digits. But she won by three percent.

Travelers' pounding on doors, Hillary's refusal to give up, "and the sheer force of her will," he said, turned the primary election in New Hampshire.

Hillary Clinton got more than thirty-nine percent of the votes, besting her husband's second-place showing sixteen years earlier. The Travelers celebrated with her as they had with him at the end of a long day working the polls.

On election night, Jeff Mitchell and Robert Rhodes admit they found a bar, expecting to cry in their beers. Hillary was supposed to

Craig Douglass does a TV interview for Hillary Clinton in Iowa in 2007.

Travelers learn the ins and outs of the Iowa Caucus in 2007. Left to right are Missy Jackson, Jerry Parker, Jo Parker, Mary Anne Salmon, Margie Alsbrook, Fran Flener, Craig Douglass, and Don Bishop.

Rep. Gregg Reep, Karla Bradley, and Margie Alsbrook work the trick-or-treat crowd at a Halloween Carnival in Iowa, 2007.

Hillary's Barbershop Singers. Shown from left to right are Myra Jones, Aaron Lubin, Lisa Powell, Jo Parker, Fran Flener, Jerry Parker, and Don Bishop.

Travelers phone bank in Iowa 2007. Shown are Myra Jones, Sue White, Shirley Montgomery, Berniece Duffey, Marie Ryan, Bob Lyford, and Vincent Insalaco.

Working a rally with President Clinton for Hillary Clinton in New Hampshire, 2008. Shown here on the front row are Vincent Insalaco and Kay Bartlett. From left to right are Peggy Turbyfill, Robbie Thomas Knight, Jay Bradford, Mary Anne Salmon, Shelby Moore, Beatrice Moore, and H. T. Moore.

Planning the itinerary with Debbie Crapo in Rye, New Hampshire, 2008. In addition to working as a Traveler, she also fed everyone. Left to right are Craig Douglass, Sheila Bronfman, Debbie Crapo, Mary Anne Salmon, and H. T. Moore.

lose by ten points, but was winning, Jeff said. They quickly got back to the hotel for the celebration, which "was a blast."

The Travelers made only two more trips for Hillary Clinton, one in Arkansas and the other in Texas.

"She wanted to show a huge win in Arkansas," said Sheila. "And we did." Clinton won seventy percent of the Democratic primary vote.

"That's not to say she wouldn't have done it without us," Bronfman added. But the Travelers shored up support for Hillary in the Arkansas primary, Bronfman said, and "got some excitement going about her." The Traveler contingent numbered fifty-eight. As in other states, they drove in vans across Arkansas over a four-day period, grabbing attention for Clinton and doing retail politics before the February 5th primary.

For Mike Malone, the Hillary trips served a dual purpose. Besides supporting her, they were an opportunity to reconnect with the Travelers. He also found it particularly useful to travel Arkansas. That has helped him in his current job with the Northwest Arkansas Council, he said. The Travelers were in El Dorado and Jonesboro and points in between, including attending church in Newport and Jonesboro. The goal of the Travelers was to help her have a strong win in the state, he said. They knew she'd win. It was just a matter of how great the margin would be.

A Russian reporter traveling with Gregg Reep in Warren "to get a taste of Arkansas and report on Hillary's campaign" taught Reep something. "As we knocked on doors, a city police car drove by," he said. The Russian visitor became concerned. He assured her the police were just patrolling and would not bother them. She told him Russian authorities "would be checking us out and would put a stop to our efforts," said Reep, who remembered to be thankful for America's freedom and political system.

The Travelers worked in a stop at Clinton's birthplace in Hope while on their Arkansas tour and made several rally stops in the state

Snow bunnies canvassed for votes in New Hampshire, 2008. Travelers were a dedicated bunch.

"Grin and spin" as a reporter from National Public Radio interviews Jim McClelland, Kay Goss, and Jeff Mitchell as they walked door to door in New Hampshire, 2008.

This group went to a restaurant to watch Hillary Clinton's debate in New Hampshire, 2008, only to discover that there was no television. As always, they made the best of it. Front left to right are Fran Flener, Nancy Richards-Stower, Senator Mary Anne Salmon, Craig Douglass, and Gilbert Cornwell. Shown in back from left to right are Dr. Richard Bronfman, Ed Fry, Ann Gilbert, Marie Clinton Bruno, H. T. Moore, Mayor Patrick Hays, and Sheila Bronfman.

Travelers stop for a photo before working in Stuttgart, Arkansas, for Hillary in February 2008. (See Photo Index for Names.)

(Above) Senator Mary Anne Salmon speaks to a rally in Hot Springs, Arkansas, in February 2008. Attorney General Dustin McDaniel, Senator Terry Smith, Representative Gene Shelby, and North Little Rock, Arkansas, Mayor Patrick Hays offer support.

(Left) Harry Truman Moore speaks to a rally in Jonesboro, Arkansas, during February of 2008. The Travelers knew how to a work a crowd.

where they were joined by Arkansas politicians, among them Attorney General Dustin McDaniel. They also worked a Pine Bluff rally for Hillary with President Clinton, providing backdrop for the event.

The final outing for the Travelers, to Texas, was both frustrating and a last hurrah for them in Hillary's campaign. The destination was in driving distance for the 70 people who participated in the weeklong outing, leaving from Little Rock and working their way to Dallas.

Texans responded to retail politics and wanted to hear about Hillary as "warm and funny and a great mom," said Alice Chamberlin, another of the New Hampshire people who traveled for Hillary. "It was an opportunity to humanize the candidate, which is increasingly a lost part of campaigns these days."

Mistrust of the media had a strange effect in Hillary's campaign, she said. "People felt like they didn't know her or thought they had a phony picture of her," Chamberlin said. Wherever the Travelers went, voters wanted to know "what is she really like?"

That Texas trip had started out with a slight glitch for the Travelers, who were given only 5,000 pieces of literature to hand out as they campaigned. That was less than 100 pieces per person and nothing like what they could distribute in one of their highly coordinated "knock and drop" efforts.

Consequently, each of the vans, unbeknownst to the others, stopped at a Kinko's or some other copy shop and printed more literature. Each van was just dealing with another situation. They paid for the copies and went on. "They knew what to do," said Bronfman.

Young people in the campaign headquarters were constantly relying on MapQuest and Google and misdirecting the Travelers. Harry Truman Moore, a van leader, was as angry as his wife, Linda, had ever seen him over an incident in Texas. The van's driver, Norman Hodges, followed the staff directions to a vacant lot in an industrial park in suburban Dallas-Fort Worth. Moore told others that in the future he would "rely on "M.A.P. instead G.P.S."

More work on the phone banks in 2008. Those very southern accents worked even in Texas. Explaining the "Texas Two Step" was not easy. Shown are Diane Goltz, Susan Siegel, and Dr. Alan Storeygard.

Former Ambassador Terry Shumaker and educator Sue Smith took off to speak to the Dallas affiliate of the National Education Assocation as surrogates for Hillary Clinton in March 2008. Travelers were always well versed on the issues.

The Travelers pack into the van to canvass Fort Worth in 2008. Shown on the front row are Fred Knight, former Ambassador Terry Shumaker, Jean Hervey, Sue Smith, Dr. Richard Bronfman, and Eileen Soffer. On the back row left to right are Stephanie Streett, Faye Rodgers, Myra Jones, Dale Evans, Rachel Levenson, and Sheila Bronfman.

One of their more unusual moments came when the Travelers, grungy from a day of canvassing Texas neighborhoods, got a call to join Chelsea Clinton at a celebrity-filled party. Despite their attire, they went and worked the crowd as requested. In her remarks to the crowd, Chelsea explained who the Travelers were and what they were doing for her mother. She shared personal stories of growing up in the Arkansas Governor's Mansion and her relationship to Ann McCoy and Margaret Whillock, two of the Travelers in attendance. Many came away with pictures of them with the celebrities that night.

Travelers served as surrogates for the campaign in Texas, too. Terry Shumaker and Eileen Soffer spoke as Hillary's representatives at a Jewish forum just before the Jewish holiday of Purim where Soffer compared Hillary "to the victorious, smart, dedicated, and independent Queen Esther from the story." Sue Smith and Terry Shumaker spoke for Hillary at a National Education Association forum in Dallas. Texas did make good use of the Travelers on these occasions.

Hillary Clinton won the Texas primary with just shy of fifty-one percent of the vote, but she came out with fewer delegates (ninety-four) than Obama (ninety-nine) after results of Texas's same-day caucus were known.

The Texas "two-step," as the electoral process is nicknamed, was especially frustrating to the Travelers.

The Obama people had organized well for the caucuses, producing a printed ticket to attend and handing it to primary voters, reminding them to come to the caucus later that night. "It was a smart maneuver," Sheila said, emphasizing that caucus participants didn't have to have a ticket.

In Texas, she explained, a voter first votes in the primary election that day, then returns that evening to caucus. A candidate can win the primary, the caucus or both. In the past, Texas normally had a big primary vote and a much smaller number of caucus participants. That changed in 2008, when the caucuses were overrun with Obama and Hillary supporters, Sheila said.

Travelers had worked at the polls from 7 a.m. until they closed, then went to the caucuses. As they realized the sites weren't prepared for the numbers of caucus voters they were drawing, Travelers stepped in to help reorganize the Texas caucuses.

Sheila and a vanload of Travelers were at a church where they persuaded the minister to open the sanctuary for a larger turnout. They had to wait, however, as a young boy had his piano lesson and caucus participants crowded up against the door. The minister had been expecting maybe twenty people, but between 450 and 500 came to that one caucus.

Clinton and Obama team members, who had been working out a plan together, were blocking the door to keep anyone from interrupting the piano lesson. They had promised the minister they would let the boy finish his lesson. Caucus-goers for both Clinton and Obama were lining up. And they were getting hostile, Sheila said. "Once we opened the doors, they stormed the place."

The Arkansas people were working with Lori Neeper, a Clinton campaign volunteer, and Obama's people to get the site organized; but it fell to a couple of Arkansas lawyers, Dale Evans and Fred Knight, to explain the rules of the caucus to the Texas attendees. At other caucus sites, other Arkansas lawyers, Bill Trice and H. T. Moore, similarly stepped up to run the gatherings. Bronfman said a lot of the people who had come to participate didn't have the right paperwork but were allowed to vote anyway. "We got outmaneuvered," she said.

In some areas, they reported the process was totally hijacked by unruly, disruptive people. In at least one case, a Traveler pulled his van team away from a caucus because of the fear of physical violence. Fred Knight said, in some cases, the Obama caucus participants had been bused in to vote "and no one was going to keep them out." It was extremely confrontational, he said.

Not all the experiences in Texas were so bad. "They loved the Clintons in Grand Prairie," said John Joyce, who had traveled with his wife, Sherry, to Texas. She agreed, "We were loved in Grand Prairie," where the Joyces worked a precinct.

If the Arkansas people were frustrated, so were some Texans when several hundred voters showed for a caucus that would ordinarily draw no more than ten. When the Grand Prairie precinct chairperson walked in, she looked at that packed cafeteria, laid the manila envelope with the caucus materials in it on the stage and just walked out, said Sherry Joyce. "She never came back. We had to take over the caucus."

Sergio De Leon, an Arkansan living in Texas, made the Travelers' experiences there better. He helped them plan their travels in Texas. He also joined them to campaign and even arranged to have a van flat tire fixed while he took them canvassing in his Suburban. What the Travelers remember most is his family's hosting all seventy of them for an impromptu home-cooked dinner in his house after a cold, wet day of canvassing. The added bonus was that the Travelers got to watch Hillary debate Obama and the rest of the Democratic field at Sergio's home.

"Their home wasn't that big, but they invited us all," said Lisa Powell. "They moved all the furniture back and put up folding tables. They turned their whole house upside down to welcome us into their home."

By early June, Hillary's quest for the presidency was over. Obama had secured the Democratic nomination and she withdrew officially from the race, publicly declaring her support for Obama. The Travelers had made their last Hillary trip in March.

One of Jean Hervey's most cherished memories is when Hillary went to the mike at the Democratic National Convention in Denver "and gracefully placed Barack Obama's name in nomination."

Elaine Lippard, of Blue Mountain, is "ready to roll" anytime for Hillary, she said. Elaine is one of many Travelers who said they hadn't understood what the impact of their work for Bill and Hillary would have on their own lives. Everywhere Elaine has gone, she tells people being an Arkansas Traveler is "a privilege I wouldn't trade anything for."

If Hillary should ever decide to make another run for president and wants their help, all of the Travelers stand ready, it seems, to go again.

20.
RECOLLECTIONS AND REWARDS

The Arkansas Travelers don't talk much about what it cost them personally to be so heavily involved in Bill Clinton's election or Hillary Clinton's bid for president. Most didn't even keep close track as they piled up bills for airfare, motel rooms, and other expenses. What they do talk about is the reward of knowing both Bill and Hillary and of life-changing experiences that come with friendship.

Some admit there was a price for their commitment, usually expressing it in a joking manner.

"I told Bill Clinton it is very expensive being your friend," said Percy Malone. "I used to have dark hair and money until I met Bill Clinton," added Mary Anne Salmon.

Over 500 individuals invested themselves in these elections, some for weeks and months and years.

Sheila Bronfman, the most traveled of the Travelers, took a year and a half off from her consultant business to volunteer for Clinton's first campaign and then ran the Traveler efforts for his reelection and for Hillary's campaign.

Other business owners lost work or missed opportunities, like lawyer H. T. Moore did. Public employees, teacher Sue Smith and state employee Phil Price among them, gave up their vacations and leave time to make the trips. So did health care professionals like Dr. Tyler Thompson and the other medical professionals who traveled.

Some Travelers are wealthy. Others are not. Most probably fit into the middle class that both Bill and Hillary Clinton have championed.

Some Traveler couples went on trips together, sharing the whole experience and hiking their costs for airfare and rooms. They didn't have to worry about paying for much food. Sheila seldom allowed time for eating.

Sometimes one spouse traveled while the other stayed home to work. Gail Goodrum traveled and helped manage the Travelers for a whole year while husband Randy made occasional trips with the group.

Other couples tag-teamed the trips or let one spouse do most, but maybe not all, the traveling. For John and Sherry Joyce, who made solo trips earlier, it was special to travel together on the last of the Traveler trips for Hillary.

Some couples swapped off trips. Those with young, school-aged children, like Joel and Debra Buckner, did. One parent needed to be home in Arkansas.

The families of Travelers were effectively drafted into the Clintons' Arkansas army, too, when mom or dad, or both, hit the road. Sometimes family members traveled together or a child might tag along. Buddy Villines had his daughter Corey campaigning by his side, building a cherished bond through their shared experience. Sisters Marci and Lila Riggs traveled together, as did Eileen Soffer and her daughter, Rachel Levenson.

The Arkansas Travelers answered when called and figured out how to pay the bills later. They had a mission.

The more important payoff on their collective investment came with Bill Clinton's election and his eight-year administration. This first president from Arkansas, though challenged personally and subjected to impeachment, delivered what his friends from home were so certain he could. At least, they don't recount any major failures.

Their faith was strong in 1992 and carries on in his post-presidency. Their faith was equally strong for Hillary. There probably isn't a Traveler who wouldn't jump at a second chance to help her win the White House.

"Being a Traveler allowed me to meet people I never would have known, go places I never would have been, and do things I never would have been able to do," said Jan McQuary. She summed up well the Traveler experience for people who lived the campaigns of Bill and Hillary Clinton.

They may have known each other casually before, but they became the closest of friends, these Travelers. "When you traveled with them, rode in those vans with them, walked through snow with them and all the rest, you really got to bond with them and to develop those special friendships," said Jan.

Being a Traveler is "more than a hobby, less than a job," said Wes Cottrell. "It's a passion."

"I got more out of it than I put into it," J. T. Rose said of the Traveler experience. Not only did he participate in Clinton's election, he also spent the night at the White House and attended events he never would have gone to otherwise.

Travelers from all walks of life of different ages, different incomes, and different education levels willingly followed Sheila's lead. They got the job done and built lasting memories, as Levi Phillips did. "As we get longer in the tooth, all we will have are memories; and some of my best memories are with the Travelers, some to be shared and some not to be shared."

The Travelers' bonds with each other grew as strong as their commitment to Bill and Hillary Clinton.

Could a group like the Arkansas Travelers successfully advance a candidate for president these days?

"It depends on the candidate, the state, and the people," said Skip Rutherford. "The campaign would need to do more with social media," he said, "but a candidate from a small state with similar close relationships could replicate the Traveler effort. The advantage of sitting down and saying, 'I know her. I know him,' is still powerful."

Not all are certain that an organization like the Travelers could work as well in today's political environment, but they're ready to try.

Interestingly, the ones most convinced that it could work are some of the newest and youngest Travelers. "One of the things that was so successful with Obama's winning campaign," Sarah Argue said, "was its reach to the micro level to ask for small donations. It is less about raising money and more about engaging people to feel a part of the campaign," she said. "The Arkansas Traveler model is all about personal connection. It is about invigorating voters," she said.

Regardless of technology advances, "nothing replaces a personal contact," Tim Giattina said, repeating the Travelers' popular pitch. "I am here from Arkansas and I want you to vote for my candidate. I flew half way across the country to ask you to vote for my candidate." It's effective, he said, although Argue noted that it is "expensive, if not to the campaign then to the volunteers."

Again, the Arkansas Travelers focused on mission, not money.

The Travelers bask in the memory of all their road experiences and what followed. There were the trips to New York and Chicago for the Democratic National Conventions and to Washington DC for one or both of Bill Clinton's inaugurations, all replete with once-in-a-lifetime opportunities to be part of the American political process and the celebration.

None of the Travelers can forget escorting the newly nominated Clinton from Macy's down Seventh Avenue to Madison Square Garden, being in the convention hall or attending an inauguration. Sid Johnson was there, a full participant, knowing he had affected the future. "This experience is just as American as it can get."

Patty Criner was there, sitting with the Clinton family as Bill was nominated. That family had been part of her life since her grade-school days with Billy in Hot Springs.

There were special events for the Travelers, like a barbeque dinner on the lawn of the White House that feted Arkansans. Peggy Nabors of Little Rock was there with her sister from Texas, thinking how incredible it was for two little girls who grew up poor on the east end of Houston to be in such company. Another White House occasion was a black-tie Christmas party just for Arkansans. Sam Perroni's best Traveler memory is of dancing with his wife, Pat, in the White House.

There were big moments the Travelers all shared and smaller ones only some witnessed. Jimmie Lou Fisher was sitting by the standard that identified the Arkansas delegation at the convention and was a little perturbed when someone came early to take it away. She asked why. It was going to the Smithsonian Museum.

The Travelers' brushes with history were numerous, the "pinch me" moments incalculable. The Travelers were a significant part of history, as Peggy Crossley of Monticello noted, "I don't think I have ever experienced anything quite like it before or since."

Barbara Hartwick, an elementary school principal from North Little Rock, also felt the tie to history. "The commitment we all had to both of the Clintons and the feeling of pride in the part we played in each election needs to be remembered."

For Rhonda McCauley, working on the campaign was the "dawning of realization that I am somebody, with the power to make a difference." What she had been taught about "government by the people" became real with the Traveler experience.

The Travelers hobnobbed with celebrities from Hollywood and from the political arena, snapping pictures for family scrapbooks all along their way. The Blue Jeans Bash, thrown mainly for Arkansans before the inaugural, was packed with celebrities, including the musicians Dee Pryor recruited to play. Bob Dylan was there. So were The Band with Levon Helm, Garth Hudson, and Rick Danko; Stephen Stills, the Cate Brothers from Fayetteville, Clarence Clemmons from the E St. Band, Dr. John, Arkansas-born Fred Tackett from Little Feat, and more, including Denny Dent, a performance artist painting portraits. It was a fun night in a fun week for all who were there.

Dee Pryor learned as a result of his campaign experience something he said couldn't be learned in a classroom, from a book, or online. "Retail politics," he said, "is a sport which can only be learned in the field." Campaigns force candidates and their operatives "to think on their feet, operate on scarce resources, and live for the moment, not the next day," said Dee.

Other Travelers' lives were dramatically changed by their campaign experience, too. Gregg Burgess was a young, closeted gay man who went on the Travelers' first trip to Florida. Exposure to "diverse and tolerant environments," he said, gave him the courage to come out. Pate Felts talked of treasured memories of Henry Woods and Ed Fry, who were among the most active Travelers and both of whom died in their fifties. As gay men, Pate, Henry, and Ed were enthusiastic about these campaigns. The Clintons "were not afraid of standing up for gay men and women," Pate said, giving us "a personal feeling of self-worth."

Participating as Travelers gave Patti and Larry Snodgrass of Lincoln a needed diversion from the traumatic loss of their son Chris in a December 1991 motorcycle accident. They unexpectedly drew national exposure during a campaign stop in New Hampshire. Clinton was speaking and recognized Larry, his former law student, in the crowd. "I was an old friend, a law student of his from twenty years earlier who was now a practicing attorney and a thousand miles from home campaigning for him at my own expense," Snodgrass said. Clinton elbowed his way to Larry, put his arm around him "and finished his speech talking about how proud of us Travelers he was." It all happened on camera and Larry's dad in Arkansas saw the clip on the news.

Many Travelers have gotten involved in politics at one level or another. Some took jobs in the White House or elsewhere in the administration. Mike Malone did. A twenty-something bachelor when he joined the Travelers, Mike married his wife, Allyson, in Washington. It was a great time to be in the capital city, Malone said. Arkansans were in vogue and the Razorback basketball team won the national championship.

Dina Wood of Fayetteville went to Washington, also to an administration job, carrying with her the lessons and friendships created as a Traveler. Most of the Travelers have stayed home in Arkansas, or come back to Arkansas as Mike and Dina both have.

For eight years, Travelers frequented White House events and participated in shaping administration policy, the way Skip Rutherford did on a part-time basis. Skip couldn't bring himself to move his family to Washington but found a way to keep a hand in White House business.

Sheila, too, cherishes her work as part of the presidential advance teams within the U.S. and overseas. And she helped bring Arkansans to volunteer in the White House. During Bill's two terms, many Travelers and others from his home state went for a week to answer the president's constituent mail and do other tasks.

Travelers have received significant appointments. George Bruno, who was appointed as an ambassador, did. Dale Evans and his wife, Sheila, got to visit Belize as Bruno's guests and be chauffeured in a stretch limo with the ambassador's flags flying. Terry Shumaker was an ambassador as well, assigned to Trinidad and Tobago. Travelers peppered the Clinton administration, including Hershel Gober, who was there, always working for veterans.

Lots of Arkansas Travelers were invited to stay in the White House, some sleeping in the famed Lincoln bedroom, as David Matthews and his wife, Mary Beth, did on her birthday. They happened to be there on a day of crisis for Clinton and stood around a White House piano with Bill and Hillary talking it through, as friends do. "I can't figure this out. Every time I have a crisis in my life, you're there. I don't know whether to thank you or blame you," Bill told David.

David was there in 1992, when Bill's candidacy was near failure. All of the Travelers were, 137 strong in New Hampshire, with more joining their ranks through all those elections to come.

"There never had been anything quite like the Arkansas Travelers," said Rex Nelson, political editor of the *Arkansas Democrat-Gazette* in 1992. "People in places such as New Hampshire were amazed that dozens and dozens of people from Arkansas would load up, pay their own expenses, and give up vacation time to campaign for their state's governor. I can tell you that it made an impression."

Their unique effort caused voters in key Democratic primary states to give Bill Clinton a second look, he said. "These voters told themselves: 'If the folks who know him best think this much of that Clinton fellow, perhaps I should consider voting for him.'" Nelson was among several Arkansas journalists to follow Clinton and witness the Travelers' work firsthand.

Another was Steve Barnes, a veteran Arkansas broadcaster and host of AETN's "Arkansas Week." He remembers the Travelers as an "indefatigable" bunch, none of them slackers or hangers-on to the campaign. They were hard-working devotees of Clinton, people who truly believed in him, including many who had always thought he would be president some day. "Here was their chance to play a part in it."

"Mother Sheila probably explained to them up front that this was not a lark. They might have some fun and get some satisfaction, but don't come unless you expect to work," he said, pegging precisely how clear her instructions were to the Travelers.

Along with the hard work came fun and friendship, as Nelson recognized. "Through long days on the road and late-night pizza, they forged personal bonds that last until this day. Folks from Southeast Arkansas became close friends with folks from Northwest Arkansas, people they never would have met otherwise. In a sense, it was like having a buddy from the armed services. You try not to lose touch, and you have the memories of a lifetime."

The analogy works for Clinton's Arkansas army and their battle-forged friendships. The Travelers are, as Wes Cottrell says, "a band of brothers and sisters." They have a real and personal history together, as they do with Bill and Hillary—all of it a continuing manifestation of the political magic that fueled the Arkansas Travelers through their historic journey.

APPENDIX A:
IN THEIR OWN WORDS:
VIRGINIA KUTAIT AND MARGARET MOSELEY (1992)

ADVENTURES OF AN FOB
By Virginia Kutait
1992

Spring was in the air, birds were singing. Flowers were blooming and our husbands were breaking their gardens. But Gayle Remer, my traveling companion, and I were packing suitcases with long underwear, earmuffs, waterproof boots, and wool socks. We were among the 100-plus Arkansas Travelers headed to New Hampshire to work for Governor Bill Clinton during the week preceding the primary of all primaries.

One may ask why a shy, AARP member would take time from a busy life to trudge the cold, wet weather of a faraway state. It was a question asked by many that week, but the answer in part was a sense of outrage at the political tripe being spread about a nice human being and, in our opinion, the best choice for president of the United States. He needed help, and we were his friends. That was enough.

The word from New England was that the weather was to be either cold or colder, that in fact there were times when there was "no temperature at all" and we should be prepared. That was good advice. By the time we arrived in Boston, it was snowing and still coming down when we reached our destination: Manchester, New Hampshire. After being picked up at the airport, we loaded into vans for the trip to our home for the next six days, the Super 8 Motel. We were briefed on the way by Sheila Bronfman, the efficient director of the Clinton volunteer activities. After a reminder that we were representing the state of Arkansas, as well as our governor, we were each issued an "Arkansas Traveler" button. How proud we were!

The first day on the campaign trail started early. Donning two pairs of long underwear, three pairs of socks, and several layers of outer clothing, we met the rest of the group in the lobby. Among the Arkansans were fellow Fort Smithians Charlie Varner, Mack Dyer, and Greg Smith.

Five vans with fifteen people to a van left headquarters for the first stop, Nashua. On the way we were given videotapes, printed material, and clipboards and told we would be "walking and talking," "knocking and dropping," and that's what we did. It was snowing, of course, and Gayle and I were the first to be dropped. Our duty was (we thought) to show the younger ones we could do this.

Not knowing what to expect, we were pleasantly surprised by the willingness of the people to open their doors, especially since we looked like a couple of bag ladies with videotapes and leaflets in a large green garbage bag (to keep its contents dry). These residents were ready to discuss candidates and issues, and so were we. Without exception, the people we encountered were polite, knowledgeable, and grateful for the economic help the campaigns were bringing to their state of New Hampshire. Not once, in all the days of walking and talking, were we met with rudeness. Not everyone agreed with our choice of candidate, but they were always polite, often inviting us in for coffee.

Working in pairs, we were able to quickly cover one area of a town and move on to another. After a short lunch break, we were back on the "routes" and by five p.m. we were loading into the vans and on our way to a rally. It was soon apparent that this was strictly GOTV (a frequently used term meaning Get Out the Vote). There would be no time for nice, long, sit-down meals. In fact, there was little time for anything other than the job at hand.

By day two, Gayle and I were mostly concerned with keeping up with the younger Travelers. However, as the days fell into a pattern much like the first, we knew that not only could we keep up, but there were times when we set the pace. We were well on our way to becoming "political junkies."

The rallies each evening provided an excitement all their own. For the Arkansas people who had been going door-to-door, the huge crowds were a great opportunity to talk with a number of people at one time. We soon discovered that a "reception line" outside the doors worked well, and we would greet the people with "hello, thanks for coming to hear our governor." As they exited, we would again form a line and ask for their support at voting time. Many remarked that this was a new approach in their primary, and they liked it.

After days of early beginnings and late endings, walking in rain, slush, and snow, encounters with dogs who were less friendly than the people, professional protesters from New York, the DAY arrived! Time for talking was past, and it was time for the vote. We were up at 4:30 and dropped at a local fire station before 6:00. For the next six hours, along with volunteers from other candidates' campaigns, we held our signs and drawled our Southern "good mornings" as the locals came to vote. Forgotten were the cold feet, freezing ears, and numb toes. A hug from the governor and his statement "I can't believe you are here," and a hug and a smile from Hillary, made all the discomforts seem mild.

After all, they had been through much more. The night the "Comeback Kid" took the stage, we stood proud and tall.

If New Hampshire was the first and most memorable, Colorado had to be the most exciting. I was slightly handicapped, in that Virginia Kelley had seen us at the airport and given me such a hug that my reading glasses (always hanging on a chain around my neck) were broken. As happy as we were, it didn't really matter, and the kind I wore could be bought anywhere.

Our van driver and leader, Rick Eoff, organized us quickly and we were "on the road again." This trip followed the format of the first, but in addition, we often met with other Democrats at their headquarters because by this time the Arkansas Travelers were a much sought-after group, and our reputation had preceded us. We did talk shows at the radio and television stations. We visited the college campuses and greeted students between classes. There were more rallies to attend, as well as receptions in private homes in the evenings. I even met the son of a friend from Fort Smith at a dinner. Were we surprised to see each other! There were newspaper offices to visit, editors to talk with, and more barbecue than I knew existed outside of Texas.

By the time Mack Dyer, Dayle Oliver, and I drove a car full of eager campaigners to Oklahoma, I felt like an "old pro." We joined others at Democratic headquarters in Tulsa for a day of parades and personal interviews. No doubt about it, these FOB's believed in their candidate, and they were willing, at their own expense, to share personal views with others throughout the country. The Arkansas Travelers made history!

MINNESOTA-WISCONSIN
By Margaret Moseley (Burris)
October 1992

Take six eager Americans;
Put in red van;
Drive through Wisconsin;
Do not feed the occupants;

Like a fully loaded supreme pizza, the six of us packed into our hastily decorated, red minivan in the parking garage of the Minneapolis Democratic headquarters. Strangers all, we had been thrown together through the caprice of a sophisticated computer, or, I rather suspect, the whimsy of Sheila Bronfman, head cook-and-bottle-washer of the Arkansas Travelers.

Two by two, the six red, white, and blue vans—adorned with the name of our governor-who-would-be-president—sped onto the midnight Minnesota highways to begin our five-day odyssey in hands-on politics. As we raced toward our first night's lodging, we tenuously began introductions.

Young Mike Malone was our designated driver—appropriately sober, serious, and responsible. A recent graduate of the University of Arkansas, Mike was currently a graduate student in Minneapolis, an avid Democrat—and I'm sure as curious and cautious about his human van cargo as we were about him and one another.

Mike's copilot was Gus Pugh who, honest to God, answered to the name of *Bubba!* Hey! My first! Silent and shy, our Bubba was a farm equipment salesman from Lake Village.

The middle seat held my traveling companion, Pam Weber from Fort Smith. Although we had journeyed to the Little Rock airport for the flight to Minneapolis together, Pam and I were strangers. I was a fifty-one-year-old overweight mother, writer, and business communications consultant, while Pam was an attractive, professional, thirty-something Junior League real-estate sales-person. Our paths had never crossed in Fort Smith but here we were—off to Oz together.

The caboose seat held civil rights attorney Margaret Reger from Harrison—my age (almost) and a dedicated Democratic campaigner. Her back-seat companion was Joe Dan Yee, a grocer of Chinese heritage from Lake Village.

Lake Village? Yes, it all begins to make sense. Pam and I were both from Fort Smith, so of course we would be together. And Bubba and Joe Dan were from Lake Village and then Harrison wasn't all that far from Mike Malone's native Fayetteville, so, yes, by George—oops, sorry—yes, by Bill, we were grouped together in a kinda geographical way.

We had very little else in common.

Except our individual determination to tell whoever would listen about our governor and the reasons we thought he should be president. That is, President. Of the United States. Of America.

Collectively, we turned into quite a little team.

I had never before campaigned, not even for a candidate for dog-catcher, and here I was, putting my money where my mouth was, campaigning for the candidate for the highest office in my country. Because my husband was, is, and will always be a newspaperman—editor of the *Southwest Times Record* in Fort Smith, I had always silently let my one vote count.

But not this time! Not this year!

I have a friend who says always vote for the Democrat even if it *is* for dog-catcher. "Cut them off at the legs," she says, "if you let a Republican win, the next thing you know he's running for the senate."

Well, I sorta identify with that sentiment, I *did* vote for George Bush, way back there in Texas when he first ran for Senate. And then again, I gotta admit, when he ran for president the first time. I like George. He's a nice guy. But, somewhere along the way, he lost touch—with me, with America.

That's what I told Bill Clinton when he and I were seated at the head table together when my husband was to introduce him as speaker at a luncheon in Fort Smith. "I don't care what you said about four years, I want you to run for president!" I'd declared to the governor during the meal.

Later I thought, what frivolous, naïve words for such a serious undertaking.

So when Bill did announce, I though guiltily, Oh, what have I done? And then, I said, "Stupid, he didn't choose to run just because *you* asked him to, but because a lot of *you*s asked him to. More important people than you."

Still though, I had asked him to run, so I better help.

First, I volunteered at the Fort Smith Democratic campaign head-quarters, passing out buttons and bumper stickers and signing up people for yard signs. Then my friend, Virginia Kutait, co-chair of the campaign, went to New Hampshire. I wanted to go. Virginia did.

Later she told me every single little detail of the exciting primary efforts.

I still wanted to go. Somewhere.

She asked if I would like to become an Arkansas Traveler.

"Sure," I said blithely. As blithely as I had asked—no, *told*—Governor Clinton to run for president.

I used the last check I received for a small contract and I paid my own way, telling the girls that they were on their own in October, 'cause Mama was going to Minnesota and Wisconsin to spend all the extra money I usually gave them for something special—their future. Neither one had health insurance. One of the things I was worried about.

Right off my traveling companions won my heart when they started calling me *little* Margaret. Margaret Reger was trimmer than I, but *I* was shorter.

Although our official Arkansas Traveler badges read "Wisconsin," our van spent the first day in Duluth, a beautiful lakeside city, proud of its heritage and eager to meet some real Clinton fans. My favorite stop there was at an old high school where we met with several combined civics classes, our first talk. As a sometime student of group dynamics, I was intrigued that no single leader emerged in our group. We all spoke equally, not as politicians, but as people who knew and respected the candidate.

A civics teacher nodded agreement when his student asked about Clinton "waffling on issues." I replied that I couldn't answer specifically on any charge he had, but that I personally respected a person who, when they had new information, was not afraid to change an opinion. "Inflexibility is limiting," I stated.

Oh, dear! Had I said the right thing?

We all studied the issues again when we returned to the van.

On to *Wisconsin.*

Hand shaking on the street. Even shy Bubba was chased out of a beauty shop by woman threatening him with a hair-dryer. We laughed. We tried to eat. We shook hands. They loved our accents. I didn't even tell them mine was a Texas one. Well, maybe after eighteen years, there's a little Arkie. We bought goodies at the bakery while doing Clinton-talk to the bakers. Bubba bought a cooler and loaded it with ice, soft drinks, and juices. Sheila said we wouldn't stop to eat a lot. Ordering food took time and our time could be better spent. Tell that to our stomachs. But don't tell Sheila you're hungry.

They say that Sheila's tough, but she's not. She's just organized.

Small towns. One after another. A group gathered on the sidewalk. Holding signs: Clinton/Gore.

Shake hands. Give out the buttons. Most don't want to talk politics. "Do you know him?"

Meeting at night with the other four vans. Hotel bars where we gathered at night and told the day's "he said and she said" stories. Buying campaign buttons at the different headquarters.

On the road again. Our white "sister" van beside us. The control van. A signal and a stop. A directive from the mobile phone. Patsy

Thomasson reports, "Sheila wants us to stop in the next town for a radio interview. You, you, and you on the radio. The rest hit the sheets." (And Bubba hit the convenience store for fresh supplies.) No time for the bucket of fried chicken.

The Lac Courte Oreilles Indian Reservation and Patsy and I are on the radio this time—a talk program beamed throughout the reservation. What about Clinton and the death penalty? I told about the time that I ran into Bill in Little Rock and he was upset at the Fairchild decision. He talked passionately for more than half an hour. "He upholds the law, but he takes each case personally and seriously," I stated. Knowing.

My van family collected an "Indians for Clinton" button for me. I don't know much more about my Cherokee heritage than I do my English or Scottish. But that's my favorite button.

More miles. We talk. And tell jokes. And laugh a lot. These five people who once were strangers and me.

There were some kids in a car on the highway. They honked when they saw our signs. They held up a handmade Bush/Quayle sign and jeered. Our redheaded Junior Leaguer reached out the window while our grad student steadily maneuvered the van onto an empty strip of highway. Going, God only knows, how many miles per hour, Pam passed them Clinton literature and campaign buttons. From car to car. And guess what conservative *little* mother held on to Pam's coattails so she didn't fall overboard. Don't tell Sheila. But I bet we got their votes.

Big Margaret and I talking to two women in a restaurant who were going to vote "like their men" 'cause they had been told to. For Bush. We gave them campaign buttons and told them about Clinton and personal rights. Wonder how they voted in private.

Our van began to look like a pigsty. Empty wrappers and Coke cans. It smelled like pork rinds.

After our only—honest, Sheila—hamburger stop, we pulled into a small town, led by a local candidate for sheriff in a vintage police car, where they had laid out a big spread of Wisconsin cheeses, sausages, and pieces of homemade apple heaven. We couldn't eat them because we were too full of junk. But we took turns telling about Bill and Hillary and why we were there.

Saw a *tamarack* tree. Had only heard about them. Weather was warm. We laughed at our cold-weather gear piled up in the back. We drove Wisconsin. And we drove Wisconsin.

We almost mutinied. The red van. Clinton was speaking in Green Bay, but Sheila said they needed us in Stevens Point. We wanted to see Clinton. But think on it, if he's in Wisconsin this close to the election, it must be an important state. Better go to Stevens Point. They need us there.

Bush country.

Joe Dan and I circulated through a definitely Republican gathering at a local school gym. Nobody wanted to meet us. Nobody shook our hand. I got a little rattled and I kept introducing Joe Dan as "Don." He didn't say a word, but shook hands as Don. Later he kidded me, "Don?" he said. "Don?" Joe Dan is as articulate as they come. He never got rattled, but loved introducing me as "Linda" after that. They were trying to dance country in the gym. "Achy Breaky Heart." We waited until we were outside to roll our eyes.

At a Wisconsin state college, we all bit our tongues to hold back the laughter when Patsy began to tell about dead chickens and chicken parts in answer to a student's question about industrial waste. She was serious and informed, but we'd had it. The red van later roared with laughter and "dead chickens" became a code word.

I got lost from my fellow travelers in a parking garage. Another van picked me up as we all had the same destination. Their van was clean. Smelled nice. They didn't tell jokes and say things like "dead chickens" or call me "*Little* Margaret" or not even *Linda*. They were very nice van people but they weren't my van people.

We wound up at a mall and I wandered around with the others, but always looking for my people. Finally, I saw Pam and Mike on an escalator and I waved off the other Travelers. "It's okay, they are my family."

Eau Claire and the last night. A surprise party. Food. And a band. We talked to the hosts and guests. More Clinton-babble. Did we still believe?

I saw Sheila smile and dance.

Talked to a man and his wife who had become engaged when he was stationed at Fort Chaffee in Fort Smith. I took their picture while they danced, but forgot to get their address.

Bubba danced with me.

We taught Mike to dance. Really dance.

The guy on the sax wanted to know if we "actually knew Clinton."

There was a family there. Man and his wife. Obvious hard workers. And their teenage daughter. Recent high school graduate and she wanted to know about Clinton's college education plan. We took turns sitting with them. The daddy danced with his daughter. They were so proud of her. She had insisted that they come to the party.

When they left, she stopped and grabbed my hand. "Will you tell him about us?" she asked.

I thought about the red van and its mixed bag of passengers. All of a sudden I knew that we hadn't been demographically or economically or capriciously placed together. We were what showed up. We were as different as day and night, but we knew we wanted the same things. Change. Something better. Something more.

We weren't any different than that family. We weren't that special. But Bill had listened to all of us. I took that young woman's hand and said, "Honey, he already knows you."

The last morning the vans were being loaded, and Joe Dan and I sat in the open van door comfortable in our "campaign" jeans and windbreakers. We thought it was funny that Quayle was checking into the hotel right after we pulled out. We must have looked suspicious as a car drove up and some suited men got out. They walked over to the van. "Good morning," Joe Dan said. "We're from Arkansas and we'd like to tell you about our governor."

I chimed in, "We're Arkansas Travelers and we've been traveling Wisconsin for Bill Clinton at our own expense. Would you like some information about our governor?"

They listened to our nasal twangs—the housewife and the Chinese grocer—and grunted in disgust. "By God, you really *are* from Arkansas."

Joe Dan and I just laughed and laughed as Quayle's advance men walked away.

Pam and I didn't get to go to Little Rock on election night, but we attended a watch party in Fort Smith at the Holiday Inn. When George Bush appeared on the large screen TV, we all said, "Goodnight George!" And when Wisconsin showed up as a win for Clinton, Pam and I smiled with ears in our eyes and said, "We did that."

Appendix B:
Iowa Newsletter (1996)

Chronicle of the Arkansas Traveler Iowa Caucus Trip
February 9-13, 1996

45 A.T.'s GO TO IOWA FOR PRESIDENT CLINTON
EDITORS' NOTE
Dear Travelers:

Was Iowa great or what?!? We had five days of no sleep, little food, freezing temperatures, and a very gusty wind. Okay, so it wasn't paradise, but we each came home feeling like it was. Maybe it was from the satisfaction of knowing we had helped our friend and President begin the path to four more years in the White House. Or it could be from the support and joy we found from the people of Iowa. Or maybe, it was that we had been traveling with 45 wonderful people where friendships were formed, reformed, or strengthened. Our guess is that it was all of the above. Well, whatever the reasons, it was a fabulous trip! Since we were separated during the majority of the time, we wanted each van to share its memories with everyone. So each van has its own columned report (some more verbose than others - some funnier than others, but each well representative of their group); plus there are a few sidebars. Hope you enjoy the first edition of the 1996 ARKANSAS TRAVELERS.
Here's to many more trips together!

Tyler Thompson, Lila Riggs, Marci Riggs

Forty-five excited Arkansas Traveler's boarded a TWA flight Friday, February 9, bound for St. Louis and then on to Des Moines, IA,. for the all-important Iowa Caucuses. This is the story of those Travelers in Iowa.

The Arkansas Travelers is the unofficial publication of the Arkansas Travelers - a group of concerned and dedicated Arkansas supporters of President William Jefferson (Bill) Clinton. The Travelers are not incorporated, not federally funded, not state funded nor are they funded with any type of tax of any sort on any level. Each Traveler DOES pay his/her own way to places as is needed across the USA to spread the good word about our friend, President Bill Clinton, because WE WANT TO!

RANDY STEALS THE SHOW FROM PRES. CLINTON *by: Lila Riggs*

Rumor has it that when folks left Northern Iowa Area Community College, they were talking about a man they had just met for the first time, a man who had stopped to shake their hand, a man who had taken time to sign countless autographs. And this man is no other than our own Arkansas Traveler, RANDY LAVERTY.

That's right, our dear Representative Laverty stole the show! While the packed auditorium anxiously waited for President Clinton, they busied themselves by waiting in long lines to get Randy's autograph. Why? Who knows! But we did learn that he can write, although he did have problems with his spelling. It seems that on one occasion, he signed his name as Randy Lavert! The funniest moment of this already funny episode is when a young boy approached Randy with his pad and pencil ready and asked him, "So, what team do you play for?" What fun we had watching scores of young people gather around Randy to get his autograph. All over northern Iowa, on refrigerators, cork boards, and in frames is a signed piece of paper with the name Y LAVERTY (or Randy Lavert)!

By the way, Van 3 had quite a hard time fitting the Now-Famous-Randy's very inflated head in the van!

DOC SAVES A LIFE (and a vote) *by: Lila Riggs*

The event at Northern Iowa Community College was over and Van3 was tired, hungry, and ready to go. But we were missing Randy

Laverty and Dr. Alan Storeygard. Come to find out, they were busy helping an older man in distress. It seems that after the President had left the stage, Randy noticed a man having problems. He dutifully ran out to find help, which he did in Dr. Storeygard. Alan assessed that the man may be having a heart attack. He stayed with him until the ambulance arrived. The good doctor called the hospital a couple days later and learned the man had made it was still in the hospital. Our hats off to you, Dr. Storeygard!

VAN 1 *by Harry Light*

Excitement filled the air as we arrived at the airport on Friday evening. Sheila said 6:00 and by God, we were there at 5:30. It was the moment we had been waiting for –our Traveler Button and our van assignment. The gasps of those assigned to Van 1 were heard among the travelers. What had we done to deserve this: Was it part of the hazing for the new guys? Was this the van for the troublemakers? I mean, we had all been warned from former Travelers – "It's a great time as long as you're not in Sheila's van." "You'll never get to stop to eat." " Forget going to the bathroom." "Don't get on her bad side!" "God help you if you are not on time!" "What's it like being in Sheila's van one former traveler mused. Well you've seen the Wizard of Oz. Remember the Wicked Witch of the West?" Little did we know that it was Sheila's twin sister, the Good Witch of the North, that had decided to come on this trip. Either that or she was putting on a good show for her niece, Mandy, the youngest traveler (we were to learn later that the real reason Mandy came on this trip was not for politics—she was looking for an Iowa man to call her own).

Apparently, Judy Robertson had been in Sheila's van before. We couldn't help noticing the sky caps struggling with her cooler of food—and was that a port-a-potty she brought along? I mean, sure, we were told to bring some food but Judy's propane stove seemed a bit much. And Miss Elmo couldn't have gotten much sleep before the trip. She brought enough home made food to feed an army – or at least the hungry hogs in Van 1. The food turned out to be much needed though to keep Peggy's and Charlie Cole Chaffin's strength up—Peggy's for substitute driving after Richard and Mandy flew back home early (I'm not the one who started the rumors.) And Charlie Cole's for helping Miss Elmo in and out of the van. Besides Judy, Miss Elmo, Peggy, Richard, Charlie Cole, Sheila and Mandy, Van 1 included Henry Woods (who joined us in Iowa from Washington – he flew in early to do advance for Sheila at the hotel—Sheila is the only non-presidential candidate who has her own advance team), Fred Knight, Harry Light, Bill Morse and Charlie Varner.

For Van 1 it was late to bed and early to rise. Fred, Harry and Henry were stupid enough to volunteer with Dee Pryor to put the signs on the vans. What should have taken 15 minutes turned into a 1+ hour ordeal. The Washington influence was felt as Henry and Dee decide each person should have a separate chore—Fred's was handing out signs, Harry's was holding signs in place and Dee and Henry were in charge of taping. It was magic watching Dee and Henry operating the tape machine—half of the tape made it on the signs and the other half ended up all stuck together. At least we did manage to get the same number on both sides of each van. 6:15 Saturday morning came awfully early. But we were on a mission to Iowa City to help the Prez (except for Mandy who was looking for love in all the wrong places) so off we went. We were watching Sheila carefully to make sure her evil twin sister didn't appear—so far, so good. Much to our surprise, we even stopped for breakfast at McD's. Our fortune of having gotten food soon turned bad as we got back into the van. For, you see, it was a windy day in Iowa and the van was long. Sitting in the back of the van was like being in a fishing boat on a rough ocean. At first, swaying back and forth was relaxing and then it started affecting our breakfast. The only one not affected was Bill who had taken a sleeping pill the night before (or should I say the 4 hours before) and thought he was still in Little Rock. On the way Mandy napped—Miss Elmo didn't.

We made it to Iowa City on time and thankfully, still with our breakfast in our stomachs. We couldn't wait for our feet to touch land again and a few Van 1 travelers were seen kissing the ground. Typically, it was an arrive early and wait scene at Iowa City. But we came as ambassadors of good will and kept a smile on our face. That is until we learned what the young democrats in Iowa City had in store for us. Half of us it seems were assigned to give out pom poms on the floor of the arena—and only on the floor of the arena because, as you know, the pom poms were needed for good t.v. angles. Judy has us in tears after the event as she relayed story after story of having to pull pom poms out of children's hands because they were needed on the floor. The other half of use were initially excited about our job—we were simply to meet and greet the thousands of waiting Iowans as they stood in line. That is until a little chap told us we were to look for Republican butons and signs and then asked to see that person's ticket. When we got the ticket we were, get this, to tear it up! Don't worry, he said, this is on orders from the secret service and they'll back you up if you need help. Being the experienced politicians that we were, we could not imagine the secret service (or the Prez's advance staff) condoning the suppression of free speech. We could just see the headlines, "Arkansas Good Will Ambassadors Wrestle Grandmother for Ticket." We then learned that the secret service had nothing to do with it—the host group just didn't want any trouble. Even though the secret service could no longer help us out, we could still find a campus security guard if we needed help. Yeah, right. The Van 1 travelers huddled and decided that we would just see if anyone had any extra tickets and then tear those in half to show the host group what a great job we did. In the meantime, we would just do what we do best—meet and greet the Iowans standing in line. We handed out Traveler cards and pictures of Mandy to eligible bachelors. We also got to act importantly by giving out instructions on how to prepare for a secret service search. We just knew there were lots of people in that line who wished they could be us.

After the Prez's rip-roaring speech, we were back at the Van on our way to lunch hosted (but not paid for) by the local group. But wait, someone was missing and had committed the cardinal sin—not getting to the van on time. Where was Charlie Varner? The tension mounted as we waited for Mt. Sheila to erupt. Nails were bitten, cigarettes were smoked. But there was no explosion. Bill, who was now with us after the effects of his sleeping pill wore off, volunteered to stay behind, get Charlie and catch up with us at the restaurant. Whew! Disaster averted, we packed into the Van knowing that with Richard at the helm we would quickly be at our next destination. We had a nice tour of a parking garage—it seems Richard was given the wrong directions (or so we were told). Thank goodness for cellular phones—Sheila made a call and got us back on track.

After an enjoyable lunch, we were given instructions on the afternoon 's activities. We would be phone banking, ugh! Apparently, the local group was operating under the impression that we had never done phone banking before—they gave us detailed instructions on what to do. We were also given a lesson in how the Iowa caucuses work—to this day I still don't understand it. With our new found knowledge on how to phone bank we were off to Cedar Rapids to make those calls. Mandy took a nap—Miss Elmo didn't.

The phone banking went by fast. We were calling supposedly registered democrats and reminding them to go to their caucuses on Monday. As usual, the lists were out of date. It was bad enough calling to ask to speak to Mr. Smith only to find out from the widow Smith that the Mr. recently expired. Even more typical was learning the person we called was the local republican chairman who told us that he did not think he would be showing his support for Pres. Clinton on Monday. On the brighter side, several calls were to people who raved about the Prez's speech. Thankfully, we finished the phone banking quickly and our thoughts turned to getting back to Des Moines before midnight, eating dinner at a reasonable hour and getting a full night's sleep. We had never seen Des Moines in daylight.

We were dreaming. You see, it just happened that we were making our calls in the office of an attorney, Bob Rush, who also happened to be running for Congress against Jim Leach. Someone got the bright idea that we should help Mr. Rush get out a mailing. We spent the next four hours stuffing what seemed like 2 million envelopes. Luckily, we had Judy—the mass mail queen with us. Had it not been for Judy's assembly lines and Charlie's dexterity, we would probably still be there. At 8:00 p.m. it was time to head for a highly recommended Amish restaurant.

We couldn't believe it. Not only were we going to get to eat dinner but eat at a famous tourist attraction as well. On the way there, Mandy took a nap—Miss Elmo didn't. Well, we did get to ear dinner such as it was. If this was a famous Iowa tourist attraction all I can say is that there must not be much to see in Iowa. The beef eaters, Judy and Harry, couldn't wait to sink their teeth into some of that renowned Iowa beef. Ours must have come from a third world country. It tasted awful. We were going to stay and relax at the restaurant for a while but Richard got into the home made Amish fruit win and we were worried we'd lose our driver. Off we went back to Des Moines.

The trip back to Des Moines took twice as long as the trip out. It seems that Richard didn't see the speed limit signs increase from 35 to 65 when he got back on the freeway. The long trip back didn't bother us though—the back of the van was full of laughs. We talked about everyone (everyone that wasn't in our van, of course). Sheila finally couldn't stand it anymore and came back to join us. Mandy took a nap—Miss Elmo didn't.

We got to sleep in until 6:45 on Sunday since we didn't have to leave for church until 7:45. You all know how great the church service was—no need to tell you again. Suffice it to say we all had tapes made and there are a lot of Little Rock preachers receiving copies in hopes that they will learn how to give a better sermon (who could ever forget Ugly Religion in a Beautiful Church). After church we had a short break and then it was off to Drake University for our second outing with the Prez. Once again we were told we were assigned to free speech suppression. Only this time Sheila told us it wouldn't be so bad—we only had to pat the person down! I didn't realize I would have to take police training to be a traveler. Luckily, we weren't needed for pat down job and got to go right to our reserved seats behind the podium directly behind the Prez (except for a few of us who agreed to hand out Mandy's picture again). At this point I couldn't believe how lucky we had been on this trip. Then I started thinking—hey, wait a minute God (and Sheila) don't work this way. Something bad has to happen. Then I realized, while looking out at 9,000 people gathered for the speech, the Travelers were all "in the line of fire." When we weren't worried about that, we worried about all the t.v. cameras pointed at us. It would be just our luck to get caught in an embarrassing slouch or scratch at the very moment that CNN was focused on us. Moreover, how were we supposed to fake a genuine laugh at hearing Sen. Harkin's instant dislike of Newt or Newtie and the blowfish jokes for the seventh time>

After the speech it was time for special meeting with the Prez. We tried to give him one of Mandy's pictures but he reminded us that he was already married. The Prez was having so much fun he got behind schedule again and Bruce Lindsey had to drag him away—after all, he might not have anything better to do but the Traveler's had to go phone bank again. Back to the hotel (and I use that term loosely) for a quick change and then off to the Iowa Clinton/Gore headquarters.

We weren't looking forward to our long evening of phone banking because there was a Mexican dinner waiting for us. Fate stepped in once again to shorten our task. It seems the local Clinton/Gore guy didn't want to discuss business with Sheila because he was trying to be on time for a date that night. Once Sheila understood his priorities, she redefined ours. Hang up the phones, its party time. Mandy and Richard had left to return to Arkansas. Bill and Charlie also had to get back to the natural state. Our van was dwindling in numbers.

I can't remember the name of the Mexican restaurant because Peggy bought us a pitcher of margaritas. I do remember, however, some long haired guy coming in and making a speech and then trying to pick up Gail. I kept wondering just how much good will a Traveler had to exhibit. Some people left early because they were tired—Miss Elmo didn't.

Monday was meet and greet the public day. Our van was assigned to the pedestrian skyway downtown. The people were friendly with a few exceptions. We did get to meet President Clinton's grandson although he wasn't from Hope but from another <u>planet</u>. At noon we were off to a retirement center. We thought we would never get Miss Elmo out of there. Monday afternoon it was off to Boone, Iowa for the Boone District Caucus. We chose this particular caucus because it was one of the 60 "fiber caucuses" around the state with a live feed to caucus central. Our caucus was to be held in the National Guard building where sometimes as many as 20 people showed up for a caucus. Peggy was then at the helm now so our driving was faster and not as turbulent. Charlie was her chief navigator and got us there quickly and well ahead of schedule.

As usual, we meekly blended in; We weren't there two minutes before Sheila had Henry and Fred decorating the room with Clinton/Gore signs. Judy, Charlie and Peggy were in charge of rearranging the furniture. Sen. Charlie was also assigned to butter up the local politicians and give a speech on behalf of the Travelers. Miss Elmo was in charge of arranging the Clinton/Gore buttons on the table. I was in charge of asking dumb questions about "fiber causcuses"—I never did understand it. The local head pol was Mr. Orville Nelson who was clutching his "autographed" picture of President Clinton. While we all took an immediate like to Mr. Nelson and Sen. Sorenson, we were soon left to wonder whether they were closet republicans. You see, at an Iowa caucus people can bring up issues to be decided by the local precinct which is then decided at the county level which is then decided at the state level which is then disregarded. Sen. Sorenson felt compelled to introduce a resolution supporting a bill that would refuse to recognize same sex marriages performed in another state. The measure passed by voice vote with only 2 dissenters. A secret ballot showed 5 dissenters and the people were staring at each other trying to figure out who the other 3 people were. Sen. Sorenson's motion was soon followed by Mr. Nelson's motion to recognize the English language as the official language of Iowa (I still wonder whether it was some dig at our southern accents). This also passed without opposition. I suspect they don't preach politics of "inclusion" in that part of Iowa. The highlight of the caucus was Sen. Charlie's speech about the Travelers. It was like seeing her on the stump again and we truly believe she could have been elected to public office that night in Iowa after her talk. After the caucus, we stopped at a local grocery store for return trip necessities and headed back to Des Moines just in time to watch the democratic election party come to a close. On the way back, Mandy wasn't there to take a nap—Miss Elmo didn't nap either. What a memorable evening and a memorable trip.

VAN #2 GO *By Sheila Bell*

The Arkansas Travelers of Van #2 who made the cold trip to Iowa in February 1996 came from the four congressional districts of Arkansas - with different backgrounds, perspectives and experiences - but all came with a spirit of camaraderie and purpose.

Early on Saturday morning, during the ride to Iowa City, the crew had the opportunity to get to know one another and to establish the rules of the road. First,"if you're late, you're gonna get your rear left behind," and "No, Jennifer, you can't get that Secret Service guy's phone number!"

The group waited outside for an hour in the brisk winter breeze before they could get into the arena to work their magic on the thousands of Iowans who came to see and hear President Clinton.

After the President's warm reception and the overflow crowd that met him in Iowa City, one of Van #2's members felt so relaxed, he found a sofa to take a nap on while the rest of the group made phone calls to the folks trying to make sure of a good turnout for Monday evening's caucuses.

The strong winds coming from the plains buffeted the van on the long trip back to Des Moines late Saturday evening, but the hot air that was inside the van helped keep it on the highway. There were jokes, stories and refreshments to soothe the tired and weary. Some even tried to sleep, and guess who she dreamed about - - - - .

Sunday morning, Van #2 was proud to have one of their own speak at the church service the entire group of Travelers attended. They didn't remember what he said, they just loved to hear him talk. "He has such a voice, and his elocution is superb," said the lawyer in the group.

At Drake University, Van #2 did some of its best work of the trip. They made sure the best seats in the house were reserved for the Arkansas Travelers. Of course, the President was overheard making some remark about the headgear one of the members was wearing while he worked the young college girl crowd outside the building.

Late that evening, someone in the group needed batteries for their camera and everyone was thirsty after the Mexican dinner, so they decided to visit one of the local grocery stores, "when what to their wandering eyes should appear but.." one 1-0- o-n-n-g white limousine, which pulled up to the front door of the store. Well, who could this be - which celebrity, which sports figure??? Without missing a beat, one of the more gregarious members of the bunch, stopped at the door of the limo and asked who they were with. They replied, PHIL GRAMM!!! And she replied, "Oh, I bet that's a laugh a minute." She did provoke a smile from the young man, but he wouldn't let her in the limo to see for sure ... She tried though and that's what counts.

An early call again on Monday morning sent Van #2 to the sky-walks in downtown Des Moines to do the campaign thing.

Two members got left behind, but they steadfastly deny any rumor that they were together. On to nutrition centers, senior citizen homes and the unauthorized guided tours of the national media center set up at the Savory Hotel.

With the caucuses just hours away, Van #2 was given the opportunity to really show some of its heretofore untapped talents - they were given the assignment of decorating the ballroom for the statewide celebration for the Iowa Democratic Party. These were the perfect people - lawyers, insurance executive, teachers, nurse, utility manager, tax collector - who better to be given paper stars, paper graffiti, and the ever-popular red and blue balloons to make a ballroom into a place for celebration.

On to the real event, the Iowa Caucuses—the group went to an elementary school where they dispersed to different precinct rooms to observe the caucus process and speak on behalf of the President if they were asked. Only someone spoke too long - and got left. Not on purpose, the group just couldn't count anymore, their fingers and toes were tired.

At the celebration back at the Savory Hotel, the group mingled with Iowa Democrats and National Democratic Chair, Senator Chris Dodd, who was so pleased to have his picture taken a thousand times with the good looking men and women of Van #2. Some of the Iowa Democrats even recognized the group - by their accents - from the phone calls they had received - and the bad pronunciations of their surnames.

On to the unofficial Arkansas Traveler Caucus room back at the hotel, where "last call" took on a whole new meaning, when the whip popped and group leader Sheila Bronfman said the vans had to be cleaned out-NOW. The usual drink cans, candy sacks and empty packages were found, but the pair of l-o-n-g black ladies stockings and socks that were under the seat were a real mystery. Once the van was clean and the packing was done, the group settled down for another good three hours sleep before time to leave for the airport.

The usual hugs and kissed followed with promises to keep in touch and the blood oath not to tell on each other - because if you told, Sheila could assign you to the van with the wild man from Berryville on the next trip.

Not to say this group was difficult to deal with, but they were the only van to have their first driver leave AND their van leader become ill. The group had to recruit one of their own as driver, who brought a while new meaning to the term, "merging traffic," and a new van leader had to be airlifted in from Washington, DC.

The fine group of Arkansas Travelers that comprised Van #2 were in no certain order, and admitting to nothing were: Jim "Elocution" Banks, Sheila "where are my leggings and socks" Bell, Senator Jerry "Headgear" Bookout, Senator Jay "where's the beer" Bradford, Weldon "napman" Chesser, Nettie "I can't walk that far" Gibson, Jennifer "he kissed me" Love, Mary "help me up" Newberry, Ann "ya'll really left me!" Price, David "because of pressing business in Washington" Pryor, Jr., group leader- Mary Ann "I really am sick, ya'll" Salmon, and last but not least Ann "this must be a nightmare" Pride.

VAN 3's MOST EXCELLENT ADVENTURE *by: Marci Riggs*

The first day of our adventure had an auspicious beginning as driver Randy Laverty had to stop and ask directions 30 seconds after leaving the hotel. Was this an omen of things to come? We hoped not.

The Travelers in Van 3 were valiantly led by Gail Goodrum and included Bernice Duffy, Lorene Leder, Randy Laverty, Joanne and Garth Martin, Levi Phillips, Lila Riggs, Vic Snyder, Alan Storeygard, and me, Marci Riggs.

In tandem with Van 4 we drove some 2 hours north of Des Moines to Mason City and the campus of NIACC - Northern Iowa Area Community College. In the high winds and low temperatures (wind chill from this Southern girl's perspective was at least 20 below!) several hardy Travelers worked the crowd lined up outside. What a great group of people! Many had started lining up outside the doors in the wee hours (3-4 AM) of the morning. In the front was a 70-year-old couple who literally spent the night out there with their lawn chairs and sleeping bags. They had never seen a President and they were not going to miss their chance.

It was a joy to talk to these wonderful Iowans (and even some from Minnesota). Most were quite thrilled to talk to us Arkansans and were all very excited and proud that President Clinton had come to their area of the world. What a joy it was to see their reaction when the President stepped out on that stage in the overflow room. When he asked them to come down and shake his hand, Phoom! 1000 people were on their feet rushing down to the front!

Sunday started with a rousing church service led by the Reverend McGill. Hey, if I'd attended such an exciting church as a child, maybe I wouldn't have complained about getting up early on Sundays.

Sunday afternoon at Drake was an uplifting experience. The crowd was great! It was worth missing the Razorback-Kentucky game to hear Senator Harkin's quip about Newtie and the Blowhards" and spend a few moments alone with the President.

After Drake, Van 3 headed off to phone bank. No one works a phone better than Levi Phillips and Randy Laverty. They just turned up that good ole' boy charm and got people out to caucus. I even heard Randy trying to convert some Republicans! As for my count - 2 dead, and one was burying his wife that day!

From phone banking, we hit "Nacho Mama's." By that time the pitchers of beer and margaritas were flowing. I'm not sure how many times we sang "Stand By Your Van," however the other bar patrons knew we were there!

Monday morning dawned bright and early for V $\sim$ 3 as we set out at 6 AM to work the UPS shipping facility. All I can say about the experience is IT IS COLD!!! Van 3 braved the cold without fear knowing we had 2 doctors on the van who could treat out frost bite - what do you do again, Dr. Snyder and Dr. Storeygard - just cut off the afflicted appendage?

At a senior center we visited we were all treated to entertainment by Dr. Alan on the piano. However, I think the good doctor need to expand his repertoire - he played Christmas Carols!

Monday night's party was a blast. Hobnobbing with Senators Harkin and Dodd. I understand that Senator Harkin was even jumping when Sheila blew her whistle! At one point in the evening as I stood beside my younger sister, over comes Senator Dodd and asks Lila if she would have her picture taken with him. Being the kind and benevolent older sister that I am, I immediately jumped into the picture also. Turns out Levi had set her up with the Senator and got him to come over and embarrass her!

For those of you who missed it, in the hotel bar Monday evening, the Arkansas Travelers plus some folks from Fox News that Sheila B. grabbed, broke into a rousing, slightly off-key rendition of "Happy Birthday" for Lila at midnight. (Yes, we also sang "Happy Birthday" at the Des Moines airport and scared off some of the press who were also on our flight. Hey, Lila, how were those four bottles of wine the stewardess gave you?)

Now for the awards presentation:

Funniest moment in Mason City (aside from the Randy Laverty Fan Club): Sue White and Joann Martin stumbling into the men's room. We know the Arkansas Travelers are supposed to go anywhere to get a vote for our Man, but did you have to take it so literally, ladies (or couldn't you have sent one of the men)?

Best store in Mason City: Kum N' Go Best quote from Drake (from a voter):

"He's (President Clinton) got my vote unless he's running against God!"

Best Truck Driver Imitation: Levi's "C'mon back" as he guided driver Vic Snyder in and out of spots. Levi also gets the chivalry award for always opening and closing the van doors and helping the passengers out. Garth Martin failed the chivalry test when he unceremoniously "helped" his wife Joann into the van by shoving her up in the backside.

In closing (finally), I have only this to say: I had a great time in Iowa and WHEN DO WE TRAVEL AGAIN!!!

VAN IV *by Tyler Thompson*

We may have brought up the rear; but because of us, the rest of you left a good final impression on those Iowa folks."

We of VAN IV were very proud to note that we all arrived together in Iowa, toured and worked the state together, and left together. There were no faces in our group that flew in from places other than our natural state, arrived late in Iowa or left early. We were a cohesive group - a real team within a team, all for IV and IV for Clinton (actually that's why we all were in Iowa in the first place -IV more for Clinton/Gore).

VAN IV was led by our illustrious lady from Conway, the incomparable Sue White. She was noted by her impeccable manners, solid direction and smooth, polite leadership - a woman with uncanny, soft-spoken yet firm leadership.

Also aboard were our two excellent van drivers - Mr. Arkansas Small Businessman, Joel Buckner from North Little Rock, and Southern Strategy Group's Ron Oliver, also from NLR (both of these men had trouble, however, finding the driveway entrances to our Iowa hotel). In addition V AN IV boasted two power couples: Fred and Pat Morrow from Little Rock, and Patti and Jamie Cox from Greenwood. Occupying the tail-gunner seat was Mack Dyer of the Dyer dynasty in Dyer; and immediately in front of him were Idavonne Rosa, RN (premier authority on home health care and aging concerns), and myself, Dr. Tyler Thompson, optometrist from Little Rock and first-timer on the Arkansas Traveler circuit.

Prior to the flight from Little Rock, everyone gathered in front of the TWA ticket counter renewing old acquaintances, making new ones, accepting packets from Sheila, passing around Arkansas buttons and pins, and generally getting pumped about the trip. Most of us headed up toward the gate, pausing briefly for a group picture on the steps up to the second level (however, we found that some of us didn't make the picture as a number were seen to be in the bar at the top of the steps). Seeing us off at the gate were a number of well-wishers not making the trip this time including Ron Maxwell and Rick and Tina Eoff (Rick was sporting a sign that read, "Bypassing the Iowa trip because of my recent triple By-pass").

On board the TWA flight everyone read the packets Sheila had given us (yeah, right), and in St. Louis for our layover the packets Sheila had given us (yeah, right), and in St. Louis for our layover most everyone did a lot of parading up and down the concourse. Again on board TWA to Des Moines we anticipated our touchdown in that capital city (note: we were acknowledged by the pilot over the intercom).

Wasn't it fun retrieving our luggage at Des Moines International and getting it all into the luggage van? Well anyway, we all saw for the first time our vans - our dromedaries of the cornfields, three gray and one blue. One of the gray ones was VAN IV. Once at the hotel we were all assigned rooms and given our marching orders by Sheila for the next morning. Vans 1 & 2 were to report at 6 AM, and vans 3 & IV were to report at 9 AM. We of vans 3 & IV lamented that we had to wait so long to get started (yeah, right).

9:00 AM Saturday morning found vans 3 & IV all chipper and ready to go to Mason City for the President's visit to North Iowa Area Community College (hereafter referred only as NIACC). The trip was straight north for about 100 miles (did you notice that all the roads and highways in Iowa are north and south or east and west? I don't know why they even have steering wheels in vehicles up there; if you want to change lanes all you have to do is let the wind do it for you). Halfway to Mason City both vans stopped off in Thornton for a coffee break and a chance to allow Ron, our driver, and van3' s driver to pry their hands off the steering wheels:

We finally arrived at NIACC about 11:30, and there was already a long line of people waiting to get into the building; note that the President wasn't to speak until 5:00 PM and the doors weren't to open until 2:30. We found out that one lady had been there since 3AM, and many had been there since 6 AM. But, burrrr, it was cold!

We were ushered into the school cafeteria where we rotated going outside to meet and greet those in line and handing out our cards. Some of us rotated more inside and others spent more time outside. I think most of us were highly impressed at the perseverance and hardiness of those Iowans who stood outside in that wind, cold and occasional snowflake.

Around 2:00 we Travelers were sent through the mags and then to the holding room outside the overflow auditorium where we were to work. The President was to speak in the gym, and our charges were to view his speech on a closed-circuit screen on the stage. As people started coming into the auditorium, we noticed a lot of grumbling from Iowans stating, "If I had known that I was going to have to see him on a screen, I would have stayed home and watched him on TV!" Soon however, a secret service agent told us that the President would drop by and make an appearance after his speech. This helped to make our job a lot easier. The most entertaining part of our waiting period for the President to show up was Randy Laverty's sudden notoriety as the "giver of autographs" (see Lila's article)—it was a spectacle that amazed, confused, baffled and amused us all. And he ate it up! He probably could have been elected governor of Iowa on the spot! Lucky for Harkin Randy wasn't running for senator.

Finally the main event started with the President, Senator Harkin and others appearing on the screen in the gym. Watching all these Iowans cheering for the President on the screen, you would have thought he was actually present on the stage of the auditorium. After the President's well-received speech, the air in the auditorium was rich in anticipation of his actually showing up in the room. A lone podium stood next to the giant TV screen, and the stage curtain was tight next to the podium. After a pregnant few minutes, the President took one step from behind the curtain and stood majestically tall at the podium. The room simply exploded with cheers and applause and contined for quite a while. Finally the roar calmed and the

President addressed the crowd. He told them that he wouldn't make them listen to his speech all over again, but that he was thrilled that they had all come and he wished them well. He could have said, "Thank you for coming and have a good day," and then gone back behind the curtain. And that crowd probably would have been satisfied because they had gotten to SEE the president LIVE. But being "Bill" (and to the consternation of the secret service), he said, "... and since you have been so patient, I want to shake hands with as many of you as I can." Well, that did it with this crowd. They stormed the stage (very politely, mind you) and many came away with comments such as, "I'll never wash this hand again" and "He touched me, he really touched me!!" After hundreds and hundreds of greetings the President left the room for the second overflow room and a series of smaller meet-and-greets with Iowa VIPs.

As we were heading out back to our vans, one of our own helped to tend to one of the Iowans in the audience who had an apparent heart attack during the President's appearance (see Lila's article concerning this).

Once in the vans we endured the Razorback-football-game-sized traffic to get out of the city and back to Des Moines. But we were all hungry and stopped for dinner before heading out (that is, we stopped at three or four places before we finally found one that our advance person agreed was our kind of place). Inside the restaurant we saw a number of people who had been in the auditorium that afternoon which wrapped up our visit in the city very nicely. The trip back to Des Moines was as bumpy and windy as it had been going up, except that it was dark, too. Kudos to Joel for getting us all back safely. Everyone was up and ready Sunday morning for the 7:15 departure to that infamous service at the Corinthian Baptist Church. All four vans attended together, and Jim Banks made us all kind of proud in his Democratic pulpit. But as we all noticed, Rev. McGill really woke us all up. Imagine Sheila in his robes using his style to enthuse the Travelers as to our next trip - Ugly Politics in a Beautiful Campaign.

After church and after a break, we (all four dromedaries full) headed to Drake University where the Pres and Senator Harkin would once again enthuse the masses (God, it gets cold in Iowa). I'm gonna pass on most of the reporting and observations at Drake since Harry did such a great job describing the scene in Van l' s report. Except that a few of us did notice a few people on the front row who showed up later at the caucus VAN IV attended on Monday night. And maybe another observation: From our vantage point on the stage directly behind the President, it was amazing to watch the people's faces head-on as they watched Bill and reacted to his comments. There was doe-eyed dedication, intense jockeying for optimal positioning to see him and be seen, rapt attention to the man who is their President, and the absolute thrill of actually being in the presence of the person who is their commander-in-chief. In addition as a Traveler myself, there was this fortuitous feeling of watching our man standing there appearing so humble and accepting this tremendous wave of appreciation for his being there with these individuals in the crowd. Naive as I may be, it almost brought a tear to my eye more than once. Now, I must admit, my butt did get tired sitting so long and I did squirm a bit. But when I realized that so many of those people on the floor had been standing for an hour or so before the President showed up and throughout the talks of the president of the college, the president of the college Young Democrats, the woman who had gone through school on federal college loans, Senator Harkin and the President, I realized that a mildly sore butt was just being petty. Some pains are merely relative, after all.

The visit with the President afterwards was simply a delight. Patti and Jamie got their official photo with the President, even though Patti had to explain to the President who Jamie was. He was a little concerned about the halftime score of the Razorback game, but was upbeat about how things were looking in New Hampshire. I'll bet that if The President had had his druthers, he'd much rather have joined us later at Nacho Mama's than doing whatever he was sched-uled to do after our visit.

After Drake it was back into the vans and another respite breather. 4:30 saw us all reporting back to the vans to go phone banking. VAN IV was sent to Harkin's campaign office (obviously an old failed savings and loan - ironic to do phone - "banking" there). Then it was off to Nacho Mama's - I defer again to Harry's report here. Can't add much to his report except to say Mama's really helped to loosen us up a bit.

Monday saw us up at 6:45 AM in VAN IV sent by Brad Knott - some to U. S. West (the Morrows and the Coxes plus Sue White) and the rest of us to the corner of 10th & Locust handing out Traveler cards and pamphlets to Iowans going to work. Other than being thrown out of parking decks, ducking gusts of sub-zero winter wind, and being ignored by uptight frozen republican insurance accountants, it was a really pleasant experience. A few of us ran out of cards and pamphlets within a short period of time, so we couldn't see ourselves just standing on corners freezing for another hour or so, so we found a coffee shop in one of the adjoining buildings and campaigned those in the shop (but mostly each other) over coffee and bagels.

Then it was on to a Mall where we tried to find a Senior Citizen's Center to do a little campaigning. Actually we spent as much time trying to find the Center as we did campaigning. We kept going around corner after corner, until I suggested (much to the chagrin of the other's of my gender in the van) that we stop and ask directions to the Center. Anyway, we made it and had quite a nice time with the folks there. Sue got on the P.A system and did her little song and dance, and Idavonne told the seniors how much the President cared for them. Job done, we had lunch at the Hall of Fame restaurant (with walls of news articles showing that it had been flooded in the great 1993 flood) and listened to Idavonne talk about her Peace Corps experiences in Afghanistan.

Back at the hotel we had some free time til 4:00 so some of us went to the Iowa capital building, some went shopping and some snoozed. At 4:00 it was off to phone banking again, this time at the

Clinton/ Gore offices (*"thanks* for calling, but I'd rather go to the republican caucus and wreak some havoc"). Afterwards, we headed to a caucus at Urbandale High School. Even saw Phil Grimm ... , er, Gramm come in and go into one of the Republican rooms. You could tell which one was him; he was the one being held up on all sides by reporters and TV camerapersons escorting him into the building. Inside the Democratic caucus rooms the action was a bit more civilized than what was reported was going on in the others. One room had in attendance some of the people we had seen earlier in the day in the front of the crowd at Drake. And also, Senator Harkin dropped by the room and made a few comments to the appreciative crowd. He even made some very kind remarks about us Travelers in the room. The Morrow's caucus assisted a lady who was there to change her party affiliation from Republican to Democrat and ended up chairing the caucus. Afterwards it was on to the victory party at the Savory Hotel where both Sen. Harkin and Sen. Dodd (Connecticut) spoke with eloquence, especially when they applauded the work and enthusiasm of the Arkansas Travelers. Harkin said we should come back and work for him (The Harkinsaw Travelers? Yeah, right). Gents from the Iowa Democratic Party handed out red carnations to many of the Arkansas Traveler ladies - nice touch. Most of us got our picture taken with Sen. Dodd - that is, most of us from vans 2, 3, & IV. Seems as though Van 1 didn't make it back in time from their caucus to enjoy the victory party. Oh, by the way, the most important aspect of the whole evening was the fact that our President won 100% of the 50,000+ votes of the Democratic caucus voting - mustn't forget that!! Results from the Republican caucuses: Dole 26%; Buchanan 23%; Alexander 18%; Forbes 10%; Gramm 9%.

Back at the hotel, most of us headed to the bar to relax and swap stories. After a while, van 1 pulled in and regaled us with their fun stories about the "fiber caucus" they attended - whatever that was. The hour was getting late, we were facing an early morning 6:30 departure for the airport, and I was getting very tired and sleepy despite the pleasant company in the bar. So I went to bed - I don't know if. Miss Elmo did or not, but she was in the vans the next morning.

Sure enough we all made it to the airport in time to check in our luggage and said our good-byes to our dromedaries of the cornfields - three gray and one blue. VAN IV was one of the gray ones.

Interesting note: We did notice some interesting special traveling companions boarding our plane for St. Louis - Dan Rather (CBS), Jeff Greenfield (ABC), Peter Jennings (ABC - who was that behind those Foster Grants?).

Second interesting note: The above luminaries (?) also noticed some interesting special traveling companions boarding their plane for St. Louis - the Arkansas Travelers.

Little Rock International Airport saw us all home safe and sound with inerasable memories in mind, unmistakable victory accomplished, and undeniable pleasures made in having served as Arkansas Travelers.

- Tyler Thompson

Appendix C:
A Complete List of
the Clintons' Arkansas Travelers
and the States They Visited

The Clintons' Arkansas Travelers

Name		Traveler Trips
Margaret (Margie)	**Alsbrook**	hIA, hTX
Vincent Cleveland	**Ancell**	pNH
Aubra Hayes	**Anthony, Jr.**	gTX, LA 1996
Sarah Ellen	**Argue**	hNH, hTX
Mauria Jackson	**Aspell**	pNH, hNH
Robert W.	**Aspell**	pNH, hNH
William Carroll	**Autry**	hIA
David William	**Bailin**	gMO, hNH, hAR
Hannah Grady	**Bailin**	hNH
Jason	**Baker**	hTX
Barbara J.	**Baldizar**	hNH
Robert	**Baldizar**	hNH
Nancy Crain	**Balton**	gIA/NE
James Henry	**Banks**	IA 1996
C. Kay	**Bartlett**	hNH
Woodson W. (Woody)	**Bassett III**	FL Straw Poll, pNH, pIL, NY Ambass
Brandi Lynn	**Baxter**	pNH
Robert H.	**Baxter**	pNH, pCA, gIA/NE, gSD/NE
Donald Ray	**Beavers**	NY Ambass, gPA, gCO, gMN/WI
Mary Frances	**Beavers**	NY Ambass, gCO
*Emilie	**Bell**	gKS
Joe Dudley	**Bell**	pNH, NY Ambass
Sheila W.	**Bell**	IA 1996
Stewart Alexander	**Bell**	pNH, NY Ambass
Joe D.	**Bennett**	NY Ambass, gMO
Mary Jean	**Bennett**	NY Ambass, gMO
Carolyn	**Berry**	pGA
Marion	**Berry**	pGA
*Cynthia T.	**Beshear**	pIL, gKY
Sanford L.	**Beshear, Jr.**	pIL, pIA/NE
Sherry Gavin	**Bird**	pNH, NY Ambass
Allen W.	**Bird, II**	pNH, NY Ambass, gGA

The Clintons' Arkansas Travelers

Name		Traveler Trips
Donald Eugene	**Bishop**	KY/TN 1996, LA 1996, hIA, hNH, hAR, hTX
Sherry L.	**Bishop**	hNH
Ralph	**Blagg**	NY Ambass, gMO
Kim Tonymon	**Blair**	pGA
Del	**Blake**	hTX
Heather Daniel	**Blake**	hTX
*Jerry Paul	**Bookout**	pIL, NY Ambass, IA 1996
Paul	**Bookout, Jr.**	pIL
Eldridge Scott	**Bowen**	gMD, gNC
Jerry W.	**Bowen**	pNH, pIL
Jean	**Boyce**	NY Ambass, gMO, LA 1996
Sam H.	**Boyce**	NY Ambass, gMO, gAL
Del	**Boyette**	pNH
Jay T.	**Bradford**	pNH, pIL, pCA, NY Ambass, IA 1996, hNH
Karla J.	**Bradley**	hIA, hNH, hAR
Herby	**Branscum**	NY Ambass, gGA
John	**Broderick**	HON
Richard A	**Bronfman**	pNH, pIL, gSC, gAL, gSD/NE, gGA, IA 1996, LA 1996, hNH, hAR, hTX
Sheila Galbraith	**Bronfman**	pNH, pIL, pCA, NY Ambass, gMO, gSC, gKY, gIA/NE, gMN/WI, gSD/NE, gGA, IA 1996, KY/TN 1996, LA 1996, hIA, hNH, hAR, hTX
Corey Villines	**Brooks**	hNH, hAR
Carol	**Brown**	hAR
*Grady L.	**Brown**	pNH
Jerry Ray	**Brown**	pGA
George	**Bruno**	HON
Marie Clinton	**Bruno**	LA 1996, hNH
Debra Sublett	**Buckner**	NY Ambass, gIA/NE
Joel Kenneth	**Buckner**	pNH, NY Ambass, gSD/NE, IA 1996
Carole Kay	**Bulloch**	pCA, gMN/WI

p • Primary   **h** • Hillary Campaign
g • General Election   **HON** • Honorary Traveler
State Abbr. • Clinton 2nd Term Trip   * • Deceased as of August 2012

The Clintons' Arkansas Travelers

Name		Traveler Trips
Ronald E.	**Bumpass**	pNH
Senator Dale	**Bumpers**	pNH
William Gregg	**Burgess**	FL Straw Poll, NY Ambass
Margaret Moseley	**Burris**	gMN/WI, gOK
Chris	**Burrow**	pGA
Bill	**Burton**	pNH, pTX
*Gloria	**Calhoun**	NY Ambass, gSD
*Robert Lee	**Calhoun**	LA 1996
Freda	**Campbell**	gMO
G.W.	**Campbell**	gMO
Lilburn Wayne (Lib)	**Carlisle**	pIL, NY Ambass, gSD/NE, gKY
*Claude	**Carpenter**	pIL, pTN, pAL, pFL, pGA
*June	**Carter**	pGA
Charlie Cole	**Chaffin**	pNH, IA 1996, hTX
Alice	**Chamberlin**	hNH, hTX
Weldon	**Chesser**	pGA, pIL, pCA, NY Ambass, gWA/OR, gIA/NE, gMN/WI, gGA, IA 1996
Courtney Robinson	**Cisne**	gKS
*Francis Charlene Orr	**Clark**	pTX
John Steven	**Clark**	hNH, hAR
Suzanne	**Clark**	hNH
*Captain John Wesley	**Clayton**	pNH
*Catherine Boler	**Clayton**	pNH
Herschel Wayne	**Cleveland**	gTX
Eleanor	**Coleman**	NY Ambass, gGA
Roosevelt	**Coleman**	NY Ambass, gGA
Margaret Villee	**Compton**	pNH, gTX, gLA
*Robert Curran	**Compton**	pNH
Glenda Johnson	**Cooper**	pGA
Sandra K.	**Cornish**	pIL
Ann Hindsman	**Cornwell**	pIL, NY Ambass, hAR
Gilbert Greene	**Cornwell, Jr.**	pNH, pIL, gAZ, hNH, hAR
Judy Fowler	**Cosgrove**	gMO, gKS

---

p • Primary
g • General Election
State Abbr. • Clinton 2nd Term Trip
h • Hillary Campaign
HON • Honorary Traveler
* • Deceased as of August 2012

The Clintons' Arkansas Travelers

Name		Traveler Trips
Wesley Allen	**Cottrell**	gIA, hIA, hNH, hAR
James Oldham	**Cox**	IA 1996
Patricia Sheilds	**Cox**	IA 1996
Larry Eugene	**Crane**	FL Straw Poll, pNH
*Rose Lynn	**Crane**	pCA, gSD/NE, hIA, hNH, hAR, hTX
Debra	**Crapo**	hNH
Patty Howe	**Criner**	pNH, NY Ambass, gCO, hTX
Lloyd H.	**Crossley**	LA 1996
Peggy	**Crossley**	pCA, LA 1996
Cathy	**Cunningham**	pNH, NY Ambass
Ernest G.	**Cunningham**	pNH, NY Ambass
Gaye Annette	**Cypert**	LA 1996, hTX
Jimmie Dean	**Cypert**	LA 1996
*Newlyn Leone	**Davis**	gMN/WI, gKS
*Sybil	**Davis**	pTX
*Taylor	**Davis**	pTX
Rene-Marie	**de Turenne**	pNH, gMN/WI, gKS
Sergio	**DeLeon**	hTX
Milana M.	**Dennis**	gGA
Martha	**Dixon**	gAL
Craig Scott	**Douglass**	hIA, hNH, hTX
Lee	**Douglass**	pIL, gGA
Berniece	**Duffey**	IA 1996, KY/TN96, LA 1996, hIA, hAR, hTX
Billie Gail	**Dunlap**	gMO
Tommy J.	**Dunlap, Sr.**	gMO
Mack Jewel	**Dyer**	pNH, pOK, pIL, pGA, gTX, IA 1996
Jackie Lonell	**Edmonds**	gMO, gKS, LA 1996
Wes	**Edwards**	gKS
David Merle	**Eldridge**	gSC
Margaret Rozzell	**Eldridge**	gSC
Elizabeth Laverty	**Elford**	gMO

---

p • Primary   **h** • Hillary Campaign
g • General Election   **HON** • Honorary Traveler
State Abbr. • Clinton 2nd Term Trip   ***** • Deceased as of August 2012

The Clintons' Arkansas Travelers

Name		Traveler Trips
Linda Jackson	**Ellington**	LA 1996, hNH
Kris	**Engskov**	NY Ambass, gKS
*Rick	**Eoff**	gMO, gCO, gIA/NE, gSD/NE, gTX, gGA
Wooten	**Epes**	gMN/WI
Marshall Dale	**Evans**	pNH, pCA, NY Ambass, hTX
Sheila Darlene	**Evans**	pNH, pCA, NY Ambass
Veronica	**Fanning**	pNH
Pate	**Felts**	pCA, NY Ambass, gGA
*Virginia	**Ferguson**	gKS
Lisa Carolyn	**Ferrell**	NY Ambass, gGA
*George Edward	**Fisher**	pNH
Jimmie Lou	**Fisher**	HON
Victor Anson	**Fleming**	gGA, NY Ambass
Frances (Fran)	**Flener**	gIA/NE, hIA, hNH, hAR
*Jerry Lee	**Flippo**	gMO, gKS, gIA/NE
*Margaret Jane	**Flippo**	gMO, gKS, gIA/NE
Sharyn	**Floyd**	pOK
David	**Folsom**	pNH, pTX
Judy	**Folsom**	pTX
Donna Faye	**Fowler**	gMO, gKS
Jimmy Ivan	**Fowler**	gMO, gKS
*Waldo	**Fowler**	gKS
*Mary Jo Rogers	**Fraley**	pGA
Tracey Dean	**Franks**	pIL, pGA, pCA, pTX
Lewis	**Frazer**	pNH
Maribeth Moore	**Frazer**	pNH, gKS
Mary Mel	**French**	pIL, NY Ambass
R. B.	**Friedlander**	pNH
*Edward Donald	**Fry II**	pNH, NY Ambass, gSD/NE, hNH
Woody	**Futrell**	pNH, pTX
Judy S.	**Gaddy**	pNH, NY Ambass, hAR
William D. (Bill)	**Gaddy**	pNH
Leigh	**Gage**	pTX

The Clintons' Arkansas Travelers

Name		Traveler Trips
Cary L.	**Gaines**	pNH
Michael Johnston	**Gaines**	pNH, gKY
Amie Lee	**Galloway**	pOK, KY/TN 1996
J.J.	**Galloway**	pOK, NY Ambass, KY/TN 1996
Timothy Joseph	**Giattina**	hNH, hAR
Marta Diane	**Gibbs**	gKS
Nettie Sue	**Gibson**	pIL, pGA, IA 1996
Ann Henderson	**Gilbert**	pNH, pIL, NY Ambass, gSD/NE, hIA, hNH, hTX
Amanda Childress	**Gillespie**	IA 1996
*Wendall	**Gills**	pNH, pTN, pGA
Patsy A.	**Glass**	hNH
Hershel Wayne	**Gober**	pNH, pIL, pTN, pAL, pFL, pGA, hIA, hNH
Beverly Fergusson	**Goggans**	pIL
Miles M.	**Goggans**	pNH, pIL
Diane L.	**Goltz**	hTX
Charles Randy	**Goodrum**	pNH, pCA, gGA, hAR
Margaret Gail	**Goodrum**	pNH, pIL, pCA, NY Ambass, gCO, gIA/NE, gGA, IA 1996, KY/TN 1996, LA 1996, hAR
Kay G.	**Goss**	gOK, hNH
Sallie Mae	**Graves**	pTX, gMO, gCO, gKS, gIA/NE, KY/TN 1996
Mary Linda	**Greenan**	pNH
Karin	**Greenberg**	gTX, LA 1996
James E. (Jim)	**Gresham**	LA 1996
Wayne A.	**Gruber**	FL Straw Poll, pNH
Brenda	**Gullett**	hNH, hAR, hTX
Robert Ray	**Gullett, Jr.**	hNH
Jose	**Guzzardi**	hTX
*Maria Luisa	**Haley**	pNH, hTX
Anna Jane	**Harbison**	gKS, hNH, hTX
Janet	**Hargett**	KY/TN 1996
*Robert (Bobby)	**Hargraves**	pNH

---

p • Primary   **h** • Hillary Campaign
g • General Election   **HON** • Honorary Traveler
State Abbr. • Clinton 2nd Term Trip   ***** • Deceased as of August 2012

The Clintons' Arkansas Travelers

Name		Traveler Trips
Ruth (Chi Chi)	**Hargraves**	pNH
Melva	**Harmon**	NY Ambass, gKY, LA 1996
Freddie	**Harris**	pGA
Jennifer Baird	**Harris**	pIL, pMD, pNY
*Phoebe	**Harris**	gKS
*Charles	**Harrison**	pTX
*Margaret	**Harrison**	pTX
Barbara Hopkins	**Hartwick**	gGA, LA 1996
Wanda Northcutt	**Hartz**	pSD, pCA, NY Ambass, gSD/NE
Robbie Jean	**Harvell**	gKS
*Patsy	**Hawkins**	pTX
Paul	**Hawkins**	pTX
John	**Haynie**	pNH, pIL, pTN, pAL, pFL, pGA
Dorothy Jeanne	**Hays**	gMO, gKS
Jimmie	**Hays**	pTX, pGA, pIL, NY Ambass
Patrick Henry	**Hays**	hNH, hAR, hTX
Ann Rainwater	**Henry**	pNH, hNH
Morriss Murphey	**Henry**	pNH, hNH
Betty A.	**Herron**	hNH, hAR
Jean	**Hervey**	pNH, NY Ambass, gIA/NE, LA 1996, hTX
Shirley May	**Hines**	gKS, gOK, KY/TN 1996
Gale Byrd	**Hinson**	hNH, hTX
Robert Ervin	**Hinson, Jr.**	hNH, hTX
David Armstrong	**Hodges**	KY/TN 1996
Marian Carole Alford	**Hodges**	KY/TN 1996
Norman Leycester	**Hodges, Jr.**	NY Ambass, gMO, hTX
B. Reid	**Holiman**	pNH
George R. (Skip)	**Holland**	pNH, pIL, pTX, NY Ambass
Cliff	**Hoofman**	gIA/NE, gGA, LA 1996
Ronald Arthur	**Hope**	pIL, pCA, gPA
*Lester	**Hosto**	pNH
James P. (Jay)	**Howell**	gNC

---

p • Primary
g • General Election
State Abbr. • Clinton 2nd Term Trip

h • Hillary Campaign
HON • Honorary Traveler
* • Deceased as of August 2012

The Clintons' Arkansas Travelers

Name		Traveler Trips
Ken	**Hubbard**	gMO
Sharon	**Hubbard**	gKS
*Bill	**Huddleston**	gIA/NE
Catherine L.	**Hughes**	pNH
Ron E.	**Hughes**	pNH
Bill	**Hurt**	pGA, pIL
Richard A.	**Hutchinson, Jr.**	gIA/NE, gKS, LA 1996
Vincent Michael	**Insalaco**	pNH, hIA, hNH, hAR
Paula Kay	**Irwin**	hTX
Melissa Judd	**Jackson**	hIA
Sandra	**Jay**	gKS, gTX
Candace	**Jeffress**	hNH
Jimmy L.	**Jeffress**	hNH
George	**Jernigan**	pNH
Suzanne Elizabeth	**Jessup**	gGA, hIA, hNH
K. Marguerite	**Joffe**	gKS
Elizabeth Elaine	**Johnson**	pTX, gMO, gCO, gIA/NE, KY/TN 1996, hTX
*Kirby	**Johnson**	pNH
Sid	**Johnson**	pNH, LA 1996
Charlotte Williams	**Jones**	gIA/NE
Clara Jean	**Jones**	hNH
James Eric	**Jones**	pNH
*Jimmie Red	**Jones**	pNH, pIL, pTN, pAL, pFL, pGA
*Myra Lee	**Jones**	pSD, pCA, NY Ambass, gSD/NE, gKY, gGA, KY/TN 1996, hIA, hAR, hTX
Susan Gail	**Jones**	pTX, KY/TN 1996, hNH, hAR
Greg	**Joslin**	FL Straw Poll
John Harvey	**Joyce**	LA 1996, hNH, hAR, hTX
Sherry Ivester	**Joyce**	gGA, hNH, hAR, hTX
Dennis Edwin	**Jungmeyer**	pNH
Delberta	**Keef**	gKS, gMO
*Jim	**Keef**	gKS, gMO

---

p • Primary   h • Hillary Campaign
g • General Election   HON • Honorary Traveler
State Abbr. • Clinton 2nd Term Trip   * • Deceased as of August 2012

The Clintons' Arkansas Travelers

Name		Traveler Trips
Aileen Page	**Kimbrough**	gKS
*Wilson W.	**Kimbrough, Jr.**	gKS
Linsley Matteson	**Kinkade**	pTX
Theresa Ann	**Kirk**	hTX
Thomas J.	**Kirk**	hTX
Robbie Thomas	**Knight**	hNH
William Fred	**Knight**	IA 1996, KY/TN 1996, LA 1996, hAR, hTX
George	**Kopp**	pCA, NY Ambass, gSD/NE, gKY, gGA
*Virginia Margaret	**Kutait**	pNH, pOK, gCO,
Mary Ellen	**Lackey**	gSD/NE
Jon Randall	**Laverty**	gMO, gKS, gMN/WI, IA 1996
Virginia Lee	**Laverty**	gMO, gKS, hIA
Billy J.	**Lawson**	NY Ambass, gIA/NE, gTX
Lorene	**Leder**	NY Ambass, gIA/NE, IA 1996, KY/TN 1996, hIA
David Paul	**Leopoulos**	pNH, NY Ambass
Rachel Ariana	**Levenson**	hTX
Harry Alan	**Light**	IA 1996
Bill James	**Linder**	pOK, pIL
Donna Sue	**Linder**	pOK, NY Ambass
Gary G.	**Linn**	gMO, LA 1996
Marie Elaine	**Lippard**	gTX, hAR
*Rick	**Lippard**	gTX
John M.	**Lipton**	pNH, NY Ambass
Rick Frank	**Lorence**	gMN/WI
*Jennifer Ann	**Love**	gIA/NE, IA 1996
Babbie Morris	**Lovett**	NY Ambass, gMN/WI
*Eve	**Lowery**	gKS
Aaron N.	**Lubin**	hIA, hAR
Robert Mays	**Lyford**	LA 1996, hIA
Diane H.	**Lyons**	gMN/WI, hNH
Donna Dee	**Malone**	pNH, hNH

---

p • Primary   **h** • Hillary Campaign
g • General Election   **HON** • Honorary Traveler
State Abbr. • Clinton 2nd Term Trip   *** •** Deceased as of August 2012

The Clintons' Arkansas Travelers

Name		Traveler Trips
Michael David	**Malone**	pNH, gSD/NE, gMN/WI, hAR
William Percy	**Malone**	pNH, hNH
Bobette Nagel	**Manees**	NY Ambass, gMO, gKY, LA 1996
*Gerald	**Markey**	gGA
Tom B.	**Marshall**	pIL, pGA, gIA/NE, gKS
Linda Lou	**Marston**	gMN/WI
Garth Armond	**Martin**	NY Ambass, IA 1996, KY/TN 1996
Joann Berry	**Martin**	NY Ambass, IA 1996, KY/TN 1996
George	**Matteson**	pTX, NY Ambass
*Gordon Crossett	**Matteson**	pTX
David R.	**Matthews**	pNH, NY Ambass
Ronald Fenton	**Maxwell**	hAR
James Ray (Jim)	**McAdams**	pIL
Skip	**McCarter**	hTX
Rhonda Jones	**McCauley**	pGA
Peggy Beisel	**McClain**	pNH, pMO, NY Ambass, gOK
Roger Hamilton	**McClain**	pMO, NY Ambass, gOK
Kay	**McClanahan**	pTX
James E. (Jim)	**McClelland, Jr.**	hNH
Jerry	**McConnell**	KY/TN 1996
Ann A.	**McCoy**	NY Ambass, hTX
Jack H.	**McCoy**	gTX
Thomas H.	**McGowan**	NY Ambass, gCO, LA 1996
*Don Loye	**McGuire**	pNH, NY Ambass
*Marcia	**McIvor**	gKS, gOK
Kerry	**McKenney**	gGA, LA 1996
Patricia (Ricia)	**McMahon**	hNH, hTX
Ted Aymond	**McNulty**	pNH, gSD/NE, gIA/NE
Jan Bickham	**McQuary**	FL Straw Poll, pNH, pIL, NY Ambass, gMO, gCO, KY/TN 1996, hNH, hAR
Vaughn Hutchison	**McQuary**	NY Ambass, hAR
William Russell	**Meeks III**	gSD/NE, gIA/NE, gMN/WI

p • Primary

g • General Election

State Abbr. • Clinton 2nd Term Trip

h • Hillary Campaign

HON • Honorary Traveler

* • Deceased as of August 2012

The Clintons' Arkansas Travelers

Name		Traveler Trips
Emily Chick	**Miller**	pTX
Gene	**Miller**	gMN/WI, gKS
Martha Marie	**Miller**	pNH
Nadine Hardin	**Miller**	hIA
Ragan Hoofman	**Milner**	gGA
Robert J. (Jeff)	**Mitchell**	pIL, hNH
Nancy Rowland	**Monroe**	pNH, NY Ambass
Thomas Ark	**Monroe, III**	pNH, NY Ambass
Shirley Ann	**Montgomery**	KY/TN 1996, LA 1996, hIA, hNH, hAR
Beatrice	**Moore**	hNH, hAR
Harry Truman	**Moore**	pGA, NY Ambass, gMO, gWA/OR, gGA, hNH, hAR, hTX
Linda Lou	**Moore**	pGA, NY Ambass, hAR, hTX
Shelby M.	**Moore**	gGA, hNH, hAR
Brenda	**Moorman**	pNH
Myra L.	**Moran**	hIA, hAR
Pat	**Morgan**	pNH, KY/TN 1996
*Fred	**Morrow**	NY Ambass, gGA, IA 1996, KY/TN 1996
Patricia J.	**Morrow**	gMN/WI, NY Ambass, gGA, IA 1996, KY/TN 1996, hNH, hAR, hTX
Bill G.	**Morse**	IA 1996
Anne Taylor Bradford	**Mourning**	pNH, NY Ambass
*Bill	**Murphy**	pMO, pIL, pTN, pAL, pFL, pGA
Jim	**Murphy**	pGA
Daniel	**Murray**	gGA
Peggy Lee	**Nabors**	FL Straw Poll, pNH, gGA, gMN/WI, IA 1996, KY/TN 1996, hNH
Gary Allen	**Neaville**	KY/TN 1996
Millie	**Nelms**	gKS
Laura Kathryn	**Nelson**	gKS
Susan	**Ness**	pNH
*Mary Alice	**Newberry**	NY Ambass, gMO, IA 1996

---

p • Primary
g • General Election
State Abbr. • Clinton 2nd Term Trip

h • Hillary Campaign
HON • Honorary Traveler
* • Deceased as of August 2012

The Clintons' Arkansas Travelers

Name		Traveler Trips
Joe	**Newman**	pGA
Lila Riggs	**Niswanger**	IA 1996, KY/TN 1996, LA 1996, hNH
Richard	**Norton**	pIL, gCO
Elizabeth D.	**Nyhus**	hNH
Dona	**O'Bannon**	gNC
James Anthony	**O'Brien**	gMO, gIA/NE, gGA
Dayle	**Oliver**	pOK, gTX,
Floy Dean	**Oliver**	pNH
Ronald Lee	**Oliver**	pNH, gAL, gSD/NE, gGA, IA 1996
*Johnnie Faye	**Owens**	pKY/TN 1996
Mary Rhodes	**Owens**	pNH, KY/TN 1996
*Ron	**Owens**	pKY
Annette G.	**Pagan**	gMO, LA 1996
Monica Jane	**Palko**	gMN/WI
Joyce McCaskill	**Palla**	hNH, hAR, hTX
Brynda Joyce	**Pappas**	gNC
Cheryl Kueker	**Park**	hNH, hAR, hTX
Brenda Sue	**Parker**	LA 1996
Jerry Dean	**Parker**	hIA
Sarah Jo	**Parker**	pOK, KY/TN 1996, hIA, hAR, hTX
Tom Vernon	**Parker**	pNH, gAL
Donald L.	**Parker II**	pTX
*Othelia	**Paul**	gKS
Jennifer L.	**Peel**	pTX
Charles John	**Penix**	LA 1996
Traci Tolbert	**Perrin**	gMN/WI
Samuel Arnold	**Perroni**	pCA, gIL, NY Ambass, gGA
James Levi	**Phillips**	IA 1996, KY/TN 1996, hIA, hNH
William Richard	**Phillips**	pNH, NY Ambass
Lee	**Pittman**	pIL
Lisa Cranmore	**Powell**	hIA, hNH, hAR, hTX
Dorothy Lynne	**Preslar**	pNH, gGA

The Clintons' Arkansas Travelers

Name		Traveler Trips
Elizabeth Ann	**Price**	NY Ambass, IA 1996, KY/TN 1996
John Phillip	**Price**	pNH, NY Ambass
Ann Lehman	**Pride**	pNH, pIL, pCA, NY Ambass, IA 1996
Thomas Arthur	**Prince**	gIA/NE
*Sydney	**Probst**	pNH, gGA
Senator David	**Pryor**	pNH
David Hampton	**Pryor, Jr.**	pNH, pIL, NY Ambass, IA 1996
Augustus H. (Bubba)	**Pugh, Jr.**	NY Ambass, gMN/WI
Joseph H.	**Purvis**	gKS, LA 1996
Susan Turner	**Purvis**	gMN/WI
John	**Raffaelli**	HON
Charles	**Ragsdell, Sr.**	pIL
Phyllis Judy	**Ramer**	hAR
James Carroll	**Rawls**	gMN/WI
Clark Everett	**Ray**	pNH, pIL, pMD, pNY
Robert Leslie	**Razer**	pIL
Robert Gregg	**Reep**	pNH, KY/TN 1996, hIA, hNH, hAR, hTX
Margaret Ellen	**Reger**	pNH, NY Ambass, gKS, gMN/WI
Robert K.	**Rhoads**	hNH
Jennifer Jane	**Rhodes**	gNC
Nancy	**Richards-Stower**	hNH
Donald S.	**Richardson**	gMO, gMN/WI
Robert Dean	**Ridgeway, Jr.**	pIL
Marci	**Riggs**	IA 1996, KY/TN 1996, LA 1996, hIA, hNH, hAR, hTX
Bobby Leon	**Roberts**	pIL
Judy	**Robertson**	NY Ambass, gKS, gSD/NE, IA 1996, LA 1996
Julie Cypert	**Roblee**	hTX
Clara Faye	**Rodgers**	pCA, NY Ambass, hNH, hAR, hTX
Steve	**Ronnel**	pIL

---

p • Primary
g • General Election
State Abbr. • Clinton 2nd Term Trip

h • Hillary Campaign
HON • Honorary Traveler
* • Deceased as of August 2012

The Clintons' Arkansas Travelers

Name		Traveler Trips
*Idavonne	**Rosa**	gIA/NE, Mitch Miller Tour, IA 1996
J.T.	**Rose**	FL Straw Poll, pNH, pIL, pCA, NY Ambass, gKY, gSD/NE
Herbert C.	**Rule**	hTX
James L. (Skip)	**Rutherford**	gME, NY Ambass
Erik	**Ryan**	gKS
Marie Jeanette	**Ryan**	hIA, hTX
Mary Anne	**Salmon**	pNH, pGA, pIL, NY Ambass, IA 1996, hIA, hNH, hAR
Victor	**Schachter**	pNH
*C. William (Bill)	**Schneider**	pOK, pIL
Cynthia	**Schneider**	pNH
Maryaleese	**Schreiber**	hNH
Mary Shoptaw	**Schroeder**	pGA, pTX, NY Ambass
Megan DeLamar	**Schroeder**	hTX
Robert William (Bill)	**Schroeder**	pGA, NY Ambass, pTX
Trey	**Schroeder**	pTX, NY Ambass, hTX
Paula Thomasson	**Scott**	pNH, pIL, pMD, pNY, NY Ambass
Berta Lena	**Seitz**	gMO, gIA/NE, gKS, gOK, hIA, hAR, hTX
John	**Selig**	pIL
Stacy	**Sells**	pIL
Lottie Holt	**Shackelford**	pNH
*Dixie	**Shrum**	gKS
Terry	**Shumaker**	hNH, hTX
Susan Goltz	**Siegel**	hTX
*Gregory G.	**Smith**	pNH, pIL, gIA/NE
Jill Coclasure	**Smith**	gKS
Kevin Andrew	**Smith**	KY/TN 1996
Othar	**Smith**	pTN, pAL, pFL, pGA
Sue Mullen	**Smith**	NY Ambass, gIA/NE, hNH, hAR, hTX
*Tom B.	**Smith**	pGA, KY/TN 1996
Alyce G.	**Smothers**	hTX

---

p • Primary   **h** • Hillary Campaign
g • General Election   **HON** • Honorary Traveler
State Abbr. • Clinton 2nd Term Trip   * • Deceased as of August 2012

The Clintons' Arkansas Travelers

Name		Traveler Trips
Larry Lawson	**Snodgrass**	pNH, KY/TN 1996
Patti Jo	**Snodgrass**	pNH
Nanalou McInturff	**Snow**	gMO, gGA
Victor Frederick	**Snyder**	pOR, IA 1996
Eileen Miriam	**Soffer**	hIA, hNH, hAR, hTX
Robert Young	**Speed**	hIA, hAR, hTX
Virginia	**Spencer**	gKS
Logan Scott	**Stafford**	pNH
Michael	**Stafford**	pNH
Beverly	**Stanley**	gMO, gOK
Don	**Stanley**	gMO, gOK
John L.	**Steer**	pIL, pTN, pAL, pFL, pGA
Amy Lee	**Stewart**	hTX
Daniel Troy	**Stidham**	NY Ambass, gMO
Jay	**Stockley**	pNH
JoEllen	**Stodola**	NY Ambass, gSC
Mark	**Stodola**	pIL, NY Ambass, gSC
Alan Robert	**Storeygard**	IA 1996, hNH, hTX
Paula Jamell	**Storeygard**	gGA, gMN/WI, LA 1996
Stephanie	**Streett**	hTX
Kimball	**Stroud**	pNH, pIL
Dorothy Davis	**Stuck**	gMO, gMN/WI, gGA
Catherine Nipper	**Talpas**	pIL
Jim	**Taylor**	gTX
Judy Kohn	**Tenenbaum**	hTX
Gayle Remer	**Thiele**	pNH, gCO
Johnna Goggans	**Thomas**	gNC
Kirkley	**Thomas**	gNC
Ben Clayton	**Thomasson**	gKS
Patsy	**Thomasson**	NY Ambass, gMN/WI
Damon	**Thompson**	pNH
Lyell Floyd	**Thompson**	pCA, gKS, gMN/WI, IA 1996
Nick	**Thompson**	pNH, NY Ambass

---

p • Primary   **h** • Hillary Campaign
g • General Election   **HON** • Honorary Traveler
State Abbr. • Clinton 2nd Term Trip   ***** • Deceased as of August 2012

The Clintons' Arkansas Travelers

Name		Traveler Trips
Thomas Tell Tyler	**Thompson**	IA 1996, KY/TN 1996, hNH, hAR, hTX
Virginia Diane	**Thompson**	LA 1996
Ray	**Thornton**	pNH
Michael E.	**Todd**	pNH, NY Ambass
Larry	**Tolbert**	gMN/WI
William Henry	**Trice III**	pIL, pCA, NY Ambass, gGA, hTX
Jodiane Cleveland	**Tritt**	gTX
*Peggy	**Tucker**	pNH, gKY
Daniel Clifton	**Tullos**	LA 1996
Peggy Nell	**Turbyfill**	KY/TN 1996, hNH
*Charles Dan (Charlie)	**Varner**	pNH, pOK, pIL, gKY, gTX, IA 1996
Larry Don	**Vaught**	pNH
Shelia	**Vaught**	gMO
Floyd G. (Buddy)	**Villines III**	gMN/WI, hNH
Wayne	**Wagner**	pNH, NY Ambass
Pamela Dean	**Walker**	pNH, NY Ambass, gKS
Mary	**Ware**	gMN/WI
Richard Taylor	**Watkins**	pIL, gPA
Pamela Roberts	**Weber**	gMN/WI
Beverly A.	**Wells**	gMO, pGA
Tommye	**Wells**	pGA, KY/TN 1996
*Carl Simpson	**Whillock**	NY Ambass, gIA/NE
Margaret Moore	**Whillock**	NY Ambass, gIA/NE, hAR, hTX
*Frank Lynn	**Whitbeck**	Mitch Miller Tour
Betty Sue	**White**	gMO, gKY, gIA/NE, gMN/WI, gKS, IA 1996, KY/TN 1996, LA 1996, hIA
*Donna	**White**	gKS
William Edwin	**Wiedower**	FL Straw Poll, gCO
Dina Nash	**Williams**	gKS, gOK
Jack	**Williams**	pIL
John Roger	**Williams**	g,MO, gCO, gTX
Lawrence	**Williams**	pNH, pIL

---

p • Primary   **h** • Hillary Campaign
g • General Election   **HON** • Honorary Traveler
State Abbr. • Clinton 2nd Term Trip   * • Deceased as of August 2012

The Clintons' Arkansas Travelers

Name		Traveler Trips
P.J.	**Williams**	gTX
Ronnie Devon	**Williams**	gMN/WI
Rocky	**Willmuth**	FL Straw Poll, pNH
Laura Bowen	**Wills**	pNH, gMN/WI, gNC
Carolyn Sue	**Wilson**	pGA
Sherri	**Wilson**	gKS
Neva	**Witt**	LA 1996
Lawrence N. (Larry)	**Wolken**	pCA
Dina Carol	**Wood**	NY Ambass, gMO, gKS
Dianne Boyt	**Woods**	pGA
*George Lucas	**Woods**	gKY
*Henry Lee	**Woods**	pNH, pIL, pMD, pNY, pCA, NY Ambass, IA 1996
Jerry	**Woods**	gMO
Judi Rae	**Woods**	pNH
*Elmo	**Woolf**	IA 1996
*Bill	**Wren**	pNH
*Judi Stuart	**Wren**	pNH
George H.	**Wright, Jr.**	pTX
Phillip Charles	**Wyrick**	pCA
Donna Kay Matteson	**Yeargan**	pGA, pTX, NY Ambass
Joe Dan	**Yee**	NY Ambass, gMO, gMN/WI
Hsing-Wu	**Yeh**	KY/TN 1996
Yun-Chi	**Yeh**	KY/TN 1996, LA 1996
Patricia L.	**Youngdahl**	NY Ambass, gKS, LA 1996, hAR
Z. Lynn	**Zeno**	pNH
Bobbie Jean	**Zimmer**	hAR, hTX

PHOTO INDEX FOR NAMES

COLOR PHOTO SECTION

The Travelers on "Comeback Hill" in Manchester, New Hampshire (February, 1992). Front row left to right are David Pryor, Jr., Linda Greenan, Patty Criner, George Bruno, Sheila Galbraith Bronfman, Ricia McMahon, Richard Bronfman, Maria Haley, Sheila Evans, Ann Henderson Gilbert, Mike Todd, Charlie Cole Chaffin, Percy Malone, Donna Malone, Ronnie Bumpass, Gayle Remer, Kirby Johnson, Virginia Kutait, John Lipton, Larry Crane, Larry Vaught, and Nick Thompson. Second row left to right are Dennis Jungmeyer, Bobby Hargraves, Ruth Hargraves, Lynn Zeno, Wendall Giles, Lottie Shackelford, Stewart Bell, Mary Rhodes Owens, Laura Wills, Sydney Probst, Paula Thomasson, Joel Buckner, Henry Woods, Ann Pride, Peggy Nabors, Cathy Cunningham, Peggy McClain, Ernest Cunningham, R. B. Friedlander, John Haney, Ann Henry, Jimmy Red Jones, Morriss Henry, Mack Dyer, Charlie Varner, and J.T. Rose. Third row left to right are Mike Stafford, Kimball Stroud, Peggy Tucker, Harry Criner, Mary Anne Salmon, Mike Gaines, Woody Futrell, Tom Parker, Sherry Gavin Bird, Martha Miller, Don McGuire, Catherine Hughes, Brandi Baxter, Ron Hughes, Floy Oliver, James Jones, Wayne Wagner, Gregg Reep, Bill Phillips, Margaret Reger, Jerry Bookout, David Folsom, Judy Gaddy, Woody Bassett, Dorothy Preslar, Bill Gaddy, Clark Ray, Jennifer Harris, Victor Schachter, Reid Holiman, Robert Evans, and Lester Hosto. Fourth row, left to right, are Larry Williams, Joe Bell, Miles Goggans, Vince Ancell, Mike Malone, Ark Monroe, Nancy Monroe, Rocky Wilmuth, Ron Oliver, Allen Bird, Greg Smith, Ed Fry, Bob Baxter, David Matthews, Herschel Gober, Cary Gaines, Phil Price, Del Boyette, Judy Wren, Damon Thompson, and Bill Wren.

The Travelers spent the day with Tipper Gore in Cape Girardeau. Front row kneeling from left to right are Dorothy Stuck, Nan Snow, Sheila Bronfman, Beverly Wells, and Jan McQuary. Front row left to

298

right are Randy Laverty, Tipper Gore, Mary Newberry, Norman Hodges, Rick Eoff, Shelia Vaught, Bobette Manees, Sue White, Annette Pagan, Elaine Johnson, Weldon Chesser, Jean Boyce, Sam Boyce, and Sallie Graves, local supporter. Back row left to right are Jerry Flippo, Jim O'Brien, David Bailin, Margaret Flippo, John Williams, and Don Richardson, Tommye Wells and Dan Stidham.

On the way to Louisville. Pictured are Travelers on the 1996 Kentucky/Tennessee trip; Don Bishop, Sheila Bronfman, Berniece Duffey, J.J. Galloway, Amie Lee Galloway, Gail Goodrum, Sallie Graves, Janet Hargett, Shirley Hines, David Hodges, Marian Hodges, Elaine Johnson, Myra Jones, Susan Jones, Fred Knight, Lorene Leder, Garth Martin, Joann Martin, Jerry McConnell, Jan McQuary, Shirley Montgomery, Pat Morgan, Fred Morrow, Pat Morrow, Peggy Nabors, Gary Neaville, Johnnie Owens, Sarah Jo Parker, Levi Phillips, Ann Price, Gregg Reep, Lila Riggs, Marci Riggs, Larry Snodgrass, Kevin Smith, Tom B. Smith, Tyler Thompson, Peggy Turbyfill, Tommye Wells, Sue White, Hsing-Wu Yeh, and Yun-Chi Yeh.

"Hope and Beyond" to Louisiana. Front from left to right are Sid Johnson, Lila Riggs Niswanger, Bob Calhoun, Jean Hervey, Melva Harmon, Annette Pagan, Peggy Crossley, Jean Boyce, and Gaye Cypert. Middle from left to right are Richard Hutchinson, Sheila Bronfman, Bobette Manees, Jackie Edmonds, Yun-Chi Yeh, Marci Riggs, Fred Knight, Shirley Montgomery, Charley Penix, Sue White, Joe Purvis, Gail Goodrum, Bob Lyford, Barbara Hartwick, Tom McGowan, Neva Witt, Pat Youngdahl, Marie Clinton Bruno, Brenda Parker, and Jim Cypert. Back from left to right are Cliff Hoofman, Paula Storeygard, Gary Linn, Lloyd Crossley, Richard Bronfman, John Joyce, Don Bishop, Judy Robertson, Dan Tullos, Virginia Thompson, Aubra Anthony, Berniece Duffey, Karin Greenberg, Linda Ellington, Jim Gresham, and Kerry McKenney.

Hillary Clinton celebrated her birthday in 2007 in Ames, Iowa. Front row, kneeling left to right, are Margie Alsbrook, Eileen Soffer, Missy Jackson, Marci Riggs, Shirley Montgomery, and Karla

Bradley. Middle row: Sheila Bronfman, Jo Parker, Nadine Hardin-Miller, Suzanne Jessup, Ann Gilbert, Hillary Clinton, Gregg Reep, Lisa Powell, Fran Flener, Sue White, Berniece Duffey, Marie Ryan, Virginia Laverty, Pat Moran, Lorene Leder, and Myra Jones. Back row: Aaron Lubin, Jerry Parker, Wes Cottrell, Rob Speed, Carroll Autry, Levi Phillips, Bob Lyford, Don Bishop, Rose Crane, Mary Anne Salmon, Vincent Insalaco, Craig Douglass, and Berta Seitz.

Hillary Clinton and the Travelers in New Hampshire 2008. Front row seated from left to right are Linda Ellington, Brenda Gullett, Candace Jeffress, Peggy Nabors, Marci Riggs, Eileen Soffer, Corey Villines, Vincent Insalaco, Jim McClelland, Chelsea Clinton, Jan McQuary, Shirley Montgomery, Beth Nyhus, John Joyce, Patrick Hays, Diane Lyons, Nancy Richards-Stower, Sue Smith, and Wes Cottrell. Second row from left to right are Sarah Argue, Karla Bradley, Peggy Turbyfill, Bob Gullett, Susan Jones, Lila Riggs Niswanger, Sheila Bronfman, Fran Flener, Hillary Clinton, Richard Bronfman, Alan Storeygard, Suzanne Jessup, Clara Jones, Cheryl Parks, Sherry Joyce, Maryaleese Schreiber, Deb Crapo, and Ann Gilbert. Third row from left to right are Jimmy Jeffress, Mauria Aspell, Joyce Palla, Kay Goss, Marie Clinton Bruno, Ann Henry, Morriss Henry, Pat Morrow, Gregg Reep, Mary Anne Salmon, Craig Douglass, Percy Malone, Don Bishop, Grady Bailin, President Clinton, Levi Phillips, Sherry Bishop, Pat Glass, Betty Herron, Faye Rodgers, Gilbert Cornwell, Suzanne Clark, Beatrice Moore, Ed Fry, Lisa Powell, and H.T. Moore. Fourth row, from left to right, are Bob Aspell, Kay Bartlett, Rose Crane, Buddy Villines, Jeff Mitchell, Robert Rhoads, David Bailin, Steve Clark, Shelby Moore, and Tim Giattina.

BLACK AND WHITE PHOTOGRAPHS

CHAPTER 14

This group recorded "Stand By Your Van." Front row from left to right are Larry Wolken, a local supporter, and J.T. Rose. Seated from left to right are Randy Goodrum, Gail Goodrum, Bob Baxter, Tracey Dean Franks, Weldon Chesser, Faye Rodgers, Sheila Evans, and Dale

Evans. a local supporter, Henry Woods, and Sheila Bronfman. Standing from left to right are Carole Bulloch, Peggy Crossley, Ron Hope, Bill Trice, Ann Pride, a local supporter, Phil Wyrick, Rose Crane, Jay Bradford, Wanda Northcutt, Sam Perroni, Pate Felts, Myra Jones, Mitchell Schwartz, George Kopp, and Lyell Thompson.

CHAPTER 16

A lot of time was spent in airports. The Travelers on the Minnesota/Wisconsin trip were Don Beavers, Sheila Bronfman, Carole Bulloch, Weldon Chesser, Nelwyn Davis, Rene de Turenne, Wooten Epes, Randy Laverty, Rick Lorence, Babbie Lovett, Diane Lyons, Mike Malone, Linda Marston, Russ Meeks, Gene Miller, Pat Morrow, Margaret Moseley, Peggy Nabors, Monica Palko, Gus Pugh, Susan Purvis, James Rawls, Margaret Reger, Don Richardson, Paula Storeygard, Dorothy Stuck, Patsy Thomasson, Lyell Thompson, Larry Tolbert, Traci Tolbert, Buddy Villines, Mary Ware, Pam Weber, Sue White, Ronnie Williams, Laura Wills, and Joe Dan Yee.

CHAPTER 17

The Georgia Travelers. Allen Bird, Herby Branscum, Richard Bronfman, Sheila Bronfman, Weldon Chesser, Eleanor Coleman, Roosevelt Coleman, Milana Dennis, Lee Douglass, Rick Eoff, Pate Felts, Lisa Ferrell, Vic Fleming, Gail Goodrum, Randy Goodrum, Barbara Hartwick, Cliff Hoofman, Suzanne Jessup, Myra Jones, Sherry Joyce, George Kopp, Gerald Markey, Kerry McKenney, Ragan Milner, H. T. Moore, Shelby Moore, Fred Morrow, Pat Morrow, Daniel Murray, Peggy Nabors, Jim O'Brien, Ron Oliver, Sam Perroni, Dorothy Preslar, Sydney Probst, Nan Snow, Paula Storeygard, Dorothy Stuck, and Bill Trice.

CHAPTER 18

Travelers for President Clinton depart for Iowa. These Travelers were on the Iowa trip. Jim Banks, Sheila Bell, Jerry Bookout, Jay Bradford, Richard Bronfman, Sheila Bronfman, Joel Buckner, Charlie Cole Chaffin, Weldon Chesser, Jamie Cox, Patti Cox, Berniece Duffey, Mack Dyer, Nettie Gibson, Mandy Childress, Gail Goodrum, Fred Knight, Randy Laverty, Lorene Leder, Harry Light,

Jennifer Love, Garth Martin, Joann Martin, Fred Morrow, Pat Morrow, Bill Morse, Peggy Nabors, Mary Newberry, Lila Riggs, Ron Oliver, Levi Phillips, Ann Price, Ann Pride, Dee Pryor, Marci Riggs, Judy Robertson, Idavonne Rosa, Mary Anne Salmon, Vic Snyder, Lyell Thompson, Charlie Varner, Sue White, Henry Woods, Elmo Woolf.

Caucus Night with Senator Chris Dodd. Shown in the front from left to right are Pat Morrow, Sue White, Gail Goodrum, Ann Pride, United States Senator Christopher Dodd, Lila Riggs, Joann Martin, and Sheila Bell. On the back row are Fred Morrow, Garth Martin, Jerry Bookout, Jay Bradford, Vic Snyder, Weldon Chesser, Ann Price, Berniece Duffey, and Levi Phillips.

Get me to the church on time. Dr. Tyler Thompson, Sheila Bronfman, Jo Parker, Susan Jones, Marian Hodges, Mayor Gregg Reep, Pat Morrow, Janet Hargett, Ann Price, Gail Goodrum, Peggy Nabors, Jan McQuary, Myra Jones, Pat Morgan, Joann Martin, Johnnie Faye Owens, Sue White, Lila Riggs, Amie Lee Galloway, Shirley Montgomery, Marci Riggs, Tommye Wells. Back row. David Hodges, Senator Kevin Smith, Levi Phillips, Don Bishop, Yun-Chi Yeh, Tom B. Smith, Garth Martin, Fred Morrow, Fred Knight, Sallie Graves, Dr. Gary Neaville, Elaine Johnson, Larry Snodgrass, Jerry McConnell, Peggy Turbyfill, Shirley Hines, Hsing-Wu Yeh, J.J. Galloway, Berniece Duffey, and Lorene Leder.

CHAPTER 19

Travelers stop for a photo before working Stuttgart. Front row left to right: Rose Crane, John Joyce, Sherry Joyce, Rob Speed, Berta Seitz, Pat Youngdahl, Margaret Whillock, David Bailin. Second row: Sheila Bronfman, Dr. Richard Bronfman, Lisa Powell, Mayor Pat Hays, Fred Knight, Ron Maxwell, Gail Goodrum, Randy Goodrum, Eileen Soffer, Myra Moran, Betty Herron. Third row: Wes Cottrell, Vaughn McQuary, Jan McQuary, Representative Gregg Reep, Judy Ramer, Sue Smith, Mike Malone, Jo Parker, Bobby Zimmer. Fourth row: Marci Riggs, Aaron Lubin, Dr. Tyler Thompson, Steve Clark, Faye Rodgers, Berniece Duffey, Cheryl

Park, Brenda Gullett, Myra Jones, Dr. Bob Gullet. Fifth row: Senator Mary Anne Salmon, Vincent Insalaco, Tim Giattina, Karla Bradley, Carol Brown, Susan Jones, Pat Morrow, Corey Villines, Gilbert Cornwell, Shirley Montgomery, and Ann Cornwell.

ACKNOWLEDGEMENTS

This book, written by a first-time author, would not have happened without the investment of time and trouble by the Travelers themselves. They helped gather the stories and arranged for interviews. A team sorted through Traveler memorabilia tucked away in the archives of the William J. Clinton Presidential Library. Other Travelers uncovered long-stored boxes of papers and photos in their own homes. The materials serve a dual purpose, informing this book and filling a new temporary exhibit in the library celebrating the Travelers on this twentieth anniversary of their creation.

Sheila Galbraith Bronfman, the Travelers' leader, and her friend Rose Crane had discussed a book project for years, wanting to capture the Travelers' story before too many of them were gone. Rose gave her interview for the book the night before she died, happily recounting Traveler stories between breaths from an oxygen mask. She was the sixty-eighth Traveler to die before their story could be written. She and many others proudly included their Traveler experience in their obituaries.

Amazingly, of the remaining 452 Travelers, almost 300 responded to an online survey designed to collect their memories. That's better than a sixty-five percent return, and some of the ones who didn't send the survey back did participate in interviews. Their collective participation in the book project is further evidence of just how much being Travelers meant to these Arkansans.

Helping to make the book happen were Travelers Mary Anne Salmon and Bobby Roberts, who were at the conference table with Sheila, the publishing team, and me from the first day.

Sheila personally invested countless hours on the project, from answering endless questions to setting up a three-day marathon of interviews with Travelers brought to Little Rock from around the state to jumpstart the reporting. Simultaneously, Tyler Thompson was recording a separate set of remembrances from the participating Travelers. His notes from those interviews fleshed out what they said in groups. Sherry Joyce did yeoman's work during the group interviews, keeping running notes to supplement my recordings. Both Sheila and Sherry and their respective spouses, Richard and John, helped edit and proofread chapters. They were the core support team, although others were also involved. Harry Truman "H. T." Moore helped Sheila select photographs and write cutlines for the book.

Political Magic is necessarily based on twenty-year-old recollections of the Travelers, but their accounts proved remarkably sharp when compared to newspaper clipping and other documentation created back in 1992, 1996, and 2008. These Travelers left a trail of newspaper accounts of their travels all across the country in those sixteen years.

Theirs is a story of devotion to Bill and Hillary Clinton, of dedication to their candidacies for president, and to "democracy in action," as Rose described the Travelers' work.

Sheila made sure the book she and Rose wanted got written and that it contained many of the memorable experiences of the Travelers. I learned firsthand about Sheila's remarkable organizational skill, her fierce determination, and her devotion to the Travelers who answered her every call.

The "bing" signaling arrival of the latest e-mail from Sheila was to me the equivalent of her whistle for the Travelers. As irritating as those interrupting bings could be, the e-mail almost always carried information I needed or had asked for and suggestions to make the book better.

Another thank you is due to Amy Eidson Clark, who painstakingly transcribed interviews and converted survey data into a more usable format for me. She worked those chores in around raising two boys, my young grandnephews, Max and Harry, who provided wonderful periodic diversion for me during this months-long project.

Thanks, too, to the Butler Center, whose forgiveness of a missed deadline is much appreciated. Life interrupted and the last of the manuscript arrived two weeks past deadline. The book is better for the patience of Rod Lorenzen and David Stricklin.

Thanks to everyone who helped in big ways and small to make *Political Magic* better.

Just as the Travelers say they'd be ready to hit the road again for Hillary, I would be as willing to report their journey. These were remarkable adventures by Arkansas people, all with a common mission. Their stories should be told.

Brenda Blagg
September 2012

ABOUT THE AUTHOR

Brenda Blagg is an award-winning journalist with more than four decades of experience covering Arkansas politics and government.

Her column on state government and politics has been syndicated weekly to several Arkansas newspapers since the 1970s.

Blagg met Bill Clinton, then a University of Arkansas professor, in 1972 before his entry into politics and was the first reporter to interview him about his 1974 bid for the U.S. Congress. She reported on his campaigns for attorney general and later for governor and covered his administrations in Arkansas, which included Hillary Clinton's emergence not only as a close adviser to the governor but also in her hands-on role in state education reform.

In 1992, Blagg went to New Hampshire to cover the Arkansas Travelers the week of the primary as the Travelers helped resurrect Clinton's first campaign for president and made him the self-proclaimed "Comeback Kid." Now she is telling the story of the Arkansas Travelers, the devoted Friends of Bill who volunteered and traveled on their own dime—first for Bill Clinton in 1992 and 1996 and later for Hillary Clinton in her 2008 bid for the Democratic nomination for president.

ARKANSAS TRAVELER WITHDRAWAL
SYNDROME CHECKLIST

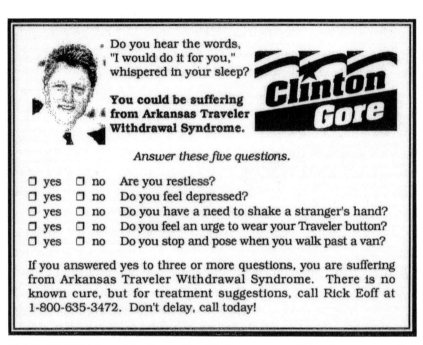

. Do you hear the words,
"I would do it for you,"
whispered in your sleep?

**You could be suffering
from Arkansas Traveler
Withdrawal Syndrome.**

Answer these five questions.

☐ yes   ☐ no   Are you restless?
☐ yes   ☐ no   Do you feel depressed?
☐ yes   ☐ no   Do you have a need to shake a stranger's hand?
☐ yes   ☐ no   Do you feel an urge to wear your Traveler button?
☐ yes   ☐ no   Do you stop and pose when you walk past a van?

If you answered yes to three or more questions, you are suffering
from Arkansas Traveler Withdrawal Syndrome. There is no
known cure, but for treatment suggestions, call Rick Eoff at
1-800-635-3472. Don't delay, call today!

Rick Eoff's "Withdrawal Syndrome Checklist" was sent to all Travelers in 1992. They
all reported suffering from this malaise. They were the ultimate political junkies.